Man in History : A Theological Study

Man in History:
A Theological Study

by Hans Urs von Balthasar

Sheed and Ward. London and Sydney

First published 1968
Sheed and Ward Ltd., 33 Maiden Lane, London WC2
Sheed and Ward Pty Ltd., 95 York Street, Sydney

© Sheed and Ward Ltd., 1968

Originally published as *Das Ganze im Fragment*
© Benziger Verlag, Einsiedeln, 1963

Nihil Obstat
Leo J. Steady, Censor Librorum

Imprimatur
+ Robert F. Joyce
Bishop of Burlington
September 14, 1967

Standard book number 7220 0535 0

Printed in Great Britain by
Compton Printing Limited
London and Aylesbury

CONTENTS

FOREWORD

Whoever tries today, in obedience to God's word, to say something about God and man has to negotiate the narrow path between two forms of titanism. The old one, dating from Constantine, which forced political power into the service of the kingdom of Christ, is today discarded, now that the Church has finally lost this power. The new one, which identifies technical progress with the growth of God's kingdom, is all the more welcomed. Both are, however, as we shall see, simply varieties of the same integralism: the one reactionary, the other progressive; the one clerical, the other secular. Both seek to provide the kingdom of Christ with earthly power, for both see this world as merging with the realm of God. The earlier age saw the visible world as symbolic of the invisible; the present age regards the invisible as the visible's dynamic source of energy. The earlier age dragged time by its hair before the throne of the eternity it claimed to administer; the present age marches with time in order to achieve salvation through it.

But the Lamb of God walked the narrow way and, by telling us to follow him along it, gave us the hope of avoiding all forms of human titanism. Neither the conservatives nor the progressives can bear the fragmentariness of existence in time. They offer formulas for how the fragment can be made a whole; perhaps, it is even seen as a whole itself. The dynamic progressives seek to harness the social program of the prophets and of the Sermon on the Mount as a dynamic force to change society, while the conservatives see the hieratic and hierarchic forms founded by Christ as timelessly and finally informing the frail material of the world.

The "program" of the Lamb, true to the earth by being truly *humilis* (i.e., close to the *humus*), can be popular with neither right nor left. It cannot be built into earthly programs; it does not offer enough for them and it cannot be exploited. If you use it as a front, it looks fine and possibly has propaganda value, but the misconception cannot be hidden forever. Thus, the medieval world regarded itself as called to administer Augustine's *"Civitas Dei,"* which meant precisely the opposite. At least, however, they were honest enough to take Augustine's "pilgrimage of the kingdom of God in strange lands and darkness" as the soul and mind for which they fashioned the earthly body.

Augustine's radical doctrine of time shall be our starting point also, so that we may avoid, at least negatively, the false conclusions and careless thinking which people ever more easily fall into nowadays when considering Christianity. The late classical point of view saw the basic philosophic question ("Wherein consists the being of that which exists? Why does anything possess the quality of being, according to the data presented to us by experience?") as indissolubly linked with the basic theological question ("What does God's word tell us of God?"). This is still a necessary position for us. If the philosophical question is no longer posed, if the only questions asked are of so-called "exact" science, which today tries to usurp the place of philosophy, then the actuality of what is presented to us is taken for granted, and no one worries about the quality of "given being."

This decline of interest in the philosophical question influences theology in this respect, that the incomprehensibility of divine revelation remains the basic phenomenon. Theology overlooks this and extracts instead the supposed "message" and immediately presses it into the service of its own (conservatively or progressively slanted) program. The "exact" scientist urges the philosopher to move on from the unprofitable question of being, while the "exact" theologian (be he dogmatist, moralist, exegete, or whatever) insists that we return to those areas of knowledge where certainty can be attained and tangible results arrived at.

The temptation to reach conclusions is particularly strong in this book. If one cannot produce satisfactory research results here, then why should he write anything? Our subject is the theology of man in history. What statements can be made and supported in this field, in view of biblical revelation, without making secret sorties into the philosophy of history? Very few and probably very tentative ones. But, perhaps, it might even be something to have refused to make such borrowings and to have warned against carelessness of method. Syntheses are easily thrown together and enjoy general popularity; breaking them up is a harder and more thankless task. For the philosopher and the theologian alike history is only a fragment; but if one does not know whether a part of a symphony is a fifth or a twentieth of the whole, then he cannot reconstruct the whole. Not even Hegel, who knew everything else, could construct the future. We, who know less than he, must abandon the attempt to establish, by means of the fragments of the world, the totality of the absolute world-transcending Spirit.

To those bent on "results" and "progress" our essay may

appear a reversal to superseded oriental ideas or to a thoroughly
out-of-date and disdained Gnosticism. But is Asia really so irrelevant to us that we no longer have any sense of its greatest spiritual
concern? Augustine, with whom we propose starting, inherited
that concern from Plotinus, considered it very seriously, and
resolved it entirely from within itself, in the same positive way
that Buber has taken Hasidism to himself. Augustine managed
to incorporate the profoundly true experience of *extension* into
Christianity by discarding the hasty and specious solution of
Gnostic identity; he put in its stead the metaphysics of absolute
love. However far we might go beyond Augustine (e.g., with
Soloviev) in giving importance to the *development* of the world,
the ultimate meaning of history is to be found where Augustine
sought it.

As with my earlier short volume, *A Theology of History,** this
book is not intended as a comprehensive treatise on the theology
of man in history. A few main themes are dealt with in a cyclic
way, with the same or similar problems being touched on frequently at different levels. The problem of time—the middle and
the end of time—crops up again and again, as does also the problem of open reason and revelation, the problem of Jews and
pagans, etc. The questions selected are aspects of the same subject: where must we look to discover, in the fragmentariness of
our existence, a tendency towards wholeness? Every separate bit
of a piece of pottery suggests the whole vessel, every torso is seen
in the light of the complete statue. Is our existence an exception?
Shall we let ourselves be persuaded that its fragmentariness is the
whole? If we did, would that not amount to abandoning the idea
of finding any sense in the fragment at all and to accepting senselessness? Thus, we are asking about ourselves, and in asking we
intend to be more than just a question. We hold that someone
must know, that there is someone who can answer our question
about ourselves.

* Sheed and Ward, 1963.

1. THE FRAGMENTARY NATURE OF TIME

THE VISION OF AUGUSTINE

With the ninth book of his *Confessions,* Augustine completed the account of his life to the time of his writing: the story of a life full of guilt and vanity, but recalled and converted by the grace of God. The account closes appropriately with the death of his mother, whose life was fulfilled by her son's conversion, and who, dying, directed her love upward to "the eternal Jerusalem," "our Catholic mother," "which thy people sigh for in their pilgrimage from birth until they come there" (IX, 13).[1]

Then Augustine transfers his gaze from the horizontal to the vertical and adds four books which, after the historical account, treat of the nature of his existence within history, lived as it was in the tension between his true home, the "Jerusalem above," and the place of his pilgrimage, the "earth," alienated by original

1

sin, guilt, and all manner of corruption. This tension is not thought of mythologically;[2] rather everything is conceived in that unity of theology and philosophy which characterized ancient thinking, especially that of Plato and Plotinus, and which was adopted by the Christian Fathers. With Augustine the investigation of this vertical dimension has a more existential flavor than with the Platonists. The question is no longer, as in the first nine books, *qualis fuerim,* but *qualis sim,* and more insistently, *quis iam sim ei quis adhuc sim* (X, 4). The basic answer is already given in the biography: I am a man turned towards the dark who was converted by grace to light and, therefore, profess the light in gratitude and reverence. But now this answer is to be expressed and justified in its theologico-philosophical dimensions: What prerequisite conditions must be in me for such a development to be possible? We are here at a crucial point for the whole of Augustine's thinking. His reasoning, uniquely stringent, proceeds in four stages.[3]

Book Ten is the book of *memory,* understood, according to Plato, as the depth of the soul's harking back to its origin. Since for the Christian this is not the world of ideas, but the living God, the inconceivably vast interior of the memory opens upon a transcendental depth: "There is something of man that the 'very spirit of man that is in him' (1 Cor. 2, 11) does not know. But you, Lord, know all of him, for You made him" (X, 5). And only through God, whom man does not know (X, 6), can he understand what he knows of himself. "Who is He that is above the topmost point of my soul? By that same soul I shall ascend to Him" (X, 7). If the soul has its origin in God, then God is in the memory of the soul (X, 24) and yet beyond it, for "all . . . things suffer change, but You remain unchangeable over all" (X, 25).

But this fundamental tension—that God "deigns to dwell in my memory," although he is not contained by any creature—is only the reflection of an immanent tension in the memory itself, which Augustine proceeds to submit to a subtle psychological analysis. "The fields and vast palaces of memory" contain immeasurable treasure—everything which the senses bring in from the world is stored up, readily available or hidden away, and can be brought to light again from greater or lesser oblivion. And I can even partly encounter there the person that I once was (X, 8), and also ideas whose truth is obvious to me as I think about them, but which I could not have known through the senses. I recognize them in my mind, although they did not exist in my memory as ideas. Yet when they were presented to me, I recognized them and said "Yes, that's right," so they must have lain somewhere, "far back, thrust away," in my memory.

To think, then, is nothing else than "to take things that the memory already contained, but scattered and unarranged, and, by thinking, bringing them together [*cogito* from *co-agito*, according to the true etymology], and by close attention have them placed within reach in that same memory: so that things which had formerly lain there scattered and not considered now come easily and familiarly to us." Much, of course, "sinks down again and falls away" and has to be collected out of dispersion. Indeed the verb *to cogitate* is named from this drawing together. For *cogito* (I think) has the same relation to *cogo* (I put together) as *agito* (I pursue zealously) to *ago* (I act). (This etymology of Augustine's may be compared with Heidegger's interpretation of *legein-logos* as collecting together, gathering.)[4]

Augustine goes on to consider more fully the phenomenon of buried memories. "I remember" means that there are things present to me which in themselves have become absent; and I myself am one of these. I remember feelings of joy and pain, anger and grief, but I no longer feel the former emotions (X, 14–15). I also remember forgetfulness in a general way (X, 16), but concretely also, since I know that I once knew specific things and now no longer know them. I can even hunt for things in my memory in such a way that I can reject what I find as wrong. When I find what I am after, I exclaim, "That's it" (X, 18). Thus, memory seeks in itself for what has escaped it; it is not therefore lost, but only buried.

How then do I seek You, O Lord? For in seeking You, my God, it is happiness that I am seeking. . . . How am I to seek it? Should it be [Platonically] by way of remembrance, as though I had forgotten it but am still aware that I have forgotten it . . . or is it by a kind of appetite to learn it as something unknown to me—whether as something I never have known, or something I have known and forgotten and do not even remember that I have forgotten (X, 20)?

Everyone strives for happiness.

But where did they know it, that they should desire it so? Where have they seen it, that they should love it? Obviously, we have it in some way but I do not know how. . . . I strive to know whether or not this knowledge is in the memory, for if it is, then we have at some past time been happy—whether individually, or in that man who committed the first sin, in whom we all died and of whom we are all in misery descended. Which of these two I do not ask now. . . . (X, 20).

Augustine adopts, in the main, the Platonic solution in spite of the theological difficulties. The point is not that everyone pursues some kind of happiness, for that happiness we all pursue is not just any sort of happiness (X, 22). And if most people imagine that they do not need the eternal joy of God to be happy, Augustine replies that everyone at least desires truth, and that full truth is identical with God, with full love (X, 23).

He does not concern himself with why the traces of former vision become effaced in our memory. Book Ten goes on instead, in Chapter 27, to examine the sad fact that it is not God who has withdrawn from man, but man from God. "For behold Thou wert within me, and I outside; and I sought Thee outside and in my unloveliness fell upon those lovely things that Thou hast made." In this diffusion unity is lost and can be regained only through disciplined self-denial, through that self-collectedness which has just been described as the essence of thought, and now is the essence of love.

For by continence we are collected and bound up into unity within ourself, whereas we had been scattered abroad in multiplicity. Too little does any man love Thee, who loves some other thing together with Thee, loving it not on account of Thee, O Thou Love, who art ever burning and never extinguished! O Charity, my God, enkindle me! Thou dost command continence: grant what Thou dost command and command what Thou wilt (X, 29).

Thus ends Book Ten with an examination of conscience which discovers that "lust of the flesh, lust of the eyes, and pride of life" still oppose this gathering love in the soul of Augustine. But the phenomenon of the self-alienation of the soul's collectedness requires profounder investigation.

Book Eleven is the book of *time*. Just as the analysis of memory was at once theological and philosophical, so is the analysis of time. It begins with a long prayer to the God of eternity, who knows the man praying and struggling in time. Both the day and the night are his; at his will "the moments flow and pass"; he created heaven and earth in his "eternally abiding" Word (XI, 1–7). It appears as if God with his eternal Word is immutable; on the other hand, his creation is changing, passing from God into the nondivine, but recalled by God's word and made still. "When from changing creatures we learn anything, we are led to Truth that does not change: and there we truly learn, as we stand and hear Him and rejoice with joy for the voice of the bridegroom, returning to the Source of our being. Thus it is that He is the Beginning: unless He remained when we wandered away, there should be no abiding place for our return" (XI, 8). To move out from God, to wander away from God: one is creation, the other is sin. But who can, in terms of our concrete consciousness, distinguish between the two? The analysis of time which now follows assumes the inseparability of the two ideas.

Thinking and loving were described in the previous book as the gathering together of that which is scattered or buried in the memory, in order to achieve a unity of direction (*in-tentio*) or a great discipline (*continentia*). With the eternal Creator there is no need of such self-collectedness. "You are before all the past by the eminence of Your ever-present eternity: and You dominate all the future. . . ." (XI, 13). But the creature does not have its being gathered together; it is "of time," whose chief characteristic is that it "tends towards non-being" (XI, 14). Future time and past time can be long or short, but inasmuch as they are future and past, they do not exist (X, 18). The moment of the present "flees at such lightning speed from being future to being past, that it has no extent of duration at all [*extenditur*] . . . the present has no length" (XI, 15).

If we do, in fact, differentiate between long and short periods of time, we obviously measure them by the feeling we have of them (XI, 16). But as we only ever know the present, which has no extent, how can we measure an extent by that which is un-extended (XI, 21)? Or is it that there are three kinds of present time, "a present of things past, a present of things present, a present of things future," the first as memory, the second as sight, the last as expectation (XI, 20)? But that does not alter the fact that we only measure time "in its passing." Compared to the vast spaces of the memory (X, 24), time appears to be extremely narrow (XI, 21). Once more Augustine turns to prayer to obtain from God the solution of this bewildering problem. It is not to be found in the Aristotelian definition of time as the most constant movement of the heavenly bodies. The difficulty is the soul's experience of duration (XI, 23), which obviously involves extension (*distentio*).[5] This is Augustine's translation of Neoplatonic thought, taken over from Gregory of Nyssa. This extended mode of duration exists even when there is no movement of the heavenly bodies. "Men could experience the duration of time even if they lived in caves, where they could not see the sunrise and sunset" (*Gen. c. Man.* I, 20; *Gen. ad litt. lib. imp.* 8), so that time can be equated with extension (XI, 26).

But what is it that is extended? In the first place, it is clear that that which is strung out must be collected in one place in order to be surveyed and measured, and that this place can only be the soul itself. "Thus it is not the syllables themselves that I measure, for they are now no more, but something which remains engraved in my memory. It is in you, O my mind, that I measure time" (XI, 27). This, however, is only possible if the mind, in its expecting, noting, and remembering, shares in the extension, but at the same time pays constant attention (XI, 28), so that it can gather together what rushes past in the present. As with an hourglass, the one container (of the expected future) empties itself through the neck into the other container (of the remembered past):

Suppose that I am about to recite a psalm that I know. Before I begin, my expectation is directed to the whole of it; but when I have begun, so much of it as I pluck off and drop away into the past becomes matter for my memory; and the whole energy of the action is divided between my memory, in regard to what I have said, and my expectation, in regard to what I am still to say. But there is a present act of attention, by which what was future passes on its way to becoming past (XI, 28).

This extended attention is not the psychological time-span in which duration is experienced directly as a unity, but it is "the whole life of man . . . and likewise the whole history of the human race, of which all the lives of men are parts" (XI, 28). Hence, historical time as human duration represents a homogeneous medium comprehensible by man, while subhuman, animal time (X, 17) and the time of the angels (*Gen. lib. imp.* 8) are also modes of creaturely duration, though measured differently.

This extension of the soul—the prerequisite for its experience of time—the Augustine of the *Confessions* interprets theologically. It is, inseparably, created time and sinful time: "I am divided up in time, whose order I do not know, and my thoughts and the deepest places of my soul are torn with every kind of tumult until the day when I shall be purified and melted in the fire of Thy love and wholly joined to Thee" (XI, 29).

But "Thy mercy is better than lives" [Ps. 62, 4], and behold my life is but a scattering [*distentio*]. "Thy right hand has held me up" [Ps. 17, 36] in my Lord, the Son of Man who is the Mediator in many things and in divers manners—that "I may apprehend by Him in whom I am apprehended" and may be set free from what I once was, following your Oneness: "forgetting the things that are behind" and not poured out upon things to come and things transient, but "stretching forth to those that are before" (not by dispersal but by concentration of energy), "I press towards the prize of the supernal vocation" [Phil. 3, 12–14], where "I may hear the voice of Thy praise" [Ps. 25, 7] and "contemplate Thy delight" [Ps. 26, 4] which neither comes nor passes away (XI, 29).

The quotation from Paul allows us to see the whole structure of extended time as something essentially *past,* and to distinguish the striving toward that which is in front and above—from which the call and pull of grace has already issued—from a future which is in time. What is called by Augustine the "old days," the Epistle to the Ephesians calls "evil days" and urges men to "redeem the time." "What does redeeming the time mean? It means to live through time, even foregoing temporal advantages, if necessary, in such a way that one is striving for and finally attains the eternal" (*Serm.* 16, 2; PL 38, 122). "To sell out time means: if someone quarrels with you, lose something, so as to remain in God and not in a quarrel. If you lose something in order to receive something, then you are buying it; what you have is bought, what you lose is the price" (*Serm.* 167, 3; *ibid.,* 910). Acquire through a loss: that is the disciplined renunciation asked of one, the collecting together of a being scattered through the formless realm of time—*colligas totum quod sum a dispersione et deformitate* (XII, 16).

To descend into time means to "wander away" (XI, 9), to "fall away" (XII, 10), to "flow away from Him into any variation or vicissitude of time" (XII, 15), to "sink" in order to "rise again" through God's grace (XIII, 7). It means, above all, to sink into the abyss which the creature would be by himself, without God's creative and grace-bestowing act, the *profunditas mortis, abyssus corruptionis* (IX, 1) that the man who forgets God becomes (XIII, 21). Thus caught up in time, the soul is ". . . dead by departing from the fountain of life so that it is taken up by the world that passes away and conformed to it" (XIII, 21).[6]

Book Twelve is the book of timeless cosmic principles. Augustine's daring combination of the philosophy and the theology of time brings him to a dangerous edge. It is not far to that theory of Maximus the Confessor which sees creation and the Fall as simultaneous, though not identical: "The moment man comes into being he departs through sin from his true origin" (*Quaest. ad Thal.* 59; PG 90, 613c); "as soon as he starts to exist he bends his mind on sensuality" (*ibid.*, 61; 628A). Augustine does not go to this extreme, however near his ontology of creaturely being brings him to it. In Book Twelve he examines the onto-theological prerequisites for existence in half-buried memory and in scattered time. He finds his speculation has a revolutionary basis in the first verses of scripture. "In the beginning", i.e., in the Logos, "God created heaven and earth," the two principles of creaturely being. The "earth" (later described as formless, void, dark, chaotic, and sealike) is pure matter, that which is almost nothing, whose fall away is stopped only by God's word recalling it, "converting" it so that, cleaving to him, it may receive light and shaped being *(Gen. ad litt.* I, 9). Strictly speaking, only matter is created from nothing; the form is coaxed forth from it by the rays of God's love *(De Gen. c. Man.* I, 10).

But matter is twofold: that from which rational creatures and that from which animals are to come *(ibid.,* 17). The first form of being and each successive one is a summoning back by the creative Word of God; the shapeless acquires form in obedience to this Word. As far as the rational creature is concerned, "Its principle is eternal wisdom, which unchangeably resting in itself never ceases through a hidden inspired call to urge each creature of which it is the principle to turn back to that from whence it came." "For turned away from unchanging truth it drifts in folly and wretchedness" *(Gen. ad litt.* I, 10). Its form of being, therefore, is a dialogue: the divine Word's summons and— by its returning—the creature's answer. But this dialogue, in its origin, is "heaven," which was created in the beginning simultaneously with the "earth"—matter. The latter did not precede it, for pure matter never existed, but was con-created (XIII, 33; XII, 29; *Gen. ad litt.* I, 29) as a basis for creaturely forms. "Heaven" is not to be understood as a mere idea (as with Maximus), but as a reality, which, Augustine goes on to say, is far above the mode of being of time, just as pure matter is far below it (XII, 11). "These two, the one formed from the beginning, the other utterly without form" (XII, 13), are outside the dimension of time.

What is, or rather, who is this "heaven"?[7] Let us listen to Augustine arguing with his opponents:

Perhaps you deny that there exists a sublime creature cohering to the true and truly eternal God with love so pure that, though not co-eternal with Him, yet it does not detach itself and flow away from Him into any variation or vicissitude of time but reposes in the utterly sure contemplation of Him alone: because You, O God, show Yourself to him who loves You as much as You command, and are sufficient unto him, so that he never swerves away from You nor toward self? (XII, 15).

This creature is seen as "created wisdom," which Jesus Sirach says was "created first of all" (Sir. 1, 4), and, thus, is differentiated from uncreated wisdom, which is the eternal Son of God himself, the principle within which heaven and earth are created. It is

created wisdom, that intellectual nature which by the contemplation of light is itself light: for this, though created, is likewise called wisdom: there is as much difference between the Wisdom which creates and the wisdom which is created as between the Light which gives light and the light that is so only by reflection, or between the Justice which justifies and the justice which results from being justified (XII, 15).

Augustine has already described this creature created in the beginning as *intellectualis*. "Although in no way co-eternal with You, the Trinity, it is yet a partaker in Your eternity. It holds its mutability in check because of the joy and delight of contemplating You; and from the moment of its creation it adheres to You with never a lapse and so escapes all the fleeting vicissitudes of time" (XII, 9). This "being" is described as *"Domus Tua,"* "a dwelling-place of Yourself, which ever contemplates Your delight without ever falling away from Your contemplation upon lesser things, a pure mind united in perfect harmony in a binding union of peace with those holy spirits, the citizens of Your City" (XII, 11). It is *"domus tua, quae peregrinata non est"* and thus, as Augustine never tires of repeating, *sine ullo intervallo mutationis*. Although capable of change, it is unchanging, and delights in God's eternity and immutability (XII, 12).

It is "the reasonable and intellectual mind of Your pure City, 'our mother, which is above and is free' [Gal. 4, 26] and 'eternal in heaven' [2 Cor. 5, 1]" (XII, 15). It is "Jerusalem, our one pure homeland" (X, 35). "Jerusalem my Fatherland, Jerusalem which is my mother: and remembering Thee its Ruler, its Light, its Father and Tutor and Spouse . . . my dear mother, where are the first-fruits of my spirit" (XII, 16). "We find no time in it, because it is fitted to gaze always upon Your face nor ever to be turned away: so that it is subjected to no change. . . . It rises beyond all extension and all the fleeting space of time" (XII, 15). It also is created from matter that has been recalled, "but mutability abides in its essence, so that it could fall into darkness and coldness unless it cohered to You in a love so great that Your noonday ever shone upon it and warmed it with its heat" (XII, 15; cf. XIII, 2; *Gen. ad litt.* I, 11).

For this reality, transcending time in the ecstasy of love, "in my pilgrimage may I sigh for you; and I ask of Him who made you that He should possess me too in you, because me too He made. 'I have gone astray like a sheep that is lost' (Ps. 118, 176), but I hope that I may be brought back to You upon the shoulders of My Shepherd, your Builder" (XII, 15). "So that I shall not turn away but shall come to the peace of that Jerusalem, my dear mother, where are the first-fruits of my spirit, from which all certitude comes to me, and there Thou shalt collect from my present scatteredness and deformity all that I am" (XII, 16). Thus, the *Civitas Dei*, which transcends time, is the horizon above, toward which are orientated Augustine's scattered life in memory and time and, hence, the *Confessions* as a whole; so much so, that the following final book overcomes the contrast between the *Civitas Dei* in heaven and Augustine in his temporal pilgrimage. He himself exists only as a member within that part of the *Civitas* which, fallen away or returning home, makes its pilgrimage through time toward its eternal reality. In this dichotomy of falling away and returning home, of sinful alienation and saving economy, lies the kernel of what will finally split the unified vision of Augustine in the *Confessions,* only for it to be re-formed, as we shall see, on a grander scale.

Not for nothing does Augustine, in this twelfth book, after treating of the transcendental *Civitas Dei*, offer a variety of possible interpretations of the first verse of scripture (XII, 24 ff). What does "in the beginning," or "heaven," or "earth" mean? The interpretations so pile up that it is as if a single sentence of God and Moses undergoes the same process of fragmentation as everything else, and even in the same half-clear way. It is a process of breaking up into pieces, since our clouded intellect can only perceive images and reflections of the one truth, and thus one interpretation follows another. But the process involves also a divinely dispensed multiplication of the one truth calling men back, through many different forms, to unity. Augustine pursues patiently, almost obstinately, this breaking down of the sentence, by tracing its hypothetical sense through endless subdivisions and shades of meaning, until, with this vast profusion of bits of meaning before him, he indicates a totally unexpected way of gathering them together:

In this diversity of true opinions, let Truth itself bring harmony and may our God have pity upon us that we may use the law lawfully, for the end of the commandment which is pure charity. . . . But let all of us who, as I confess, see and say truth in these words, love one another and likewise love You, O Fount of truth to those who thirst for truth and not for vanity; and so let us honor Moses Your servant, the dispenser of Your Scripture, as to believe that when under Your inspiration he wrote these words, he had in his mind whatever is most excellent in them by the illumination of truth and their fruitfulness for our profit (XII, 30).

Because truth has fragmented itself, this maximum of excellence can be a connection between or a unified view of the different fragments. Augustine, putting himself in the place of Moses, says "Certainly—and I say this fearlessly and from my heart—if I had to write with such vast authority I should prefer so to write that my words should mean whatever truth anyone could find upon these matters, rather than express one true meaning so clearly as to exclude all others, though these contain no falsehood to offend me" (XII, 31). What is uniformity of meaning when it comes to the eternal word of God, proceeding, as it does, from the home of truth, which transcends time and space? How can exegesis, whose thinking proceeds along the path of temporal, fragmented truth and simplifies in accordance with it, lay down rules for God's word, which speaks from within a totally different unity of truth? And even if Moses or another sacred writer had a fragmentary truth in his mind when he wrote the text, it is not he, but the Holy Spirit of the scripture that truly knows its contents, which are, ultimately, eternal and infinite (XII, 32).[8]

Book Thirteen is the book of the pilgrim Church.[9] It is concerned with the word of revelation which descends into the multiplicity of the "flesh" and through it issues its call. This book ambiguously reads creation history as salvation history, interpreting the first account of creation ecclesiologically. It cannot be called "allegory," because it is not "something different" that is being talked about, but is the same thing. Later Augustine will be analyzing his whole view and dividing it into two sections: cosmology, or account of creation, and the theology of man in history, or account of salvation. His cosmology (as well as anthropology) he will develop in the commentaries on Genesis; his historico-theological account of salvation he will elaborate in the books about the *Civitas Dei*.

The first sign of this differentiation is that the mysterious time-transcending realm of being of the *Confessions* becomes in the Genesis commentaries quite clearly the angelic world of pure spirits (spiritual matter), divided by the *firmamentum* from the whole corporeal world (corporeal matter), whether heaven or earth (*Gen. c. Man.* I, 17). The second sign is that the structure of time (as extended) is ascribed more clearly than before to the good purpose of the good Creator. Already in the *Confessions* he writes:

You made all things: and this not as drawing them out of Yourself in Your own likeness, the form of all things, but producing from nothing a being utterly unlike You and utterly without form, which yet could be formed in Your likeness, by a recourse to Your unity in the measure ordained by You and given to each being according to its kind: and that all things are very good, whether they abide close to You, or else, at various degrees removed from You in time and place, they cause or undergo all the lovely changes of the world (XII, 28).

Hence, he praises constantly the surpassing beauty of the universe and its harmony which is made up of many different things (XIII, 28 ff.). The later commentaries emphasize this: "Certain beings who have moved beyond all temporal mutability persist in the fullest holiness under God; others, however, remain in the mode of their temporal existence in time, inasmuch as the beauty of cosmic time is woven out of the passing away of things, generation succeeding generation" (*Gen. ad litt.* I, 14). The materiality of corporeal things thus acquires its full cosmological aspect. That the distinguishing between day and night is put into the mouth of God himself "means that God leaves nothing unsettled, that even formlessness, which is necessary for things which pass, through change, from one form to another, is part of God's plan; and the decrease and increase of creatures, by means of which they succeed one another, contribute to the beauty of the universe. For night is ordered darkness" (*ibid.*, I, 34). In this completed cosmological conception of time the old idea of the *Confessions* has obviously been modified: the structure of time as such involves an existential alienation, but super-time (the *Civitas-Mater*) embodies a form of duration without this alienation, a continuous resting in chosen love.

Choice is, in fact, essential. It is necessary to be "endlessly and unfailingly united to You" (XII, 11), to have an unchanging will like the angels. They are full of the choosing of God and, thus, of the "renunciation of self" (X, 2; XII, 11): "They ever see Your face, and in Your face they read without syllables spoken in time what is willed by Your eternal will. They read it and they choose it and they love it; they read it without ceasing, and what they read never passes away. For by choice and love they read the very immutability of Your counsels" (XIII, 15). He who loves once and for all transcends time, because whatever the future holds cannot be different from the present or the past: namely, the beloved object, which leaves room for surprises, but not for the end or the alteration of love. This timelessness which the beloved object bestows on the person who chooses it is at the same time that freedom which Augustine never tires of praising as the work of grace.

At this apex of the world, where the creature declares itself for God in an inviolable act of love, the *fiat lux* of the Creator is fulfilled. The timeless day that now supervenes is not simply the first in a series of creation days, but the one day which embraces all others. In the archetypal *conversio* to eternal light all temporal things down through all the lower material orders turn to the light as well, and thus physical light comes into being. When God says, "Let there be light,"

these words are spoken not only soundlessly, but without any movement in time of created mind. They are impressed by the eternal Word on the reasoning mind, and accordingly dark, inchoate, corporeal nature turns to the form of beauty and thus becomes light. It is admittedly difficult to understand how created mind translates these spiritual words, impressed on it by the wisdom of God, to the lower beings, and how these words become, in the temporal beings which are to be formed or directed, movements in time (*Gen. ad litt.* I, 17).

Such a cosmology, however, explains why Augustine in the last book of the *Confessions* always understands the light, which descends into the world of men, in a spiritual and ecclesiastical sense as well.

The Church, here, is two things: ascending *matter*, longing for conversion (i.e., man, who in his aversion from God had turned away, in guilt, to his materiality and is now struggling towards the light), and also *light*, descending from the heavenly Jerusalem of love. Concretely, the Church is the ever-increasing mutual penetration of these two elements, which were "created in the beginning" as "heaven and earth." Together they are "the spiritual and carnal members of His Church" (XIII, 12), because both, living in the same continuing peril, "forgetting the things that are behind, [they stretch themselves] forth to those things that are before" and sigh for the bridegroom above (XIII, 13). Over both is spread the "firmament of the authority of scripture," that earnest of the realm above time given by God's revelation of love to the Church on its pilgrimage (XIII, 15). In the word of God the *sea* (of bottomless passions) is collected and has limits set to it, so that the dry land might appear (the soul thirsting for the loving word of God) (XIII, 16–17). And now begins the work of the awakening of inner life and light in this soul through the influences of the eternal word as embodied in scripture and the Church.

The work of spiritual distinguishing is between darkness and light, flesh and spirit, so that the "earth may bear fruit" and "our light break forth as the morning . . . and . . . we, established in the firmament of Your Scripture, shine like lights in the world" (XIII, 18). The chosen lights are those Christians, who following the precepts of Christ, choose the true light and, abandoning everything else, transfer their treasure and their heart to heaven (XIII, 19). The word, in turn, multiplies itself in the symbols of the sacraments and parables and in preaching, so that, poured out and broken up through the abysses of materiality, it may work as a fisherman's net, gathering us home (XIII, 20–21). Thus, matter is tamed and becomes a "good beast" that serves the spirit. The spirit is created in the image and likeness of God and is therefore in contact with God, and, if it is truly spirit, it commands all the beasts of the earth, i.e., "judges all things."

Now in the earthly *Civitas Dei* there is the distinction between the clergy and the laity, which corresponds to that between the sexes (man leads, woman is led), but in the spiritual man this difference is overcome, just as that between Jew and heathen, slave and freeman (Col. 3, 11) (XIII, 22–23). Again Augustine speaks of the variety of sensuous symbols and of the spiritual aspects of the Church. These minister to the needs of bodily life as well as to the productivity of spiritual life. The blessing of God on growth and increase of life enables a thought to be expressed in many different ways and different languages, and permits, in turn, a parable or word to be understood in many different ways (XIII, 24).

Finally, summing up, Augustine says that this "very good" world was created in Christ.

In Your Word, Your only-begotten Son, were *heaven and earth*, signifying the head and the body of the Church, predestined before all time, when as yet morning and evening were not. Then You began to work out in time what You had predestined outside time, that You might show forth things hidden and bring order into our disorder: for our sins were *over* us and we had gone away from You into the *abyss* of darkness, and *Your good Spirit moved* over us to raise us up in due time. And You *justified the wicked* . . . and gathered [them] together . . . into a society of one mind (XIII, 34).

Here the mystery of the time-transcending origin appears as the total Christ, Head and Body, bridegroom and bride. The world and its falling away were created for the sake of this origin and this goal. The time-transcending contemplation of the "higher Jerusalem" is then at once the "eternal covenant" which surpasses and at the same time justifies time. It is the bridal love in the divine and human being of Christ as the measure of all things (as it will be described in the *Enarrationes in Psalmos*).

The whole conception of these last books of the *Confessions*, while avoiding the danger that emerges with Maximus the Confessor, could fall into another, namely that of Origen. For him, also, there was a real "heavenly Jerusalem" at the beginning, the gathering of all created spirits in the light of love, and a falling away of the spirits through love growing cold. There is the same strange parallelism between creation history and salvation history within the one descending and ascending economy. But the differences outweigh the similarities. For Origen, at least in his systematic early book, the emphasis of the doctrine of man lay in the freedom of neutrality. Hence, he conceived the doubtful idea that after the return of all creation to the original unity of the heavenly Jerusalem there could be continual new moves away from and descents into temporality. For Augustine, the emphasis lies in a love that is beyond all neutrality and cleaves to God, untouched by any temptation. He filled out this idea with the biblical bride "not having spot or wrinkle," and had he lived a few centuries later, he could have made it even more concrete and real with the immaculately conceived virgin mother and bride Mary, as the essence and kernel of the Church. That is why Origen, in spite of his even closer linking of the form of the world and the form of sin, misses the essential point: that the extended structure of time can only be dissolved *vertically*, by being reenfolded in the freedom of transcending love.[10]

The idea of a vertical resolution of the whole structure of time, and hence of history, by a regression to its origin is not new: it corresponds, formally, to the Indian idea of escaping from the revolution of the wheel of time (sansara) into the timelessness of nothingness (nirvana), and to the escape of Gnostic systems out of the emptiness of time into the fullness of God (pleroma). But the essential difference with Augustine is the idea of elective love. God himself is this love, this mercy which predisposes and chooses in ways we cannot understand, and it is for man to respond to this love in an irrevocable act of choice. The philosopher has nothing but a mortal existence which searches for immortal love and, in the form of eros and *philo-sophia*, thirsts for the unattainable, at best something once grasped and now lost, now longed for. The Christian, with Augustine, can know that which is longed for as the reality of agape, which is *theologia*, the self-communication of eternal love, which has received, in grace, a time-transcending, fully true answer. It is the pedal note which lasts through all the confused music of the world's time.

THE UNFOLDING OF HISTORICAL TIME

The Personal Dimension

Conversio *and Creation.* Augustine's understanding of time is strongly influenced by, and at the same time is vastly different from, that of Plotinus, who represents the last of Greek philosophy.

For Plato, time is the moving image of immovable eternity, its best possible imitation, created at the same time as the world and, passing away with it; its motion is circular and governed by astronomical numbers.[11] If space is the extension of that which belongs together, emphasizing distance, time is the pure, complete image of that which is gathered in unity, which is why Plato, as later Augustine, denies the dimension of time to disordered chaos.

Unlike Plato, Aristotle does not understand time primarily from its relationship to eternity, but as the inner form of the process of becoming. Since everything is constantly coming into being and passing away, the superior, comprehensive measure of all these smaller times is found in the revolution of the heavens, which move constantly, but transcend the processes of birth and death and are therefore eternal. Thus, this superior time is beyond time.[12] Every moment, as the midway point between "was" and "will be," is by the same token the eternal now of this time-eternity.[13] But thinking, as the self-comprehending of unity, is beyond time. On the other hand, the question arises of how, and indeed why, movement comes to exist. The answer to this lies in Plato's idea of eros: the eternal (God) moves the sphere, and hence everything within it, as a beloved, yearned-for object.

Thus, Plotinus, building on both classical philosophers, is able to ask the question neither of them did, namely, whence comes the distance between the eternal and the temporal, and what is its measure? Instead of just setting one order off against another as original and copy (Plato) or as eternally moved and unmoved (Aristotle), Plotinus asks about that movement which has caused the distance between the eternal and the temporal. In the One there is no time. In the mind an eternal movement from thought-content to thought-content is possible, but always within the total presence of truth; there is no resistance to be overcome; the mental movement is an expression of pure plenitude and, hence, transcends time. It is with the soul and its own particular movement that the problem of distance from the eternal arises. "Its busy nature, which desired to be independent and belong to itself, chose to seek more than the present. Thus, it started moving, and so did time also, and they set out toward that which was after, that which was later, that which was not the same." The growth of life, compared with the gathered contemplation of the mind, consists of an extravagant latitudinal pouring out of the One and the loss of itself through its progressive advance.

At this point Plotinus catches up with his master Plato again: this pouring into a void, which is the distancing activity of the soul seeking independence, is what makes time an "image" of eternity.[14] Moreover, the (horizontal, cosmological) circular movement of Aristotle's sky is now made dependent on a (vertical, onto-theological) circular movement of the soul which has "fallen away" from the One and is striving to get back to it.[15] For the quest and longing created through the soul's "falling away" and entering time can turn only to the One. The Platonic and Aristotelean eros is immanent in all movement here as well; but as "longing upwards," through turning round (*conversio*), it clearly acquires the sense of a return home to a lost origin.[16] Time is the existential distance between departure and return, but distance within the same continuum. Plotinus rejects any idea of creation as the free positing of the *other*. That is why the returning *conversio* is performed by the mind's reflection, or rather, by contemplation's grasping in reflection unreflected unity. At this point Augustine, the Christian, steps in to give Plotinus' whole scheme of time a basically different character.

He takes over, in particular, his view that the dimension of time is limited to noneternal being and that its origin lies in the soul and in its distancing itself from its eternal origin and goal. For Plotinus as for Augustine the distance is twofold: vertical and horizontal. Vertical, because the soul in its "fall" measures in itself the distance between its origin-goal (eternity) and its present moment in time; it measures it by the paradox of the memory, that remembers the origin, but only as lost and buried, i.e., remembers it only through the nonoriginating medium of passing time. Horizontal, because the soul, having lost its origin, remains in an essential, ineluctable vacancy and vanity: the transient, evanescent quality of every moment in time is one of time's chief characteristics. Augustine cannot, however, take over Plotinus' idea of the identity within which all distances (between the One, the mind, and the soul) are contained. The world is created, and so is man who is also personal. This is an idea not found in Plotinus, whose only substitute is the idea of a temporarily assumed personification or "role." If the creature is personal and faces the infinite and eternal person of God, then the relationship of alienation and return cannot be a matter of mere intellectual forgetting and remembering, or of questing activity and longing turning back, but primarily a matter of love and faithfulness.[17]

In Augustine's writings the ancient biblical concept, propounded also by Origen, reappears: "Thus the soul is guilty of fornication when she turns from You and seeks from any other source what she will nowhere find pure and without taint unless she returns to You" (II, 6). If the distance is taken as a rejection of eternal love, a second concept, which constitutes a major theme of the *Confessions,* necessarily follows. For the first time in the anti-Pelagian controversy it is drawn out of the heart of the faith: one who has rejected the love of God can only return to loving through the free loving-kindness of God through which he will feel a nostalgia to return to love.

But that is not the only change that Christian thought brings to the idea of creation. For Plotinus, time is basically the measure of the distance from the One—of the alienation and return—while for Augustine the distance from the Creator to the creature is itself a good creation of God. In this view of creation, time is neither evil nor sinful. Time results from the radical not-being-God of the creature and, for Augustine, that means that it is rooted in its (bodily or spiritual) materiality. Time is the principle of total differentiation from God and all similarity to God originates in what calls the creature back to God, the power of the Logos drawing form out of material substance. Precisely because matter is not in opposition to God—which Augustine vigorously maintained against the Manicheans—and indeed is the definite basis of all the good created works of God, creaturely time is good in itself and does not express a fall. The creature called from the realm of nothingness into being by God has this longing for the source of being, the transcendent (and, therefore, extratemporal) being of God.

This kind of ec-static existence seems to fit equally well into both Plotinus' and Augustine's idea of the unending but temporal being, but their understanding of it is different. For Plotinus, it is a return of mystic ecstasy into identity; for Augustine, it is cleaving to God in love: prayer is worship, thanks, and supplication. Only as prayer is creaturely love combined with eternal, divine love does it transcend its temporality, itself, and even its own soul, in order to cleave to God, beyond all possibility of change, in absolute love. But such transcendence, as Augustine grasps ever more clearly, is the work of the unfathomable elective grace of God and is the answer it elicits.[18]

And yet, both before and after the *Confessions*, time is also for Augustine the medium of the good and beautiful deeds of God. Music is resounding nothingness; into the pure nonidentity of time the wonderful works of measure, number, and order are written, whose very slipping away into nothing is the source of their beauty. Even more important is the observation that language, which is the self-revelation of a person, is committed, like music, to this medium of nothingness. It must flow away, syllable by syllable, until the meaning of what is said, distilled like an essence out of what has vanished, can be understood by the listener.

With language, however, as the free communication of persons, when and as they like, the temporal moment acquires an historical character. Something unique in time—the person—expresses itself uniquely through language as word or as deed, and creates something unique in time. Thus time, even as a void, not created or controlled by the creature, offers the necessary "space" in which mind can clearly reveal, express, and perfect itself. Even the indeterminate character of an empty extension is the occasion for self-determination; the boundless is the occasion for that positive setting of bounds which is the nature of history. With Plotinus there was no history of any philosophic importance, neither earthly nor mythical.[19] With Augustine all events between God and the world are written into the medium of history. The conversion of the individual, Augustine himself, is historical; the wanderings of the *Civitas Dei* through the medium of transient time will also be historical.[20]

And history not only occurs between the eternal and earthly spirits; the beings of nature also share, according to their fashion, in historicalness. The biblical account of the six days of creation presents, in figurative terms, the history of nature. When Augustine, as a natural philosopher, endeavors to understand its meaning, he does not need to grant the whole element of the time-reckoning to a mythical use of language. Indeed, God is himself above time, and time exists only within the world (as Plato had already stated in the *Timaeus*). And so God creates everything at once. That does not mean, however, only that the

First Cause is above time and "simultaneous" with any moment of the world's time, but also that God was able to place in the beginning the bases of everything's being, which lay in matter at first "invisible, potential according to their causes" (*Gen. ad litt.* 6, 10), in order to come to the light of realization "in the due succession of time" (*Gen. ad litt.* 5, 45).

The history of nature thus acquires an analogous share in actual spiritual history, and when man is expressly described as being hidden in the *rationes seminales,* then it is perfectly possible to represent the history of nature as an embryonic anthropology. However, although Augustine saw second causes as thus endowed with power by the Creator, he did not want to rob the latter of the freedom to realize his work anew at any moment. The unfolding of the world from its causal seeds is rather, for him, only the basis for a true, freely conducted historical dialogue between God and creature.[21]

If that is so, then the finiteness of time is also implied. It results from the finiteness of creaturely being, and is, in fact, identical with it. The finite creature moves *before* God, but it cannot move anywhere except out from God, who created it, and therefore back to God, who is its delimiting measure and calls it home again. That the finite creature is measured by eternal being implies directly that its time is also measured by timeless eternity. With its being the creature is also given a path, a necessarily finite, seminal *ratio,* which unfolds, and a sense of direction, which engages it in purposive movement toward a goal. And according as the being advances, its duration unfolds and its time comes into existence. In order to continue this time, the creature is given being by the eternity of God, which at once posits and pervades it, leaves it free and delimits it. The transcendence of this eternity immanent in time permits it to make its presence felt in it at any time as the "other," the eternal, and to reproduce a dialogue between time and itself.

This secret of time's being held, transcendently *and* immanently, by eternity (which not only lets the temporal unroll, but also accompanies it in its development of sense and direction as an "ordering providence") makes the antinomies of finite time appear no more important than the antinomies of finite, creaturely being itself. How can the latter return to God, from whence it came, without becoming itself God? How can the analogy of being prove a true upward movement (*ana*) to God (as *ano*), and yet remain eternally ranged before God as measured from above? The first aspect shows creaturely time as vertical and cyclic. But in the second its true freedom and independence emerge, which allow it to return, personally and lovingly, to its origin as its goal and to bring itself, as the fruit of its pilgrimage. Finite time is then truly, in the words of Irenaeus, "the ripening of the fruit of immortality" (*C. Haer.*, 4, 5, 1). One can see that the ancient myth of (horizontal) cyclic time as an eternal return is, in fact, a pallid version of the true nature of time. Each completed cycle marks the track of finite time, but with its quantitative repetition the unique vertical movement away from the infinite God back to the infinite God is transferred to the horizontal and thus into empty, hopeless infinity.

This whole consideration of creation and time, however, remains unreal insofar as we know both only in the modality of falling away and being brought back through grace. Or perhaps not? That first glorious creature, which the *Confessions* described as the heavenly *Civitas Dei*, our mother and home, has never fallen away. Dark and temporal at its root, because drawn from matter, it lives above itself (like all creatures) in the eternal light. This vision is enough to be able to say that for Augustine even the "natural" order of creation, if freed from guilt and fall, cannot exist otherwise than in a vertical relation to eternity. Even here the nothingness of the creature in time exists only because of its loving suspension in the eternal. The possible fruit which it produces during time ripens in order to be bestowed at the same place in the eternal kingdom of God. Here, too, horizontally extended time exists only in relation to vertical time.

Sinful Time and the Time of Grace. The autobiography and the concluding reflections of the *Confessions* have shown also how indissolubly the experience of nothingness is bound up with sinful alienation from God. The memory, lost in the night of created being (I, 6), cannot recall any youthful dawn, however faint, that is not already marred and darkened by this alienation (I, 7). Sin, which "I do not want [to do]" (Rom. 7, 15), stands like a strange power between man and God. It was the overpowering sense of this which drove Augustine into Manicheism; but a dualistic metaphysics does not solve the problem. He gets to grips with it in the eighth book. The division is closer and more interior: it lies in the very heart of the will. It is "a sickness of the soul to be so weighted down by custom that it cannot wholly rise even with the support of truth. Thus there are two wills in us, because neither of them is entire" (VIII, 9). "It was I who willed . . . , I who was unwilling. It was I. I did not wholly will, I was not wholly unwilling. Therefore I strove with myself and was distracted by myself. This distraction happened to me though I did not want it" (VIII, 10). "My two wills, one old, one new, one carnal, one spiritual, were in conflict and in their conflict wasted my soul" (VIII, 5).

It is just these ideas of "old" and "new" which are to be significant for his experience of time. Already his heart is more in that which he approves and yet does not do than in that which he does and no longer approves of. Already the call of God, "Sleeper, awake!," is so strong that to hesitate and continue to lie lower, agreeable though it is, makes one feel uneasy. That which he had firmly held on to is already vanishing into the past; it is gone and finished with. That which is to come has not yet been grasped, but it is a future that is approaching so quickly now that it is already coming into the present. In this experience of the inevitable approach of conversion, he has a completely new experience of time: the whole person, turned away from God and turned sinfully towards creation, experiences itself in its nothingness and vanity as something belonging totally (together with its present and future) to the past. And the whole of the present time offered by God's grace to the convert comes in and takes the place of this time, which has passed away, as a true, continuously arriving present. This present, however, is no longer the fleeting one of natural time; it is, in a quite new sense, the divine, i.e., eternal, present, offered as an earnest and a pledge. In converting a sinner, grace also changes his time: his sinful time sinks into the past, the "grace" time given to him rises into the present. This is the point at which Paul (and, following him, Augustine) distinguishes between the "old" and the "new," the "flesh" and the "spirit," the "outer" and the "inner" man: "Though our outer nature is wasting away, our inner nature is being renewed every day" (2 Cor. 4, 16).[22] This temporal "every day" refers to the two things: to grow old and to be renewed are one process, which can be observed, indirectly, in creaturely time. Something changes within the uniformity of time, something is achieved: "For salvation is nearer to us now than when we first believed; the night is far gone, the day is at hand" (Rom. 13, 11–12).

This is the breaking in of the time that God has fashioned for man into the lost time that the sinner has fashioned for himself. It is the reconstitution and surpassing of the original verticality of time, which neither affects the structure of creation time as suspended in nothingness, nor simply cancels out the structure of sinful time, but rather transforms it. Sinful time, in contrast to creation time, leads sooner to death. The *Civitas Dei* will speak of this immanence of death in every moment of corrupted time in the same terms in which the *Confessions* had spoken of the ungraspable fleetingness of the present in the stream of time. When does one die? As long as one is moving toward death one has not died; but neither does the dead man die. Death is a point as indivisible as the point of the present between the future and the past. And "you cannot say that someone is dying because you cannot be dying and living at the same time." Or can you? Namely, inasmuch as death dwells in every moment of mortal life. "For what else takes place in the single days, hours and moments, which hurry past, until dying has stopped, and now the time after death begins, whereas the time before life disappeared was a time in death? . . . Was not man simultaneously in life and in death?" (*Civ. Dei,* XIII, 10).

It is the sense of time in the *Enarrationes in Psalmos* which imperceptibly and inevitably passes from the sense of creation time to the sense of sinful time. If time is here first of all a Platonic "image and as it were shadow of eternity" (in Ps. 9, 7), with its fragility emphasized (Ps. 62, 6), it is that which does not store itself, but slips away (Ps. 65, 12), that which comes, not so as to be there, but so as not to be there (Ps. 89, 6), i.e., that which is a "stream" (Ps. 65, 11, Ps. 143, 2), a "rushing torrent" (Ps. 57, 16, Ps. 123, 6–7), "rivers of Babylon" (Ps. 136, 1), "breakers" (Ps. 129, 1), "sea" (Ps. 142, 11). Life in mortal time is altogether "sickness" and "corruption" (Ps. 102, 6); "everywhere there is weariness, everywhere weakness, everywhere decay." Hence, the psalm says, "My soul thirsts for you, as manifoldly also does my flesh" (Ps. 62, 5–6). And everything that we long for from the future we must also fear, because as it comes it supplants us, just as pampered children, when grown up, ask their parents to retire from the scene (Ps. 127, 15).

This devouring "abyss" of time (Ps. 103, 6) is not closed by grace. Man dies just the same. Only the sense of time and death is changed. Here the personal dimension of time transcends itself and opens into the social and universal. For grace does not change the meaning of death (and hence of time) from the outside, but rather from the inside, by becoming flesh and descending into death. Only in this way, through Jesus Christ, is there offered to the individual man who is converted a salvation which is something different from a "flight from time."

The Universal Dimension

It is surprising and yet logical that the personal time dialectic of the *Confessions* should be seen ultimately, *yet logically,* within the framework of a social and universal view of time. *Memoria* does not lead to the remembering of a prenatal existence in heaven (although the origin of the soul remained an unsolved problem for Augustine all his life), but to the heavenly *Civitas Dei.* It is the pivot of individual existence; to know this heavenly mother is to understand oneself. She is the unbroken unity of men with God, that unity which existed for a moment in Adam, before it was shattered by sin. Augustine has not hesitated to adduce the myth of the scattered and re-collected original man in order to d:scribe the cosmic dimensions of fall and salvation.

He "shall execute judgment and justice in the earth." Not just one part, for he has not redeemed one part only; he shall judge the whole, for he has ransomed the whole. You have heard the gospel, where it says that at his return "he shall gather his chosen ones from the four winds." He collects all the chosen ones from the four winds, that is, from everywhere in the world. For Adam means, as I have often told you, "the whole earth," according to the Greek. His name consists of four letters: A,D,A and M . . . Anatole is the east, Dysis the west, Arctos the north and Mesembria the south. . . . Thus, Adam is spread over the whole earth. Once he was in a single place, then he fell, was split into fragments and filled the earth. But the mercy of God collected the pieces from everywhere, melted them in the fire of love and fused together again what had been broken. The artist is able to complete this work, let no one be discouraged. True, the work is great, but remember how great the artist is himself. He who once fashioned it has refashioned it, and he who formed it has reformed it.[23]

The *Confessions* had already mentioned this fall of Adam, from out of whom the whole bitter sea of restless, surging humanity flowed forth (XIII, 20),[24] a pouring out which only another Adam will again gather in, by means of another healing influence: *"tamquam in uno quodam nomine diffuso orbe terrarum, et succrescente per volumina saeculorum."*[25] Until then, however, the world time is smitten unto death by the sickness of being, which was not part of creation time: *"morbo quodam ... factum in illis est ut illa in qua creati sunt stabilitate amissa, per mutabilitates aetatum irent ad mortem."*[26] The experience of the essential "oldness of days," that quality of being past which pertains to them, becomes an experience of the whole of humanity: *"Ecce veteres posuisti dies meos"* (Ps. 38, 6, according to the Septuagint).[27]

Here one could adduce the doctrine of the primeval state held by Gregory of Nyssa and the young Augustine, according to which man in paradise would not have reproduced himself at all, or else done so in a nonsexual manner unknown to us.[28] It is jejune to dismiss this tentative speculation as Gnosticism or Manicheism, as puritanical fear of the flesh, for it is based on quite different, profound, and exact considerations. Sex means death, as the whole natural order both before and outside Paradise shows. To deny paradisal man death, but leave sex, is at least as incredible a speculation as the other. In the time-transcending *Civitas Dei*, which cleaves to God, love is such that there is neither marrying nor being given in marriage (Luke 20, 35), for the whole order of marriage belongs to temporality. Hence, the lovers in the Song of Solomon comprise a self-sufficient unity, which is not disturbed by purposive considerations of offspring. If the question is raised of why marriage does not belong to the guiltless natural order, then it may be equally asked whether and in what sense death belongs to this guiltless natural order, if, as according to Paul, it came into the world through sin? The lines of such a natural order are nowhere to be discovered, which is all the more painful. Thus, the shape of the inner, most intimate structure of our being is undecipherable.

Here one must remember that Augustine presents no elaborate theory of the original *Civitas Dei,* but only, as it were, makes dotted lines converge above: the idea of that pure point above time is developed from Hebrews 12, 22–24:

But you have come to Mount Zion and to the city *(Civitas)* of the living God *(Dei),* the heavenly Jerusalem, and to innumerable angels in festal gathering, and to the assembly of the first-born who are enrolled in heaven, and to a judge who is God of all, and to the spirits of just men made perfect, and to Jesus, the mediator of a new covenant, and to the sprinkled blood that speaks more graciously than the blood of Abel.

This *Civitas Dei* is thus the "heavenly Jerusalem," that Paul calls our mother (Gal. 4, 26), the bride and wife of the Lamb (Apoc. 21, 9); since she is "without blemish" and "glorious" (Eph. 5, 27) she has her true symbol in Mary. But she is equally the assembly of the first-born, that is, of the countless hosts of angels, of which a part have fallen from a duration, not describable in terms of time, into another equally indefinable duration. Since these spirits are described by Paul as the rulers of the cosmos and its elements, the material temporal power could have been disrupted and destroyed by them right at the beginning, even before the fall of man in Paradise.

The first human pair, protected in Paradise by their innocence, had shortly to come into contact with tempting disorder—in the symbol of the snake. In their state of innocence the first men (as the "heavenly Adam") were of the same order as the "assembly of the first-born" and all predestined beings, as "those whose names are written in heaven," and as "souls of the perfect just ones." These are (as in Eph. 1, 3–14) considered as having a vocation transcending time; they were chosen "before the foundation of the world, (to be) holy and blameless before him." This present state of being is a presence in eternity, not affected by "being there yet" or by "not being there yet," but at the same time is a being chosen among the chosen and the loved—"Jesus, the mediator of a new covenant" and his blood "that speaks more graciously than the blood of Abel" (Heb. 12, 24; Eph. 1, 7).

The Church, the angels, Adam, those predestined: they are all in heaven[29] as chosen in him, as redeemed through him, as married to him. So much so that Paul (1 Cor. 15, 44 ff.) sees Adam as on the earth in order that the "last Adam," as the "man from heaven," may be given the decisive, time-transcending task of reunion. But this last Adam is already always the one who has bled, "the Lamb slain before the foundation of the world" (Apoc. 13, 8) in an "eternal redemption" (Heb. 9, 12), and who speaks louder with the event of his blood than any murderous events within time (the "blood of Abel"), as they were judged by "God, the judge of all."

Thus, the sequence of events within time—fall, sin, lost being, and lost time—is always already contained in the first predestined man, who is also the last Adam, the Alpha and Omega of all times, and expressly in his blood, which blots out everything else, that is, in his passage through time and death. The time-transcending point as the point of Christ lies not only "over," "before," and "after" time; it transcends it in such a way that it simultaneously contains it. It contains it, however, not in the way that God's transcendence is immanent in all creatures; rather, by the event of his incarnation, death, and resurrection he has taken time into himself. This descent of the Son into the eternally "beneath" of the earth, in order to ascend from there into the eternally "above" of all the heavens (Eph. 4, 10), is the comprehensive measure of all vertical time, that measure within which alone every individual reversal of time (*conversio*) can take place. This is necessary for the establishment of true, fulfilled time.

Through Christ's coming in the flesh,[30] his becoming present in time, he brings plenitude into a void, which he fills with future time, without destroying it as a time form, but by making its emptiness and its cause—sin—a thing of the past. This is the ultimate result of his descent into the "underworld," which thus (as rightly sensed by Schelling, although speculatively obscured) was made an "eternal past."[31] That element which cannot be built into the synthesis of Christ, that which is discarded once and for all in each individual life and in the total life of the world, hence that which is irrevocably lost—this never-again is the true past. Those who once built their present on this past now begin their lament:

And the kings of the earth, who committed fornication and were wanton with her, will weep and wail over her when they see the smoke of her burning. . . . And the merchants of the earth weep and mourn for her, since no one buys their cargo any more. . . . "The fruit for which thy soul longed has gone from thee, and all thy dainties and thy splendor are lost to thee, never to be found again!" . . . And the sound of harpers . . . and trumpeters, shall be heard in thee no more; and the light of a lamp shall shine in thee no more; and the voice of bridegroom and bride shall be heard in thee no more. . . . (Apoc. 18, 9 ff.).

That which thus sinks irrevocably into the past is that which cannot be chosen by God. It is evil; it is like the great whore of Babylon who is the epitome of everything which has whored away from God's love and, *being* alienation, is by her nature not capable of turning back. Therefore, it ends in "outer darkness" (Matt. 8, 12), whose burning can only be observed "from afar" (Apoc. 18:10, 15, 17). That which is not irrevocably gone can obviously be brought back, even if it is past in time: it can be brought back in the vertical time-reckoning of Christ, even if, in empty, horizontal time it seems irrevocable. Thus, Israel, if it repents, is promised "restoration" to its original condition (Jer. 15, 19). Peter refers to this in his discourse to the Jews, when he promises them the "times of restitution of all things" and with it the return of Christ (Acts 3, 21). The "future of God" in the incarnation of Christ does not mean that God, descending into the stream of time, was swept away by it like everything else coming and going in time. If he is truly in time (so that he must suffer and die), he is still the eternal one, who enters time, and thus brings his eternity with him into time and transience. But eternity is incommensurable with temporality; hence, even when it has come, it retains the temporal mode of that which is to come, of the future. The incommensurable state of being offered to temporal creatures by the one eternally coming and present is expressed in the biblical idea of "today."

"Today" is the present of vertical salvation time, which "in itself" is presence for man and the world, but is taken hold of by man and the world undergoing *conversio* and must be changed into a "for-itself." The vertical "today" is suspended in and over the horizontal "now"; it cannot be anchored in it as something future which is at hand (for horizontal time passes away and cannot be anchored), nor can it be regarded as something timelessly suspended above it, for the "future of God" is not a timeless idea, but an event of divine freedom breaking in. This "today" (Heb. 3, 7; 4, 7), this "now," this "acceptable time" (2 Cor. 4, 2; Is. 49, 8), can be grasped by transferring one's heart there "where neither moth nor rust consumes and where thieves do not break in and steal" (Matt. 6, 20). This "sursum corda" is the renewed practice of cleaving in love to God, where the heavenly Jerusalem lives. It is cleaving to the one being ascending, Christ, and only vertically is the shattered old Adam integrated into the all-comprising new one.[32] The *conversio* of a man as a reversal of the direction of his time—that which Max Scheler has described as "repentance and rebirth"—is an act which is understandable in terms of the philosophy of religions, because it is truly, as Augustine's *Confessions* show, an act of man as such. But this insight into the reversability of time and of the judgment upon us which it involves is only understandable if it is on God's initiative; otherwise God would be compelled to forgive because man repents.

We must, however, at this point, remember that the reversal of historical time took place through grace in the person of Christ, who is not a "principle," but a single "man" (1 Tim. 2, 5) who, as such, entered sinful time with all its inner futility. Vanity had to affect his earthly existence and work, not only as the common lot of man, but especially in that, obedient unto death, he had to descend to the bottom of the abyss of time. Thus, it was not a case of reversing futile time, as it were, bit by bit in order to impart significance to it bit by bit; rather he had to take upon and into himself the total passage through the absolute past in order to achieve from the other end the reversal of the whole. Apropos of this the Fathers occasionally say that Christ appeared when the world's guilt had reached its fullest measure.[33] Only in regard to the full measure of the alienation from God's eternal present, to the full measure of going astray into the eternal past, does the Savior live through transient time. His steadfastness in the unsteady is his filial faithfulness to the father: the important thing is not that it is eternity intervening in time, but that it is obedience through love. The point of greatest antithesis—between sinful time run to its end and spotless eternity—becomes the place of the most intimate loving union between Father and Son. Thus, the antithesis between the eternal God and the temporal creature also achieves its ultimate significance. Thus, creation time and even sinful time become, through the freest grace of God, the vessel of the self-manifestation of eternal life. What it truly means to transcend time by cleaving to God is seen for the first time in the life of Jesus, and it is made possible by him for us. Because it is the act of elective love, it eludes mythical or Gnostic interpretation and is an essential element of a Christian understanding of time.

Choice of the beloved and of his will, choice out of pure, unconditional love in the frankest, most boundless *yes* (2 Cor. 1, 18–20), is, when the beloved is God, elevation to absolute freedom: nothing can pass away which does not remain forever; nothing can come but that which was always there, freely given.

And all is rapturously crowned when this choice can be the answer to having been already chosen oneself in love; then the mutual sinking into each other becomes itself eternity. M. F. Sciacca distinguishes here correctly between *scelta* (choice as deciding between various alternatives) and *elezione* (choice as a unique, unrepeatable election).[34] The latter is what Augustine described as *legere-eligere-diligere*, which constitutes for him the fundamental act of the gathering Logos. In the Logos become man, however, it is a gathering election in the "nothingness" of futility, thus a persistence (*con-stantia*), patient enduring (*patientia*), remaining here below, while everything dissolves or collapses above one[35]—all this as a loving "to the end" (John 13, 1).

From this point Christ, living in time, is able to state his christological present: "Before Abraham was, I *am*" (John 8, 58). The other *ego-eimi* texts are to be read in the light of this one: John 8, 24; 8, 28; 13, 19. His present is not only the abstract existence of eternity in time, but also eternity won from time: the planting of eternity through elective love in the heart of futile time running towards death. The uniqueness of Christ's loving choice also makes his "now" and "today" unique: in this the *hapas* of the New Testament (Heb. 6, 4; 9: 7, 26, 27; 10, 2; 1 Pet. 3, 18) and *ephapas* (Rom. 6, 10; Heb. 7, 27; 9, 12; 10, 10) is distinguished from all Platonic prefigurations of the idea *esaiphens* as eternity breaking vertically into time. It is the presence of incomprehensible freedom, but of a freedom through love, which, it is true, disposes in advance of its own future, but only inasmuch as his own being was "given" and "poured out" in sacrifice (Luke 22, 19–20). His sacrifice disposes freely of the sinner's past in order to place him, through forgiveness of sins and awakening from the dead, in a new present time; it disposes, in fact, of his own total past in death in order through the resurrection to "take his life again" (John 10, 18). Now at last the "descent" of Christ into time is complete; now he can train men for eternity through his own faithful heart. Thus, the problem of

the analogy—with the ambiguity of *ana*, which seemed to have
two irreconcilable meanings—is solved. It now becomes clear
how time, even lost time, is able to flow into eternity, not by its
being destroyed, but by its being fulfilled, and not only from
without and from above, but also by contributing itself from
within to its own eternal fulfillment.

Through Christ "Jerusalem" itself has also come down into
time. He is himself essentially this Jerusalem: he, with his bride,
whom he lets pass out from within him, and who cleaves to him
through grace; he as the Head and she the Body, the Head in
heaven and the Body on its earthly pilgrimage. The last book of
the *Confessions* had already introduced this transformation of
Jerusalem into the Church; the books of the *Civitas Dei* describe
the nature and the destiny of the kingdom of God on its pilgrimage. It is a pilgrimage because the time up to death is the
vessel of salvation time. But time up to death cannot be dammed
up, and the kingdom of God "grows" through this void, not
visibly, but through removing treasure and laying it up in the
kingdom above, away from moth, rust, and thief. Therefore, it is
impossible to apply to the kingdom and the Church the idea of a
temporal evolution. The kingdom is built up in the vertical and
the essentially invisible, and the whole ethics of Christ and the
apostles is a training in enduring patience, which, through all
earthly doings and workings, knows the profound necessity of
such removals.

The life of the Church is like walking on the spot; it is journey-
ing in the darkness of faith (John of the Cross), in that subterranean chiaroscuro which renders vain all calculations of progress. The constantly self-realizing point of intersection between
transient time and salvation time causes the duration of the
Church to appear as an ever-present dramatic event which, precisely because of the indwelling of the eternal in it, can never
be seen as a whole. How pregnant of events this time is is shown
in the powerful images of the Apocalypse. But all these images
are suspended within the point of intersection itself and are

neither exclusively horizontal (as a description of the dimension of world history) or exclusively vertical (as a mere paraphrase of an eternal conflict between heaven and earth). The very fact of its figurative nature is evidence of this strange suspension.

Augustine sees the kingdom of God on its pilgrimage within this suspension. To be in historical time means to journey in a foreign land. Not because God has not providentially impregnated everything with his presence, but because the form of temporality itself, by its lack of unity, is an absence of the creature from unified eternity. Its positive side is that it is the place wherein movement forward takes place and where hope extends itself. Yet, as the place where movement away is constantly renounced, it is negative, and this, seen from the point of view of God, is judgment. It is a continuous judgment on that which is insufficient in order to be the guide of that which is sufficient. Thus, in immanent judgment itself grace is always immanent, which allows us to leave behind everything that seems mere appearance, according to the law of "Decay and Growth." This grace is so deeply interwoven in the structure of time that one almost thinks he can come upon it without needing to look back to the grace-bestowing judge; and yet, as it shines through, it manifests even more profoundly his hidden, eternal present.

Just because the constant removal of time is grace and has salvation significance, the journey in the void must also have significance in terms of direction. Thus, it prepares a harvest which must be gathered. This necessity implies final value. Two things become final simultaneously: the emptiness of time as death and the significant element in time, which is its being enfolded by the eternal. Both—death and being enfolded—are inseparably immanent in passing time. And so the wonderful thing is that the harvest cannot be brought in unless time stands still, and that in the harvest the entire salvation content of the time-*form* is also enfolded. The image of ripening remains only an image, for in one sense time never ripens, and the fruit piling up with the judge is not to be judged simply by the visibility and the extent of that which is ripening. It ripens away from itself toward God, but in this secret openness it *does* ripen.

The just men of the Old Testament, who lacked this openness to the eternal, had to be satisfied with the earthly image and died, if grace sustained them, "in a good old age and full of years" (Gen. 25, 8; 35, 29; Job 27, 17). For the Christian this fullness no longer exists, neither for the individual, nor for the Church on its pilgrimage. Augustine denies the Church any final state on earth that would be qualitatively different from its other states.[36] The eternal does not become any more revealed in the course of time; the form of time reveals it only in its hiddenness. And one cannot lay hold on eternity in time by leaps out of time, but by obedience and acceptance of the renunciation which is imposed upon him. Blessed are the poor in spirit, for theirs is the kingdom of heaven; blessed are the meek, for they shall inherit the earth.

Notes

1 From *The Confessions of Saint Augustine,* in the translation of F. J. Sheed, copyright 1943, Sheed & Ward, Inc., New York.

2 Cf. *De Gen. c. Man.* I, 17, on the separation of the upper from the lower waters by the firmament: *et ideo fortasse supercoelum esse dicuntur aquae invisibles* (i.e., the realm of angels), *quae paucis intelliguntur non locorum sedibus, sed dignitate naturae superare coelum. . . .*

3 Including these last books of the *Confessions,* Augustine wrote four commentaries on the beginning of Genesis. In the following a number of phrases are taken from the later commentaries if they express the ideas of the *Confessions* in a particularly concise way.

4 With a correction brought forth by Walter F. Otto (*Der Mythos und das Wort,* in *Das Wort der Antike,* 1962, 357): "The original meaning is that of 'choice' (and, therefore, of gathering), also of paying attention, of thinking it over, of considering it."

5 The central importance of *distentio* in Augustine's conception of time and of its being overcome by *intentio* is well treated in G. Quispel's *Zeit und Geschichte im antiken Christentum, Eranos-Jahrbuch,* 1951, 115, 140.

6 The picture of the turning "wheel of birth" is known in the bible ("the cycle of nature," Jas. 3, 6). The origin of this concept could be Indian or Orphean. G. Kittel (*Die Probleme des palästinens, Spätjudentums and das Urchristentum,* 1926, 141–168) thinks it could have spun off from late Jewish

thinking and been passed on harmlessly to the Christian authors: it retains in that case its existential coloring which throughout cannot be disposed of as "mythical"; we find it again in Augustine as well as in Origen.

7 For this form of the question, cf. my essay *"Wer ist die Kirche?"* in *Sponsa Verbi., Theol. Skizzen,* II, 1961.

8 Modern exegesis, more *nolens* than *volens,* more *nesciens* than *sciens,* has honored again these exegetic principles of Augustine by demonstrating the various perspectives within a single text (e.g., von Rad with Genesis) which even at the time when it was first written down already contained different strata of meaning and, as well as that, in the course of time can acquire further shades of significance. Augustine would not have been surprised by these discoveries.

9 Cf. the newest study: A. Hull: *Die welt in Zeichen bei Augustin, Religions phänomenologische Analyse des 13. Buches der Confessiones,* 1963.

10 Already in Plato the yearning for the lost origin had the characteristics of *eros;* in Gnosticism all thinking is conceived as nostalgia (cf. Norden: *Agnostos Theos,* 4th ed., 1956; Reitzenstein: *Mysterienreligionen,* 3rd ed., 1927). V. Jankelevitch shows to what extent this longing can influence a philosopher even today (*L'Eternité et la première Impureté,* in *Archivio di Filosofia,* 1959, 25–34; *La Purification et le Temps, ibid.,* 1958, 11–17). Augustine purifies and exalts the yearning of *eros* to *eros* for the original *agape,* which is not only, as with the Gnostics, feminine as *sophia,* but is (hiddenly marian) the real-ideal immaculate, virginal-maternal woman. The motif of the purification of fallen love, through the maternal love of Monica, to the love of the marian "Jerusalem above" is not to be mistaken, even if it is not explicitly shown by Augustine.

11 *Timaeus,* 37d–38c.

12 *Phys.,* 251 b 13.

13 *Ibid.,* b 17–23. This, combined with the idea of the cosmic cycle, means that there is no absolute before or after. The Trojan War was "before," but what has been can come again in the cycle and thus come "after" us. Aristotle agrees with the words of Alkmaion that men only pass away because they were unable to join up their end with their beginning. *Problemata,* XVII, 3 (916, 18–39 Bekker).

14 *Enn.* III, 7, 11, Bréhier, III, 142.

15 *Enn.* II, 2, Bréhier, II, 20–23.

16 Arnou: *Le Désir de Dieu dans la Philosophie de Plotin,* 1921.

17 J. Guitton: *Le Temps et l'Eternité chez Plotin et S. Augustin,* 3rd ed., 1956, 125.

18 Cf. *Enarr. in Ps.* 38, 1–3; 41, 8; 61, 14; 76, 9–12.

19 It has often been attempted (e.g. by W. Nestle: *Griechische Geschichtsphilosophie, Arch. f. Gesch. d. Phil.,* XLI, 1932, 80–114) to attribute to the Greeks a "theology of history," but they have none, unless it is Hesiod's idea of decay from age to age. Cf. E. Bréhier: *Quelques Traits de la Philos. de l'Histoire dans l'Antiquité classique, Rev. Hist. Phil.,* XIV, 1934.

20 Here Augustine differs radically from Gnosticism, with which one might perhaps superficially compare his theory of vertical *intentio*. The Gnostics, for whom the antitheses world and God, time and eternity, are absolute, assign no positive value to time or history. Time is not an image of eternity, but a caricature of it. Thus, if revelation descends vertically, then past time can only be rejected (Irenaeus, C.H., 4, 13, 1: *contrarietas et dissolutio praeteritorum*). Time is anxiety and lostness; the temporal, as such, cannot be made eternal. Nothing is more foreign to Gnosticism than the Christian "resurrection of the body," as Tertullian rightly pointed out. For the whole problem, cf. Henri-Charles Puech: *La Gnose et le Temps, Eranos-Jahrbuch,* 1931, 57–113.

21 Thus, Augustine distinguishes between what scholasticism later calls natural and obediential potency, the latter signifying the plasticity of the creature in the hands of God. *Gen. ad litt.* 6, 28–29; 9, 32.

22 Cf. *Enarr. in Ps.* 38, 9.

23 *Enarr. in Ps.* 95, 15. De Lubac gives further patristic references in *Katholizismus als Gemeinschaft,* 1943, 339–340.

24 Similarly *In Jo.* tr. 9, 14; tr. 10, 11.

25 *Enarr. in Ps.* 118, 16, 6.

26 *De Peccat. Meritis,* I, 16, 21. Cf. further texts in Irenee Marrou's *L'Ambivalence du Temps de l'Histoire chez S. Augustin,* Vrin, 1950.

27 Cf. his fine commentary in *Enarr. in Ps.* 38, 9, with the "leap across" from the old days to the new through faith in Christ.

28 Texts in Michael Muller's *Die Lehre des hl. Augustinus von der Paradiesesche und ihre Auswirkung in der Sexualethik des 12. und 13. Jahrhunderts bis Thomas von Aquin,* 1954.

29 Cf. H. Schlier, *Epheserbrief,* 1957, 45 ff.

30 Heinrich von Neustadt calls one of his spiritual epics *The Future of God.* In it he portrays the first and second comings of Christ.

31 Schelling: *Die Weltalter,* 1946.

32 *Sermo* ed. Mai 98 (Morin 347–349; *Sermo* 91, 7–8 (PL 38, 570–571); *Sermo* ed. Morin I, 20 (Morin 504–506).

33 *Letter to Diognetus,* IX, 1–6; and especially Gregory of Nyssa, *In Diem Nat. Chr.* (PG 46, 1132); cf. De Lubac, *Katholizismus als Gemeinschaft,* 229.

34 *Scelta ed elezione,* in *Filosofia e Vita, Quaderni trimestriali di Orientamento Formativo, anno 3,* no. 4, 1962, 7–9.

35 Eric Przywara: *Demut, Geduld, Liebe, Die drei christlichen Tugenden,* 1961, 30–44. Przywara compares, somewhat one-sidedly, Christian patience with the Platonic-Aristotelean idea of virtue. Patience, however, as the stoical endurance of all suffering, is the basic virtue of Odysseus and of many figures of classical tragedy.

36 Texts are to be found in my selection from *De Civitate Dei, Die Gottesbürgerschaft,* 241–260.

2. THE PERFECTIBILITY OF MAN

CONTRADICTORY MAN AND RELIGION

The Imperfectibility of the Creature

Man sees himself as the sum and perfect image of the cosmos. All the realms and genera of living things converge in him; no animal species is alien to him. He contains them all, as superseded and discarded forms in which he can mirror himself and, as in fables, recognize the features of his own character. Even scholastic embryology made the discovery that in his ontogenesis man recapitulates the stages of the natural development from which he emerged, which is confirmed by modern paleontology and biology. In this respect the man of today is no more and no less closely bound up with the natural cosmos and the universe than the man of mythical ages and of antiquity, who also thought of himself as a *microcosm*.

If this is so, however, it is obviously not as the result of an

43

external summation of separate cosmic realities: he is, as their epitome, neither plant nor animal nor anything else apart from himself. "Micro" also suggests a kind of concentration, which both makes man the synthesis of the world and raises him above it. In this exaltation above the immediate he is that which mediates itself to itself; he is mind and person. He looks openly into the openness of being in general, which, of its nature, is bounded only by nothingness. Although he is always a single individual, his nature is orientated toward being in general. He receives his freedom from it and in relation to it: freedom from any constraining bond of special being appropriate to his individuality. These appropriate elements do exist, of course, but only so that they may be illuminated and liberated in the whole.

This openness of his situation and the directing of his gaze inward does not detach man's mind from the ground of nature, but enables him to make his roots in it stronger, profounder, more intimate. Animals are swept away by the waves of sexual drive which ebb and flow like the sea, whereas man can experience *eros* in a more inward, sublimated way and, through love, make for it a lasting abode in his enlightened heart. He can also do the opposite (as the German romantics well knew), and transfer the infinities of spiritual dimensions to the dark maternal forces of nature, thus giving back to them, through his spirit, the dignity that nature had accorded him. For nature was never without spirit in man, just as the human child never ascends up from lower nature to become a spiritual being, but always awakes out of profound mental depths to consciousness and freedom.

How can such a being be perfectible? Man, as the epitome of the world, would be perfectible only if the world fulfilled itself with him and in him. But inasmuch as he transcends the world as spirit and is open to being in general, the fulfillment of the world is not enough to bring about his perfection. Man is personal, transcending the world and its being. The personal is more than being, which is predicable of a multiplicity of things; it is unique. It is that which existentially justifies the unrepeatable finality of exclusive love. Although every man is a person, and thus possesses this quality of incomparability, it cannot be predicated of him as a quality of his being. As spiritual beings men have in common many qualities which are of the species; but in those same spiritual beings, inasmuch as they are persons, these qualities are so different that subsumption under one generic term is impossible.[1]

If the question of perfectibility is asked—at this stage, purely formally—then one thing is certain: the person does not disappear into the race, however the total final purpose is interpreted—statically or dynamically, or in terms of a materialistic, biologistic, or even theologico-mystical evolution. Such a subordination of the person to the world's being is as equally inadmissible as the contrary "acosmistic" (Scheler's word) conception of the person, which sees its perfectibility as something which is possible only beyond the world's being (and hence, logically, beyond its own corporality).

The nature of human love shows how indissolubly intellectual being and the personal are bound up with each other. Both in his natural being and in his personal being man finds his completion and his happiness only in communion with another human being. This is the basis of the sexual difference (in which the profoundest wisdom is revealed), devised by *natura naturans* for the most intimate encounter and unity. It lies at the heart of the nature of the species, and roots it in *eros;* through the natural difference itself it shows man the eternally unbridgeable, unimaginable difference between one spiritual being and another. And again, this—rightly—exlusive love does not exhaust a person's relations with the world.

Man (as a cognitive, conative being), in spite of any individual tie to another person, remains open to the whole world, that is, to a world of work, a world of research, a world to be built up and realized in the human community. In addition, in order to remain open to the world, he remains open to the whole realm of being beyond it, which he misunderstands if he tries to embrace it as the quantitative sum of "world material" and thus undertakes interplanetary expansions of his area of habitation and power. He makes this "technical" plunge into the quantitative only because a philosophical plunge into the qualitative is doomed from the start. The search for the eternal "realm of spirits," the epitome of the qualitative personal, was a dream that Leibniz, Herder, the young Schiller, Hölderlin, Novalis, and Hegel dreamed, but, obviously, did not carry into their waking thoughts.

Neither the other person as the beloved, chosen one, nor the universe as a place of work and achievement, nor the unattainable totality of all persons answers man's deepest needs. Ultimately, it is only Absolute Being, itself spiritual and personal, that can do that, beyond the difference between spirit and nature, beyond the even profounder difference between the personal (as absolute uniqueness) and being (as absolute universality and totality). Within man no transition is possible between the two poles.

Don Juan tried to bridge the gap by starting from the person and thus destroyed his very starting point: the fidelity and exclusivity of the love between one person and another. The pantheist tries to do it by starting from the universe to which he transfers personal love; this can lead only to an illusory intoxication. The average man resigns himself early to a compromise between the two halves of life which can never be completely integrated: friendship and study, family and the office, private and political life. In renouncing the possibility of ever making his life whole, man can draw a certain satisfaction from the fact that these two spheres, although never fully penetrating each other, can complement and enrich each other. This unresolved tension can engender a sense of life which saves him from narrowness and rigidity and always offers him the possibility of a new departure.

This unbridgeable gap in man's nature affects also his relationship to God. Wholeness would be possible if the inwardness of the natural and spiritual love-relationship and the sovereign freedom of the abstract knowledge and shaping of the world could be united within an inclusive third relation which would be not only the origin, but also the final goal, of the other two. Quasi-infinite love is possible between two finite beings only if infinite love is operative in the ground of their nature, that is, if that which the lovers swear to each other is not necessarily an intoxicated exaggeration, or a "trick of nature" (for which she subsequently offers a cynical explanation), or else *hubris* (which causes a tragic fall). Equally, if a spiritual being loses himself in the abstract demands of a political or technical world of work, it is no betrayal of his mind to a mere anonymous, antlike existence, made palatable by promises of a utopian future, not for man as a person, but as a species. The individual will maintain mental honesty if, behind and above the objective spirit to which he has to sacrifice himself, there is an infinite mind toward which, in all the activities of his freedom, of his control and service of the world, he is moving, with the same or even greater intensity of love than that which he has experienced in the bosom of parents, family, marriage, and friendship.

The happiness caused by such a momentary vision of the possible wholeness of life within a religious relationship, the unimaginable promise it seems to contain, fades into inadequacy as soon as we try to reach for it directly. It is not enough to indicate the place where the higher third entity must find itself if existence is to be completed; for the question remains whether, as it is constituted, it *can* be completed. If, however, it cannot be completed in its totality, according to its whole basic structure, then all partial, fragmentary fulfillments avail it nothing. Any partial significance is constantly combatted and, rightly, negated by the lack of meaning of the whole. The man, who doubts and despairs, who constantly exposes any partial significance of love or knowledge or virtue or achievement as meaningless because of the overall meaninglessness, cannot be refuted. If, however, man is merely a fragment and as such incapable of completion, then it would be better if he did not exist at all, and he has no other

choice than to curtail and reduce his own contradictory being
to the point at which the contradictions fall away and he can
achieve, on a lower, more modest level, some kind of completa-
bility.

Nor is this disquieting problem solved if man imagines the
idea of an infinite god as the horizon toward which his finiteness
can integrate itself. It only seems to become all the more disquieting. How could God, infinite, hence in need of nothing and bliss-
ful in himself, help the integration of this creature which, from
the whole structure of its being, is obviously incapable of being
integrated? For its being is not only finite and in the world; it is
mortal. Death, it would appear, is the great rock thrown across
the path of all thinking which might lead to completeness. Even
if one regards its terrible aspect as something which was a subsequent development in original nature, the ending of man's
earthly life poses one insistent question: How can a natural
being, which must necessarily die (as he must as part of a genus
and a race), be conceived as united, to the point of identity, with
an infinite spiritual and personal being with infinite claims of
knowledge and love?

The question is not answered by saying that man is made up of
a "mortal" body and an "immortal" soul; the division is—as has
already been shown—a different one: that between the cosmic
mind-soul of nature and the "super-cosmic" person in direct
relation to God. It is also a falsification to see the cosmic soul,
with Origen, as a state of self-alienation of the spirit. The acts in
which the mind-soul experiences, knows, and loves in the world
have at least their uncorrupted, purely creaturely side, by virtue
of which they contain eternity and are unrepeatable. However indissolubly (according to Augustine) vanity and futility may have
become involved in the form of creation, thus making earthly
life forever a mystery, the pure original shape of creation, now
unreconstructable, was itself a hieroglyph.

The centaurlike being, man, manifests something uncompletable which points beyond himself to a manner of integration—undiscoverable to him by himself alone—which is formally indicated in the relation to God. But the manner of integration is left open and, indeed, must be left open, if the relationship between God and man is to be determined and shaped in dramatic dialogue by God alone.

The Contradiction of Death

In death the uncompletability of man becomes obvious to the point of absurdity, because his descent into corruption destroys any vague remaining hope of integration. When the beloved face loses its color and starts to decay, a curtain is lowered which separates forever: a unique being has gone, irrevocably. No transmigration of souls, no reunion on "other planets," is a satisfactory substitute for continuation. But death, attacking the sense of life at its core, is not simply an external catastrophe, the Fates cutting the thread. It seems to reveal a whole gradient in life that falls away in the opposite direction from wholeness.

Death is neither an external accident, nor is it comprehensible —in its opposition to the sense of life—as a constituent element of being, however desperately one may try to show this. After all, one cannot swear eternal faithfulness with a time limit set to it. The only reason that hearts do not constantly rebel against the dark omnipotence of death is that its fateful wind has always bent the trees of the soul toward it, that the powers of infidelity, of injustice, of betrayal, of spiritual debility and physical illness and infirmity are familiar to us from childhood in all their destructive strength. They are forces that are not only above us, but in us, with whom we seem inexplicably to have made a compact, voluntarily, yet against our will, at a time and place we can no longer remember.

This is Kafka's problem: How do these alien forces, the worst of which is guilt, first come to us from without, then penetrate us layer by layer, until we are "compelled" to acknowledge them as our own corruption and declare, "I am guilty"? The horror of their alienness nevertheless remains. Therefore, the heart that has to confess itself as sinful—not adventitiously, but by reason of its very nature—is always close to rebellion against the existence that has been forced on it. It casts around for a tribunal to release it from this sentence of doom which can only have been spoken by a "God."

But in the meanwhile these powers claim the whole man; let him turn which way he will, he cannot escape them. He has been unable to awake to the consciousness of his dignity and his mission without already finding the worm in him that gnaws at the kernel of his freedom and love. He recognizes a moral imperative, not just as an indifferent law to which he is subject, but as that which will lead him to his true freedom. But he also feels an unwillingness to follow this lead, a laziness that weighs him down, a sluggishness of the heart that would rather abide by itself than embark on the strenuousness of love. Love means self-conquest, and so even as a child one seeks a way of having the pleasure of love without self-conquest. He wants to win the affection of the world without exerting the self; this is the essence of nonlove disguised as love; this is lust.

This fateful sense of not being able to do something and not wanting to do it, from which the child who starts to experience sin for the first time tries violently to escape, is a prelude to the inexorable objective forces, whose deceitfulness the heart detects at once. Learning that radical protest is useless, the heart is finally overpowered by their crushing weight. The world of the adults is right, and wrongness is obviously an integral part of this world. And I myself am moving towards this world of adulthood, and therefore must come to terms with injustice. There may be attempts in this world, both in the private and in the public sphere, to dam in the destructive powers; to associate oneself with these attempts will be noble and praiseworthy, but nowhere, either privately or publicly, will man be able to deal finally with the hydra. He carries it around with him as his enemy; it grows with him, and often it seems to him as if, with the growing effort to conquer it and transform the world into a paradise, the snake head doubles itself after every blow.

In the region where he imagines he can register something like real "progress," in the organization of a moral world order, this so-called progress seems only to open up apocalyptic abysses. Measurable progress, not only in the technological, but also in the cultural and social fields, can, of its nature, take place only within the natural order of humanity. But the depth of a person's individuality, whose home is in the eternal, resists being reduced to a means within a type. The progress of optimism of a technological culture has to make so much noise because it has to drown ever more desperate cries of the ravished person. Even such an anti-socialist as Nietzsche, who appears to have been concerned only with single outstanding individuals, in the critical moment, reassessed all personal values through nature and reduced them to biology. The superman has to be "bred," and for this purpose are all moral valuations (which disclose in us a profound incapacity for good, what Kant called the radically bad) to be dissolved into a real biological strength. That Nietzsche's ideas lead inevitably to those of his bitterest opponents, history has shown and, thereby, indicated also that the problems Nietzsche was rightly concerned about can be solved only on a basis other than his.

The Answer of Religion to the Conflict

Man would not be man if he were not constantly aware of the essential conflict, which the increasingly grave state of the world only renders more acute. Sucked ever more sinisterly into optimistic, hopeful schemes for world improvement, for unraveling the mystery of man, and dominated ever more fully by the collusive and apparently inescapable forces of economics, world politics, and world technology, he sees with horror the danger to his last remaining shreds of freedom and of personal feeling. These powers in a dreadful conspiracy offer him, instead of true joy, true suffering, true fidelity, and true self-sacrifice, only bogus versions the validity of which rests on a tacit betrayal of the eternal person.

The critical world situation, however, is just a frightening illumination of what it means to be human. If it emerged from the foregoing that man can become finally whole and integrated, that his nature can be given a formal expression, but never a specific content—because the requisite synthesis of the elements cannot be achieved in an observable way—then this is infinitely more true of man in his fallen condition. The idea of wholeness which he can conceive of himself not only surpasses his nature; it contradicts it. However he may put this idea into practice, there will always be one forgotten element that has to be included, because the conflict is rooted indissolubly in the very nature of the man seeking wholeness.

I shall offer a short survey of the possible ways to wholeness which, insofar as they are conceived by man, can be reduced to two main ones. The third way, which overcomes the conflict, can only be conceived and offered by God and as such is correctly called "revelation," however much the other ways may claim this designation for themselves. Many men, indeed whole peoples and cultures, can believe them to be "revelation," inasmuch as they truly demonstrate an aspect of the process of becoming whole, with a clarity unattainable by the common run of men. They do not, on that account, need to be true "revelations," because, being rational, they are adequately explained by the rational faculty of man. In fact, they cannot ultimately be "revelation" because they do not unravel the Gordian knot of life; they cut through it.

This is not to say that, at the level of a preliminary conception of redemptive revelation, they do not, purely formally, adumbrate the revelation which is to proceed from God. It is a defining of the area in which the event must take place if man is truly to be the recipient of such saving revelation. The human imagination will seek to fill this formal framework with concrete preparatory conceptions, with myths of saving deities, which make clear what is to happen, and to transfer them from the region of mere thought and phantasy to the sphere of reality. It is not, however, accidental that such myths fail to emerge on the stage of actual human history. Thus, they retain an aesthetic element which is part of their magic, but also, because they are magic, they retain part of their incapacity to provide salvation. The fact that such myths exist shows the impossibility of man's achieving wholeness for himself purely anthropologically. Nor does it help to disregard myth (as a self-alienation of the spirit) in order to seek the solution in finite existence. There is no way back behind myth, but only forward beyond it, so as to arrive at the reality, which at the same time provides the integration, the possibility of which myth had hoped for.

HUMAN WAYS OUT AND THE CHRISTIAN WAY

The Way of Appearance

If the paths that humanity has taken toward salvation, i.e., toward a relationship with God, are examined, the first thing to be noted is that both in their inventive conception (theory) and in their existential living out (practice) they represent the boldest conceptions and most exalted endeavors of the human spirit, borne through history by individuals and peoples prepared to sacrifice their lives for them. On no account are they to be condemned *a priori* as deceptions of the devil or is the mind that conceived them to be branded as a *fabrica idolorum*, even if these paths prove, in the event, to be fragmentary and unable to provide total, objectively indivisible salvation. They are, therefore, in a sense ambiguous. As serious attempts to discover salvation, they may contain redeeming grace hidden within them, yet as human creations they may involve man still deeper in his corruptions. What we see here is not how God directs the heart of the individual, but how the objective attempt is related to the objective problem of humanity.

The first way consists in a soaring movement of the heart, which leaves the whole of contradictory earthly existence beneath it in order to seek a home in the region of a supraterrestrial divine power. The basic idea is a very simple one: all multiplicity is opposed to unity and has in some mysterious way fallen away from it; only unity can be true being. Thus the difference between God and the world, between unity and multiplicity, is the same as that between true and untrue being, between being and appearance. Time and space confirm at every moment the inability of things to exist in place side by side and the readiness with which they change into one another. They are Sansara, driven by the power of Maya and Tršna, the unquenchable thirst for the other. The way of salvation demands an inner renunciation of worldly differences: theoretically, in the act of seeing through them all to their identical divine ground; practically, in the act of renouncing satisfaction through a finite, particular being.

What in this system can still be called love is fidelity to the *thou*, not in its difference, but in its ultimate identity with the loving self. The person loves, not out of the differentiating point of selfhood, but out of the world-transcending identity of God, only experiencing deep "compassion" for the still imprisoned individuality. But compassion, too, is robbed of its real content, because there can only be true compassion so long as the compassionate being exists together with the object of compassion in the world in a condition of differentiation. Leaning back from regained identity into the sphere of differentiation can only have symbolic value. The ways of salvation that operate with the idea of appearance, that is, with the unreality of the fatal conflict and hence of death itself, certainly bear witness to an exalted intrepidity of the spirit, which challenges the totality of the world and its laws in order to negate them with sovereign freedom. But this negation is directed against the very nature of man, who saves his truth (in the absolute) only by abandoning his whole worldly reality.

India has been the most radical exponent of this way and has declared all individuality, all separateness, mere appearance. But even the salvation ideas of the Greeks also, even if they stop short of the ultimate Asiatic conclusion, tend in this direction: the monism of Parmenides as well as the dualism of Plato (which abandons corporeal existence in order to save only man's "immortal soul"); the central cosmic fire of the Stoics, of which the individual is only a spark which has leaped out (*scintilla animae*) and is striving to get back to its center; above all, the Neoplatonic ideas of the lessening of being by emanation, whereby the salvation of man can be conceived only as either a dissolution of the degrees (*Nous-Psyche-Hyle*) in the supraspiritual one (*Hen*) or as the giving back at death of all the separate elements of man to the appropriate sphere.

All these forms of salvation, however different they may appear to be, have one thing in common: they endeavor to rescue something "immortal" in man by abandoning the rest to the devouring powers. That which is rescued is called the "real," that which is abandoned is called the "unreal." However beautiful and sublime this may seem in theory, practice throws a rather different light on it, because it is no longer worthwhile committing oneself finally and responsibly to the transient. Moreover, insofar as these systems place the "immortal" element on the side of the divine, they are basically Asiatic: a reciprocity of love between God and man is not a serious possibility. It is only possible for as long as man in the conflict of existence is different from God, for as long as he can experience God as grace from the divine sphere, a hand reached out to him, and (with the Stoics) rids himself of those resistances which prevent him from attuning himself to the great law of the universe.

If the renunciation of finite pleasure is attractive in its heroism, we must remember that its purpose is to overcome the conflict and thus get rid of pain. But perhaps the renunciation of pain, from the point of view of the possible wholeness of man, is more dangerous than the renunciation of pleasure. The Greeks felt this and therefore preferred, at least in the classical age, to accept ultimate contradictions between a logically thought-out metaphysical anthropology and the particular conditions of earthly life. They did not, in the cause of achieving human wholeness, want to draw out conclusions which ultimately cancel out man. Their thinking remains so close to reality that the metaphysical perspectives do not ultimately throw doubt on this reality, but rather impart to it something like a transfiguring halo. Thus, the relation between transient and eternal existence remains curiously unresolved.

Only on this basis was tragedy possible. Man is committed, to the point of sacrificing himself, to the order of the gods, but the order of the gods remains committed to man and is often, on his account, drawn with him into conflict. If the world is "appearance," then it is appearance which is beloved of the gods themselves. The tragedy of conflict is not overcome, as in India, by denying it, but is the necessary prerequisite for the purification of the heart (*catharsis*). Thus, all remains in a dreamlike fashion with the understanding that the question of ultimate reality cannot be raised.

The Way of the Tragic Conflict

This brings us to the second possible way. The contradictory nature of existence is so fundamental that the problem of salvation must be concerned with it. It cannot be left out of account in trying to solve the question of salvation. The way which called it appearance canceled out the good as well as the bad. What makes life profound and noble, if not suffering and tragedy? What steels man and polishes the hidden jewel, if not suffering? And not just some external, contingent and avoidable suffering, but the essential suffering involved in being man. In mutual exaltation of nature and spirit—in spite of all the mutual threat —lies that incomparable sublimity that neither animals nor "God" can achieve. This incomparable quality of being set about with abysses is what makes us shudder in Shakespearean tragedy at the sight of the monstrous thing that is man. Or in Faust, who both says and does not say to the passing moment, "Tarry a while, thou art so fair," and ultimately, in his eternal striving, is already redeemed.

Even more than Greek tragedy the world of the Germanic heroes shows man's tragic situation as that which most perfectly characterizes him. It is not the modern idea of man's being divided against himself, but a sense of grandeur, which is imparted, not only by the tragic downfall, but by the indissolubility of fidelity and loyalty. However meaningless it may appear in view of the downfall, through the downfall it gains its eternal lustre, which makes it continue as an inspiration, to be celebrated in song, in the memory of following generations. The mythical realm of the gods which arches over such a picture of the earth can itself be only a reflection of the most sublime earthly qualities. Even the realm of the eternal ones is riven by mortal struggles and is full of battles and cataclysmic downfalls which cannot be smoothed away by ideas of astronomical cosmic cycles and philosophical theories of an eternal return.

But the distinguishing human quality would not emerge from this view of the world if in the values of loyalty (and of its opposite, treachery) the ethical did not everywhere prevail and was not stronger than sheer vital energy. Here, too, man stands within the framework of that which is the right of the order of the clan; thus, it is the fight between right and wrong that is transposed into the absolute.

Hence, one cannot condemn outright dualistic systems, however meaningless they may ultimately appear to be. Marcionism, for example, which makes the biblical opposition of law and grace (as of the Old and the New Testament) an absolute one between two divinities, reflects within the conceptual framework of Gnosticism an ubiquitous anthropology. It can receive different emphases. For it may be that man, by nature the creation of the dark god of the world, rebels against his mortally contradictory laws and precisely thus—with the grace of the supreme god—is able to break through into the realm of freedom and the spirit. Marcionism, then, is only a dramatic form of the way of salvation, already discussed, from multiplicity to unity.

It may be, however, that man becomes the victim of the struggle of the two divinities, and only in death is able to wrest himself away from the god of the world and fly to the arms of the paternal god of grace and freedom. This is that fascinating mixture of Gnosticism and Christianity which crops up in many Protestant variants—at its purest, perhaps, in the poems of Blake, but also quite clearly in the dramas of Schiller, where the tragedy of breaking through a realm of right, now superseded and thus put in the wrong, into a realm of freedom reveals the shape and meaning of existence. However much the tragic hero by his breakthrough makes life in this realm of freedom possible for the generations that come after, this secured freedom still remains insignificant and wearisome. All human greatness is concentrated in the struggle of the breakthrough, in which death and birth form an indissoluble unity.

It is never far to Parsee and Manichean-Catharist dualism when the situation of a struggle and breakthrough is taken as the primary condition of man. Such systems of metaphysics can only be meant as foils for an aristocratic, heroic view of man. If one makes absolute the struggle which is at the very heart of existence (important also in great pre-Socratic philosophies such as those of Heraclitus and Empedocles), and is to be conceived and carried out as a supreme idea, he requires a man who, tried by suffering and resistance, has learned to love the furnace of pain which is purifying him and despises any cheaper harmonizing process.

Nietzsche, who opposes any eschatological elimination of suffering with his "eternal return" which eternally reintegrates it, sees in this an antipessimistic ideal which affirms everything that' strengthens one: "In pain there is as much wisdom as in pleasure; they are both among the chief forces which preserve the race"; "pain is a necessary ingredient of all activity; there is a will to suffer at the basis of all organic life." Unlike the way of appearance, which in the first place seeks to eradicate suffering and thus sets about destroying "thirst" (concupiscence), the way of the tragic struggle never loses touch with historical reality. It offers no suspension in empty space, but ensures that the foot that kicks against the stone knows it is kicking against that which is truly real, of which it partakes.

The Provisional Nature of Both Ways

No one, however, was foolish enough to proclaim the way of suffering as the way to God, as if the more pain one endured, the closer he came to the absolute. Pain remains, at best, an episode; only in its purifying and tempering power in the comprehensive whole of life in this world, which is taken as the uncrossable horizon, as the "divine," is it to keep its assured place. "Divinity is day and night, winter and summer, war and peace, being satisfied and being hungry; it changes like oil mixed with perfumes" (Heraclitus). Therefore, this way of the "immortal struggle" (Plato) is basically not a way, but a self-knowledge by self-contained man, who creates an image of God out of his own highest possibilities.

One need not say that this second conversion is therefore less religious than the first. In the first man strives away from himself (as contradictory multiplicity) toward the unity that he is not. In this second one man is self-sufficient and fashions his god according to his own measure. The first way is not, as might superficially be thought, optimistic because it affirms the One as primal light and primal radiation. It posits the One at the cost of the radical denial and dissolution of all worldly reality; it is, therefore, radically pessimistic. The second way, which at first appears pessimistic, because it does not seek to overcome the tension of the opposites, is more deeply affirmative of reality, if only with an heroic emphasis. Thus, it foregoes any other (transcendental) salvation and contents itself with the healing forces which exist in life as it is.

Both ways, however, are seldom found in a pure and separate form; they are generally found combined with either one or the other predominating, but neither wholly absent. Even the mystical ascent to the One demands, in its way, the suffering of a heart that renounces, and the heroic struggle implies ultimately reconciliation. They complement each other, even in their image of god. If the god of the first way is not to be simply an indifferent, heartless void, then emanation has to be understood as "gratuitously self-radiating goodness." If the tragic struggle is to have a divinely significant basis, then the fact that the gods are subject to destiny reveals a vulnerability, a knowledge of their own responsibility, a sharing of the divine ground of things in the fate of the universe.

The world of myth is rich in concepts which foreshadow the true relation of God and the world, in which the elements are mixed and set off against one another in an almost infinite number of ways. Whatever the mixture, whatever images may be used to convey it—from the most primitive African, American Indian, and Polynesian legends to the subtly poised Gnostic myth—the ingredients always yield significant, symbolically profound pictures, which there is no need to classify here. Mythical religions always combine these elements: a sphere of earthly justice, which embraces both the private and the public spheres, in which a provisional ethical catharsis is attempted through renunciation, discipline, suffering, and expiatory, reconciliatory sacrifice. But this is always projected onto a transcendent horizon of heavenly grace, of the promise of salvation on the basis of a covenant relationship to a merciful god, so that the ethico-political order of the earth with its active virtue is made possible by a transcendental relationship to a believed, hoped-for, and (in the loyalty to the god promising it) loved salvation.

Nevertheless, the idea of its emergence on the historical plane —of salvation there from the entanglement of existence—is intensely envisioned, but remains only a vision (a god whose reality is more than mythical is to be found nowhere in history). Hence, the salvation which depends on this contact with the real, mortal world remains always a potential, unfulfilled idea. The more spontaneous the influence of the mythical image in the world, the more the earthly order—of peoples and of persons—can be shaped by it. But with the coming of the age of philosophy, the mythical, magical power of religious images declines, and then the naked helplessness of historical, contradictory man becomes again apparent. Into this situation comes the third way of the bible and of Christ.

Before we proceed to consider this third way, it is to be noted that the transcendence of human existence, which expresses itself in the search for wholeness in conceptions which are irreconcilable ideas, is an essential law of its being. It is more than an "ideological superstructure" above that which is ultimately fragmentary; it is the movement of the fragment towards its whole. This transcendence expresses itself in the consciousness of the "immortality of the soul," which is the best available expression for the ontological postulate of totality. Inasmuch as "soul" means the "very heart of man's being" which cannot be destroyed by the fact of time's existing in extension, a philosophical insight is expressed here which can be arrived at by man himself and is not achieved only with the Christian revelation. Only this insight itself points to the void, because "immortality of the

soul" does not suffice to guarantee an assumption of time into
the eternal, which is unthinkable if one makes man the starting
point. The mythical imagination must here make up what is
missing and what cannot be provided by philosophy. No rational
speculation—e.g., concerning the universalization of the soul
separated from the single body by its relation to the total cosmic
material—can offer sufficient foundation on which to base a view
of the wholeness of the human fragment. Here lies the grain of
truth in the refusal of Karl Barth to accept the "immortality of
the soul" as a demonstrable truth. If it can be proved philosophically, it only contains once more a fragmentary answer to
the question of the wholeness of man, which receives its full
answer only through the way of revelation.[2]

The Third Way of Love

Similarities and Differences. The biblical Christian way could
appear, to the superficial gaze, as one of the many variants of
the myth, which combines in a particularly happy way the poles
of the first and second ways. From the first way it apparently
borrows the formal framework of the world's going out from
God and returning to God, and according to this structure interprets Christianity by Alexandrian theology (the influence of
which continues into Scholasticism and the Renaissance). God
the Father is absolute unity; the Son is the potential multiplicity
of the world of ideas and the point where the subsequent incarnation takes place; the Holy Ghost is the gatherer of the many,
through the ideas, back to the absolutely One. The creation of
man and the incarnation of God then appear mainly as the "self-
exteriorization" of God, a conceded stooping of the higher to the
lower. The ways of the return are mainly those of seeing through
multiplicity to its divine ground of unity.

From the second way, however, the Christian one apparently
borrows the importance of the painful struggle, which places the

cross in the center, as the reconciliation of the world through pain and as the superheroic fight of the "Lion of Judah" with the powers of chaos and of hell. Through the cross the contradiction of sin is overcome through the contradiction of expiation whereby, as in myth, the cathartic sufferings of the crucified man are placed within the realm of the divine. By the cross the "sufferings of God" reveal to the world his involvement in the fate of his creation. Christianity can be interpreted according to this basic structure, just as convincingly as the Alexandrians understood it according to the first one: e.g., by Luther, Pascal, Böhme, and Baader.

The decisive difference, however, has still not been mentioned: namely, that the salvation event, by means of which man achieves a redemptive relationship to God, occurs in history, that God does not set a sign or speak a word to man, but uses man in all his existential doubtfulness and fragility and imperfectibility as the language in which he expresses the world of redemptive wholeness. God, therefore, uses existence extended in time as the script in which to write for man and the world the sign of a supratemporal eternity. Hence, the man Jesus, whose existence is this sign and word of God to the world, had to live out simultaneously the temporal, tragic separating distance and its conquest through (Augustinian) elective obedience to the choosing will of the Eternal Father, in order to realize mysteriously the essentially irrefrangible wholeness within the essentially uncompletable fragmentary. The question of how that is possible and what form such a life takes will be discussed in the last part of the book. So much is clear, however, at this stage, that if this has happened, historical existence, without being devalued by being regarded as mere appearance and without one's having to turn his back on it, has been put in the movement of returning to God.

The christological synthesis here achieved is fundamentally different from any synthesis of the mythical imagination; its force and effectiveness lay—beyond all expectation and imagination—in the resurrection of the dead. Since Christian teaching from the beginning concentrated on this one point and interpreted everything else—the incarnation, life, teaching, sufferings and ascension of Christ, along with Pentecost—strictly according to this central doctrine, it must be understood as the core of the kerygma. It is impossible to elaborate here on all the illuminating truths which this central idea gathers up and radiates out again. For our subject it is sufficient to note that Christianity, with its declaration of the resurrection of the dead, claims to offer the only complete and satisfying solution of the anthropological problem, and thus to be superior to all the religions and philosophies of the world—only, of course, if it is not understood as a superreligion or a superphilosophy, but as a pure act of God's grace. That the fragmentary ways of thinking found in the humanistic religions—the mystic and the mythical, the monistic and the dualistic—have their value at the level at which they were conceived, has already been suggested. But none were able to place the finitude and temporality of historical man in the lap of God's eternity. This was only possible through Christ's resurrection from the dead.

It remains a mystery which, though inexplicable, is proclaimed as experienced by witnesses in the middle of history and is accepted in its continuing inexplicability, and yet is seen at the same time as the only valid solution of the mystery of man. So much so, that even if one were to feel impelled to reject the reality of the event as too extravagant, one could still see its possibility and its value as the adequate answer to the question of existence. The Resurrection is not a fairy-tale postscript to the life of Jesus, but is its obvious conclusion and sum. This sum is not, as with other men, at the most a living legacy, a "spirit" which continues to have an influence through time; the "spirit," in the case of this man, is so much alive that it testifies to his total mental-physical reality being alive and present. In the "memory" of his death, as the community of the faithful celebrate it, he is always among them as he who lives forever.

One might consider for a moment what Christian teaching (giving reasons for it as well as drawing conclusions from it) sees together with this fact: that this crucified and resurrected man is in a special sense God's Son. Anthropologically, what distinguishes him from all the mystical sons of God is more important: namely, that he is, in an historical sense, the "Son of Man," a man who was really born and really died, a man who like all men, lived and suffered and then rescued this finite reality of flesh and blood for eternal life, opening up for all his brothers the way out through the portals of Hades. Thus, the first contradiction is overcome: namely, that man is at once nature and spirit, and that the claim of spirit bursts the bounds of nature without being able to do without it. In Christ eternal love and loyalty become possible, without the laws of the physical and mortal heart condemning this love as imagination and as falsehood.

The Revaluation of Death. Now we can see that, in order to remove the second and profounder contradiction, the death of this resurrected man had to be revalued and seen as a voluntary death out of love. Through his death the corruption of all hearts —their sinful incapacity for love—is overcome, because it is expiated, borne away, and freed from the paralyzing pressure of fate. We can understand that such an historical existence could only be lived if the human heart, awakened to the fullness of love, was from the beginning enfolded within the heart of God who, by involving himself lovingly in human destiny, sought to overcome that destiny by suffering its conflicts through to their very root. It is not the absolute heroism of a human heart alone which through the conquest of existing fate gives birth to the God (in Rilke's sense) in whom temporal and mortal men are ultimately enfolded and redeemed. Such purely "intransitive love," which by its sheer intensity warms the coldest cosmic nights, had to be divine in the first place in order to be able to perform this work.

However intransitively the love of the man on the cross, abandoned by God, experienced itself—Rilke has here found something which was lost and is nearer to Christianity than he ever thought—it streams directly into the boundlessness of divine love and is a full and complete answer to it. Out of the abyss of total futility and abandonment this love corresponds to the absolute gratuitousness of God's love for the world, which ultimately can find no other argument for itself than itself. Futility and abandonment as the mode of being in the guilt of disobedience become the articulation of the word of faithfulness and innocence; in death itself they have attained the superdeath, the state of being on the other side, within the sheltering womb of eternity. The predatory gesture of voracious death is overcome by the gesture of surrender of the dying man. And this too has its measure in the self-giving of God to the world out of love.

Now at last the aspirations of mysticism and of myth can be fulfilled by there being a true "appearance" of God as the salvation for man. As he pursues the way of salvation, he makes the world transparent for the divine to "appear" through it. This appearing is now no longer a turning away from bleak historical reality—as mystic negation of finitude or as its mythical translation into images of the imagination—no, reality is the place and the material within which the living God appears. In the identity of the Son of Man with the Son of God, not only must the truth of man appear at the same time as the truth of God, but man's love for God must also become identical with the love of God for man. Thus, necessarily, the love of man for man (if it is love which comes up to the Christian standard) must become identical with the love of man for God. It must also be evident that in the tragic, expiatory suffering and death of the one man who at once was man and God, God himself goes into death. He places himself in humble and humbled love in the power of the fate which rules the human world, so that he might be henceforth no longer just the fulfillment of the first divine image of transcendent unity but also the fulfillment of the second, in which the gods as well are drawn into the tragic struggle. But the unity of both images is not to be found in merely seeing them superimposed on each other. This unity is to be discovered in something unexpected, something unrealizable by man on his own, something granted him only as the free self-revelation of the innermost heart of God: that the spirit of God is above all conflict and all fate at precisely that point at which his heart, in the ultimate humility and defenselessness of love, is able to be above all blasphemous attacks, all conflicts, all hate.

The Old Testament's Idea of Man. The Old Testament is the preparation for this wholeness. In the history of Israel God not only performs "mighty deeds" for his chosen people and thus shows himself as the true God as against the impotent gods of other peoples, but takes his historical covenant seriously and, when the bride entrusted to him breaks the covenant and behaves like a harlot (Ezek. 16; 23), reacts like a deceived and outraged lover. As Lord he must threaten punishment and judgment, but as a lover he cannot help showing the "weakness of love" almost to the point of self-degradation, promising not to leave the truant where she is, but to bring her back and redeem her forever in a new and eternal covenant. In the face of this revelation of the loving heart of God in making this covenant, man is able to ponder his incomprehensible paralysis of heart, his involvement in an immemorial guilt, and to make it intelligible as an ancient falling away from an original covenanted love, which is the only reason for the existence of creatures at all in the reality of the world. The primal legend of Paradise, of original sin and of the punishment of subjection to the powers of death and pain, and of enslavement by the anguish of living may be clothed partly in mythical elements. But it is the expression of that existential difference between the heights of the demands of love and the impossibility of satisfying them which man carries round with him always as a dark mystery, whose reality as "original sin," however, becomes intelligible in the face of the fulfilling of the covenant by the other partner, God.

Reflection on the reality of the covenant which constitutes the history of Israel with God, deepens two truths from century to century, truths which reflect each other and reveal ever further depths. The first truth is that the heart of man fails before God, not just occasionally and by chance, but, if dependent on itself alone, by its very nature. The second is that the heart of God never, under any circumstances, fails man, not only in single events, but always on the basis of his inner necessity to love and his free love involvement with the chosen lover. Therefore God can inspire in the man who fails him the power of love to remain *faithful.*

The Trinity and the Holy Spirit. The presence of the self-revealing God is what illuminates man's inadequacy for him; that is why it is impossible for him to take himself just as he finds himself, in his glaring contradictions, as the measure of his self-appraisal. If he attempts it, he can get as far as establishing the existence of this conflict—between the "sensual" and the "suprasensual" man (whom Kant calls the *homo noumenon*). Perhaps he can even identify the "radical evil," which prevents the assimilation of the former to the latter, because the requisite freedom to do this is paralyzed. The suprasensual man formulates a resounding categorical imperative, which does not promise the absolute happiness of man if it is obeyed but, in order to be comprehensible, postulates the (unverifiable) idea of man's wholeness, of his freedom and immortality with God. That is as far as the philosophical man can get; but that does not solve the anthropological question. It is only posed in its most acute form. Viewed from it, man is incapable of being whole and, at a more profound level, because of "radical evil" he constitutes a refusal even to start moving towards such unattainable wholeness.

But now this "negative" philosophy is taken up into the

"positive" philosophy of revelation; man is no longer interpreted within the area of his own mystery. He is to be understood within the space prepared by God's love, in which he is already affected by love: trained by it, directed toward it, freed and fated for it. In this discovery the mystery of the Son of God and of Man is freshly illumined. For if this Son were not orientated toward something above him, then he would not have been man and he would have no followers. If, however, like the others in their inadequacy he had been orientated toward an ideal of himself, then he could not be the redeemer from inadequacy. Here the inner nature of God is revealed to us. What, in self-alienated man, must be a looking upward to God, must be prayer, obedience, faith, hope, and love, in the self-collected Son appears as something absolutely ultimate, something which corresponds to the depths of God. Within God himself there is the original of that of which man's relationship to God is a copy: room for love between Father and Son—for God in the mode of creative giving and for God in the mode of created receiving and giving back in full measure—in the unity of the Spirit of love which alone emerges from the double fount of love and, as the eternal fruit of love, unites and distinguishes the Father and the Son. These unplumbable depths of the springs of life in the eternal God are seen as the only sufficient condition for the historical appearance of the Son of God and of Man, since he, appearing in the middle, points behind and above himself to the Father who sent him and promises the Spirit which is freely given to the world and is easily known by it when the "life of the flesh" that leads to death ends, and the "life of the spirit" that resurrects from death begins.

That the Holy Spirit has become freely available to man means that the existence of the Savior, who resolved the conflict of life and liberated men finally from the power of fate, is not suspended as a purely transcendental idea above the man who follows him. He need not despair of the attainment of the idea in the same way that he was torn apart by the discrepancy between the claims of love and the incapacity of loving. That would be the case of the relationship between the sinner, who contributes nothing to his salvation, and the Savior, who in place of the sinner obtains and prepares all that is asked of the latter, as if this situation were the last word. If it were, it would still remain an "as if" situation, a purely external accounting of the merits of the Son of God to the meritless sinner, hence a relationship which would not overcome the tragic discrepancy in man himself. If that were the doctrine of radically interpreted Protestantism, then it would lack the dimension of the Holy Spirit.

The sending of the Spirit after the completion of the Son's deed of redemption is, again, something quite new: the unique historical deed becoming interior to the narrow, finite consciousness of man. It is force, pressing up from inside man's deepest depths, encouraging him, and empowering him to enter on the venture of Christian love. The Spirit poured out into the hearts of men, of which Paul speaks, and the drastic language of the Church's teaching of the "infused virtues," i.e., strengthening, of faith, hope, and charity, show that the tragic discrepancy in man is led by God the Spirit himself to final annihilation. This tremendous exertion of man in the Holy Spirit—of the individual and of all men—and with the microcosm of the macrocosm assigned to him, Paul describes in Romans, 8 (and John in the Apocalypse, 12), with the image of the birth pangs. According to Paul the Holy Spirit of God not only shares in bringing into being the new man and the new world, but his sighs and groans are the real driving force which imperatively demands the impossible of man and through its divine strength achieves it.

Man's way to unity with God is now no longer separate from the way of the man with the bleeding heart. His heart broke on the cross and poured itself out for all men. His Spirit daily opens up that heart and pours from it into all who give themselves over to his guidance. In Christianity man is neither dominated by God (as in the way of union)—he is taken seriously in his difference from God, to the point of God's becoming man himself—

nor is he absolutized in his tragic difference by becoming the "battleground of the gods," because the divine Spirit becomes part of him and enfolds his discrepancies (perfecting, preserving them) in the loving differences within God himself. What vastness there is here, what great seriousness of love God reveals when he lets the tragic and apocalyptic differences between God and the world, God and hell, be fully expressed within his own all-embracing differences.

This becomes clear in the first place in the creative work of the Father. In its whole potential and actual falling away, in its tragedy and fatality it had to be not only answered for, but also carried through and supported, in the heart of the Creator. Otherwise, the creating God himself would acquire demonic character—either of a sublime indifference or of being drawn himself into the workings of fate. A God who, out of his own inviolable beatitude, let his creatures suffer and related these sufferings back to his own glorification, would not stand to his creatures in the relationship of original to copy.

This becomes clear in the second place in the work of reconciliation by God the Son, who does not expiate the sin of the world from the separating distance of the (pharisaically) "pure." Because he is the pure lover, he unreservedly identifies himself with the guilt and the fate of his fellowmen. He does not set beside the tragic discrepancy another untragic one. He takes the tragic one into himself and lives it through to its very ground, but with the longer breath of love, which allows him, out of the darkest, most hellish abandonment by God, to be resurrected to the Father and to the world.

This becomes clear in the third place in the redemptive work of the Holy Spirit, who overcomes the remaining sinful discrepancy in sinners, not with the easy superiority of God, but with the infinite labor of one who goes into the bleakness, the narrowness, and the stupor of finite and fallen consciousness in order to open it, together with him and on his conditions, to infinite love. In this humiliation of love the divine Spirit of love reveals its true being. We can see this from the warnings of Paul not to grieve the Spirit, not to extinguish it (as if it were unspeakably sensitive and a tiny delicate flame which is in danger of going out).

The Spirit obviously does not alienate itself in this redemptive work from its own divine nature, but rather places itself inside the heart of the creature. He who "searches the depths of the Godhead" is he who truly knows and has to do with those ultimate possibilities, which lie in God himself, of creating something which shuts itself off in enmity from God and encloses itself in itself with no way out. These are possibilities which cannot have any Christian significance if seen as the draconian measures of a Marcionist Yahweh and a Blakean Urizen or as the (related) hellfire decrees of the God of Tertullian, Calvin, and Jansenius. They become Christian possibilities only through the doctrine of the Holy Spirit, who in its love is beyond these tragic conflicts. This brings us, however, to the Catholic doctrine of the Church.

Notes

1 The mystery of the difference between spiritual being and the personality was seen with great clarity by Anton Gunther; all his thinking revolves constantly around it. Unfortunately, however, he made the mistake of equating directly that element in the personal which transcends nature with the theological supernatural. Thus, he remained caught in the idealism that he was combatting. It is true that the uniqueness of the human person can have its root only in the uniqueness of having been created and called into being by the absolute uniqueness of a personal God. In this sense personal man stands in an immediate relationship to personal God: it does not, however, necessarily follow that the infinite freedom of the personal God will reveal and offer to share the intimacy of his divine being with personal man, though it is true that the created person only becomes truly aware of his personality through the call of God's revelation.

2 Cf. the comprehensive investigation of Ansgar Ahlbrecht, O.S.B.: *Die bestimmenden Grundmotive der Diskussion über die Unsterblichkeit der Seele in der evangelischen Theologie, Catholica* 17, 1963, 1–24. Cf. also M. Schmaus: *Unsterblichkeit der Geistseele oder Auferstehung von den Toten?* in *Pro Veritate, Festgabe für L. Jaeger und W. Stählin,* 1963.

3. THEOLOGICAL REFLECTIONS ON HUMAN WHOLENESS

MAN BEFORE THE MEDIATION OF THE CHURCH

The Church as Human Wholeness; Mary

The Holy Spirit anticipates all the tragedy of the sinful world, not only by being beyond it in a cloudless heaven, but also by being in its innermost heart. Thus, the divine Spirit which implants itself in humanity can have infinite compassion and, through love, infinite knowledge, without necessarily on that account succumbing to the tragedy of not-loving. It is precisely the freedom from all not-loving and paralysis of the heart which makes possible that intimacy and ultimate knowledge and involvement which characterize the Spirit.

If this is so, then the conquest through the Holy Spirit of man's tragic incompleteness in the ordering of existence is truly ensured if the Spirit does not stand out against impotent humanity as the one fully potent force. Rather, he is the spiritual measure of human potentiality, a humanly sheltering "mother" to whom the children of God are born and by whom they are carried until they are of age. The nature of this achievement is necessarily feminine, and it is necessarily related to the incarnation of the Son of God in the primary physical sense, as well as the self-continuing eucharistic and ecclesiological one.

Hence, this is the role of Mary, overshadowed by the Holy Spirit and impregnated with the Son of the Father, in an event that involves the total act of faith in the word of God, in which the action of the "daughter of Zion" concludes and the action of the "bridal Church" commences. The Immaculate Conception is that necessary piece of the logic of revelation which first makes possible the doctrine of the Incarnation. There is a real mother who nevertheless must not transmit to the child anything guilty or corrupt. As well, it makes possible the doctrine of the Church, which the Son presents to himself as a "glorious bride without spot or wrinkle" and which in turn guarantees beyond all tragic ruin the Christian life of love. This *mater purissima* is also a human guarantee to the individual believer of the primacy of an immaculate existence in love. She remains to the end of the world, at the same time, *mater dolorosissima,* as is revealed not only by the vision in the Apocalypse, but also by reflection on her union (founded in the "overshadowing" and never sensed) with the Holy Spirit which groans in suffering hearts. She stands, both as an individual person (Mary) and as a creaturely "total person" (*ecclesia*), under the cross. She is "under" the cross because she is together with all sinners, in anonymous solidarity with them, and, thus, she is not in the least in competition with the unique crucified one. But she is truly under "the cross" (and not under sin), because only in the figure and the experience of the cross was sin transformed, and continues to be transformed, into pure love.

Augustine envisaged this reality of Mary and the Church when he sought the point in which the easing of the tension of fallen time is suspended, not as the pure eternity of God and of uncreated wisdom, but as the super-time of created wisdom— gathered together in elective love—the first creature which is the basis of all other creatures. This first creature is not, of itself, subject to the uselessness of the easing of the tension; the useless emptiness of time did not flow from it, but it enfolds in its heart this element of dissolution. It descends with it into time, without ceasing, however, to cleave directly to eternal love. It is broken up compassionately with fragmentary creatures in order to share with them the wholeness it never loses. "I have become all things to all men"; many other sayings of Paul are spoken in its spirit.

As the mother chosen for the birth of the Son and freed in advance from the corruption of original sin, Mary is necessarily the object of love which adequately corresponds to the Son and is presented by him to himself (Eph. 6, 27) as that "bride" and (seen eschatologically) "wife," who concludes in advance for all and in all the love contract between God and the world, between the eternal and the created heart.

Authority in the Church

It is against this essential background that we must understand everything ecclesiastical which seems to be an external construc- tion or a positive "law" and creates difficulties for the religious man. That there are such "laws" is due to the fact that the community which answers the historical Son of God must have an historical shape; it therefore exists in time and space. As a community with its forms it precedes the individuals assigned to it and growing in its womb. It must in its visibility as in its precedence have something of marian normativeness. That is true especially of the official functions, whose "givenness" must certainly go back, originally, to the historical Christ (as commis- sions, which necessarily imply authorization). But insofar as the Church is inspired by the Holy Spirit, these functions can operate only according to the norm of this Spirit of love as it exists in the maternal and bridal Church. Christ did not leave any other Spirit to the world. It is not possible to set up the "Spirit of the office" as a kind of "paternal authority" over against the "Spirit of Church love" (which pervades the charismata and thus the structure of Church life), claiming that the Spirit of the office "functions" on the basis of Christ's promises even if the Spirit of love is absent from the Church. Such a statement destroys the trinitarian unity of Christ and the Spirit. It fosters a conception of the Church against which the critique of Tertullian and Joachim of Flora, even of Luther, would be unanswerable.

The teaching office of the Church (together with its "infallibility") has no such immediate relationship to the teaching Christ that it does not need as part of mother Church to follow the *manner of* Christ's teaching: namely, in the unity of word and life, of truth and love. If the Holy Spirit inspires the pure bridal Church with precisely this unity and teaches it to her children, then "infallibility" cannot go back, beyond "immaculateness," i.e., the bridal character, to Christ, but must be the necessary form in which the holiness of the Church-bride presents herself historically—through necessarily imperfect, sinful men. In that case the authority of the Church cannot, under the pretext of humility—of not wanting to be confused with the one redeemer and, therefore, of not even wanting to suggest an identity of office and love attainable only by him—limit itself *a priori* to a purely "formal" authority, with which would be contrasted dualistically a charismatically attested, Spirit-filled authority of, say, the saints.

Such an ultimate dualism cannot be the last word about the nature of the Church. All that is deficient in the administration of the Church must always be criticized from that identity that lies in marian grace. In other words, all authority can only be exercized out of and in the direction of (suffering) love and, as far as man is able, also in it and as its expression. This is shown quite clearly by Paul's exercise of his office, the only one of which we have any adequate account in the New Testament.

The Transparency of the Church's Shape

If the "bride" is the refashioning of the form of the Son and bridegroom through the Holy Spirit in humanity, then it cannot possess any shape of its own which is independent of the Son. What might appear as such is the shape of the answer, made possible by the Son, to the taking shape of God in the world through the Son. This answer is made possible in the last act of the self-sacrificing love of the Son, who gives his flesh and blood for his own and in this utterly real act of devotion (as "thanks" to the Father, *"eucharistia"*) builds the Church in the realtiy of his flesh and blood: in the sacrament of the Eucharist. Here culminates the Christian synthesis of both ways humanity has taken toward a solution: this sacrificed flesh and blood itself is the way of the union of all in the Son and toward the Father (John 17). This union is accomplished precisely in the most extreme mortal tragedy of a sinful creature abandoned by the infinite God.

The Church comes into being in the remembrance of this central event from which all else flows—"Do this in memory of me." And as the Eucharist is one with this unifying death, so also are the other sacraments: especially baptism, which implies being baptized once and for all into Christ's death (and thus is the entry into the community of the Church); confirmation, the fulfillment of baptism, in which full positive status in the Church is imparted to the Christian who has come of age; confession, which signifies the renewed immersion of the sinner into the total confession of the sins of the world on the cross and in the total absolution of the Father at Easter. It would not be difficult to show the same thing in the case of the other sacraments.

It is essential that such mediative practices of the Church be understood from their origins. Therefore, they should be presented and performed in such a way as to become transparent and show their birth. That is, these various systems of laws need to be understood by going back to the original situation of the Church, just as the Church can be made credible to the world only by going back to Christ. But Christ offers himself to the understanding in such a way that he constantly dissolves the particular synthesis (the laws) and makes it transparent to the Father and to men. Thus, he does not present himself as a third being between God and the world (Arianism), but as the one who makes their encounter possible. This is the sense of the christological dogma, finally formulated by the Council of Chalcedon: the "nature" of God and the "nature" of man, not brought together within another nature, but mediated through the fluidity of *one* person (hypostasis). If the God-man is already a pure reduction, how could the Church, as his Mystical Body, be anything different?

On this reduction depends the "comprehensibility" of the mystery of revelation, whereby the mystery character is not dispelled, because it has always to proceed in two directions: as interpretation of God and as interpretation of man. The interpretation of God comes first, for only in the presence of absolute love is man brought into his truth (and hence comprehensibility). But that God reveals himself to man out of his own free divine initiative is the basis of the actuality of Christianity and of the lasting involvement of human self-understanding in this freely creative act of God. Both the different paths of salvation worked out by men prepared the way, even if negatively, for such a divine act. That is why the fulfilling, positive, divine act is not exterior to human action and being. Despite its wonderfulness, it is at the same time the filling of the empty space, the solution of the insoluble problem. God is ultimately never that which is absolutely exterior to man, totally different from him. As the Creator and ground of man's being he is the *not-other* (*Non*

Aliud, as Cusa says), so that God, in revealing himself to man, is also of necessity revealing man to himself.

The dual resolution of the fact of Christ in the direction of God and in the direction of man, and the simultaneously theological and anthropological importance of this fact, is shown in what Christ made the chief commandment, explaining all the other commandments by it and relating them to it. John expressed it by saying that he who does not love his neighbor cannot love God. The identity of the love of God and the love of one's neighbor is not something that is merely formally laid down, but is identical with the hypostatic identity of God and man in Christ. As he loves us both as God and as man, he who loves him gratefully in return loves both the God and the man in him, without differentiation. This is—beyond all possible aspirations of humanism—the supreme honoring and ennobling of man. Hence, the whole civilization of the West and of the world that truly stands on this Christian foundation (and not on things which have falsely claimed the name of Christ) is not only supreme religiousness, but also supreme humanity.

THEOLOGICAL REFLECTIONS ON HUMAN WHOLENESS

Philosophical or Theological Wholeness?

Christianity has shown man an unexpected way of achieving the perfection that was formerly always impossible. But it is a way that requires belief in the resurrection of Chirst and thus is a stumbling block to reason and is a constant challenge to it. The two thousand years of Christian history are a continual and ever more intense struggle with the problem of man and his relation to God. More precisely, it has been a struggle with the respective priorities of the self-understanding. As a being endowed with reason, man owes himself and endeavors to achieve self-understanding in the activity of philosophy. But he has also self-understanding through faith, revealed to him directly by God as the ultimate truth about himself.

This dualism, always present in Christian history, has deepened in the course of the Church's thinking about itself as the earlier somewhat hasty attempts at harmonization proved to be inadequate and as philosophical questioning became more aware of itself in conscious polemical opposition to theology and sought to distinguish itself from the latter. True "secularization" of man and his culture is only possible in a "post-Christian" era, for the cultures of antiquity are by nature religious and in this sense theological. Christianity has so polarized this universally diffused religious feeling around its new center that now the decision for or against Christ becomes a decision for or against the religious significance of existence and culture. Every attempt to reestablish the old, naturally religious atmosphere—most spectacularly in the movement of the eighteenth century called the "Enlightenment"—retains more or less the flavor of a polemical and hence tendentious, negative undertaking.

Religious feeling in the ancient world was so strong (see Paul's discourse in the Areopagus with its mention of the "unknown God" and the poetic quotation "For we are indeed his offspring" Acts 17:23, 28), that the Church Fathers, after the necessary combatting of polytheism, thought they could adopt the classical image of man without much alteration, only with the necessary changes of emphasis. There was no occasion to separate philosophy and theology in the world outside the bible, for man considered himself perfectible only through transcendence into the divine sphere, and the regions of divine epiphany continued both cosmologically and theologically from the absolute into our cosmos. Thus, the Church Fathers were able to regard the pagan (philosophical) theology as an insufficient, but still usable model for the theological self-understanding of man from biblical revelation.

The fact that certain discrepancies became apparent between

the anthropology of antiquity and that of the bible—touching the composition of man out of body and soul—is less important than the fact that the basic Greek idea, that man was destined to a salvation which transcended his earthly existence and was to be found only with God, was confirmed and made more profound by Christianity. If one starts from the strength of earthly, mortal existence, this salvation simply is not possible without divine help. Without a self-manifestation and inclining of the divine, man cannot achieve salvation by himself. It lies, moreover, in a "heavenly" sphere which is closed to earthly existence; in this sense, salvation is "supernatural."

This idea of grace and of the supernatural did not need to be discarded, but only fully illuminated, in order to receive its biblical and Christian sense. The new element was the free personality of the infinite God, who revealed himself through Abraham, Moses, and the prophets, and finally in Christ. He granted man, in gracious mercy, the salvation he could not obtain for himself by admitting him to the inner heavenly reality and essence. What ancient peoples dimly tried to realize in their myths and divine epiphanies, their religious state feasts and sacramental cult dramas, darkened and obscured by many misleading details, was in fact granted in biblical times truly by God as grace, without any anticipatory human interventions and in full transparency. However, this grace demanded a radically penitent, sober rethinking on the part of man.

Thus, the "seeds of truth" (*logoi spermatikoi*) in the pagan world were able, after due purification, to pass into Christian theology. The basic conception that concrete earthly human nature is, individually as well as socially, perfectible only beyond itself, only in the sphere of God, and thus "supernaturally," was comprehensive. It supplied the only possible meaning of the problem of existence, so that the question of man's perfectibility without passing into the world of the divine would have appeared totally absurd and could not have been asked. The grace quality of the self-revelation of God, the essential gratuitousness of his self-giving—what personal love does not have this quality of grace and is not always experienced in this way?—still prevented asking the question of what would have happened to man if this grace had not come to him.

This is still the case with St. Thomas Aquinas. He attributes to human nature a single, supernatural goal. The natural goal of which he sometimes speaks, he regards as the best that a mortal man can achieve in this earthly life, but one which would never suffice to justify the existence and the particular nature of mankind. As an Aristotelean he does not even hesitate to ascribe an inner sense of direction to "nature" which informs it about its own powers and possibilities in relation to something which is essentially unattainable by it. St. Thomas even sees in this apparent disproportion a mark of the dignity of man: "that nature is of a nobler kind which can attain the perfect good, even if it needs help from outside to do so, than that nature which cannot attain the perfect good but attains only to an imperfect good for the achievement of which its own powers are sufficient" (*Summa* I–II, q 5, a 5, *ad 2*).

Whoever writes like that is thinking in a Greek as well as a Christian way. He is thinking like a Greek, because man is regarded from the start as part of a comprehensive whole (both divine and cosmic), within which alone his perfection is imaginable. His thought is Christian, because this obvious dependence appears at once as the gracious openness of God which, indeed, grants man true transcendence with its promise of salvation. Yet, it is possible to examine with St. Thomas, whose thought comes at the end of the Middle Ages and the beginning of the modern world, man's own powers and to ask how far man is able to look and move toward God by his own nature, and what chance he has of apprehending a personally self-revealing God by himself with the aid of his own created intellect.

The answer St. Thomas gave was adopted, in essentials, by the

First Vatican Council. The Council declared that the human mind can and must understand of itself that the world is not God, that it has a transcendental origin and a transcendental goal in the Absolute (the Christian term for which relationship is free "creation"). The Absolute in itself is "incomprehensible" and "inexpressibly above anything which can be conceived outside it." But it is obviously the basis and goal of all creation (i.e., that which is not necessary, but contingent).[1]

To ask this is not, for St. Thomas, to ask the later question raised by Michel de Bay (Baius, born 1513). In de Bay's opinion, perfection through grace belongs to the integrity of human nature; thus, the supernatural is something owed to nature (at least originally in Paradise), something which is bound up with it, and in this sense is "natural." In the reaction against this view, which was condemned by the Church, baroque theology deepened the gulf between the "natural" and the "supernatural." The element of the gratuitousness of grace (as participation in the divine nature) could now apparently be salvaged only by contrasting with man actually called and raised to the supernatural (to the ultimate goal of the immediate vision of God) a "pure nature," which is admittedly only *possible*. This "pure nature" never existed as a reality—since the first man was created immediately in grace—but it certainly could have existed, if grace really is grace.

It was now tempting to trace the outlines of this hypothetical "pure" human nature, for such nature did exist as a real element within the totality of the actually existing human being. Further, one could ask what would be a purely natural goal which was not the vision of God; he could ask whether or not the resurrection of the flesh, i.e., the perpetuation of earthly human wholeness, would have belonged to the goods of "pure nature." This was a speculation which had serious consequences, for under the pretext of serving Christian theology it gravely endangered it. Not only did this idea of a so-called "pure man" beneath the Christian nature directly serve post- and anti-Christian thought, it also made the supernatural orientation of man toward the God of elective love appear as an inessential, even dispensable, addition and superstructure. What theology pondered here in a purely experimental and abstract way was soon, in English free thought and in continental enlightenment, to become the actual model of humanity. It lay in the nature of the case that the Adventlike openness of late medieval philosophical theology could no longer be reestablished, and that now in enlightened anthropology the original doubts about the nature of man became far more acute.

Either man is once more to be redeemed (from matter) to spirit, by renouncing his unique personality (thus Hegel and his predecessors and successors), or else the tragic dualism remains the last word, which heroically sees imperfectibility (as the eternal return) as absolute (with Nietzsche), or else the fragment experiences in its "failure" (Jaspers) and in its "determination to accept death" (Heidegger) a gleam of wholeness which one sees and shares in only in renouncing it. It follows that, faced with this impossibility of completion, man denies his spiritual nature altogether. Consequently, either he sees himself biologically as a member of a species (vitalism, Marxism), the significance of whose existence is only an anonymous evolutionistic one, or else he sees himself, to his ruin, in shallow, decadent existentialism as the eternal self-cancelling question mark.

Christian theology has never wanted to give the idea of a possible purely natural integration anything but a completely hypothetical significance. The question can be raised whether the hypothesis—making a statement in the abstract without any content was unknown in the whole course of early theology—is a necessary part of Christian thinking. It cannot fill the gaps of concrete human existence: man, in fact, remains most painfully imperfectible by himself. It should satisfy reason to establish his dual character.

Even Adam, according to the legend of Paradise, although

created in the fullness of God's grace, had an unsatisfied longing until God had given him Eve. Adam transcended and sought through the whole of nature—naming and hence knowing it—looking for that which would bring him fulfillment and completion. He did not find it. It is strange that human nature, obviously quite different from the animals which were already created two by two, has to long for the other. The other is not simply there, but is brought to him by God, as a grace, which harms him as well as fulfills him. For Eve was taken from his side—he has her within him, and yet she is more than he is and cannot be arrived at from him—in sleep, in defenseless *ekstasis*, which, according to the old theologians, foreshadowed the cross. Why should not Adam's dialogue relationship to God, in which he received through grace a share in the nature of God, have just as much and even more—beyond his natural capacities—awakened him to and given him the power to attain that for which he had always been intended by God?

We dismissed above the equation of spirit (as that which is above nature) and God's grace (as the supernatural), which is the basis of Anton Günther's system. The encounter of human beings in love and knowledge is above nature, but not supernatural. The Garden of Eden was already in "converse" with God; thus, that language was already a reality for Adam. But man (whether thought of as an individual or as a couple) is not wakened to language except by being addressed by the absolute Word. Only by answering love he has experienced does he find his way to words. Human speech can never "develop" from animal noises. With the problem of the origin of language, the distinction between that which is above nature and the supernatural becomes so difficult that any idea we have of the former collapses without the latter. The theological demand of a possible purely natural man, of whose innermost being language would be a part (Aristotle), without his being engaged in a (two-sided) dialogue, is a rational impossibility.

With the relation of Adam to Christ comes the ultimate idea of Christian anthropology: the "first Adam" is created and endowed for the sake of the second one. He is the image and likeness of a figure of fulfillment who is still to come and, therefore, cannot be fully interpreted by himself. He is intelligible only in the final figure of the dying and resurrecting Son of God. The transcendence of Adam's sense of life, according to which he can find the meaning of his humanity only in the repossessing of all his own powers and only in the flight of grace carrying him to his ultimate goal in God, is, then, the beginning, the inchoate foreshadowing of that which gives purpose and sense to the existence of the man Jesus. He does not exist otherwise than in being taken up and over into the person of the self-revealing Word of God, in a degree of surrender and of being taken over which—itself unique and boundless—is yet the form given for all human beings.

If this is so, then the whole question of the relation between "philosophy" and "theology" in the modern sense appears superseded. For the ancient and the medieval consciousness both "sciences" were either identical, or else philosophy was one element within a comprehensive (natural and supernatural) theology. The concern is always to illuminate reality through the reason, and reality, both for pagan and for biblical-Christian man, is constantly such that divinity has always revealed itself out of itself, and is thus both natural and supernatural. Integrating significance, however, can come only from the supernatural, from that which is ordained by God. Hence, this significance is the ultimate concern of philosophical reflection; existence must be interpreted according to it. In Christian terms this would mean that the final and, hence, the first idea of the Creator in making the world and making man was "to unite all things in him (Christ), things in heaven and things on earth" (Eph. 1, 10). Thus, everything outside this ultimate synthesis remains fragmentary and not capable of being fully understood. But if this is the supreme intention, affecting the whole of creation as such, though grace is owed to no one, then all the laws and forms within creation must stand in the range of this comprehensive grace. There is no need to ask the question of any possibility outside it; it then becomes so shadowy that any valuable statement about it is impossible.

Man in Freedom and Hereditary Guilt

From what we have already said some light falls on this, the darkest area of theological anthropology. There is a double light: partly from the origin of human creation, partly from the goal which is the fulfillment of man's significance in Christ.

If Adam, from the beginning, in the act of his first creation, was chosen, beyond his total natural human strength, to love the eternal God and to achieve supernatural perfection in the measure of this love, then God gave this "first" man, who serves all those following as a model and an idea, the power to live his life in loving dialogue with him. One can also say that God, who inclined toward his new-born creature with infinite personal love, in order to inspire him with it and to awaken the response to it in him, does in the divine supernatural order something similar to a mother. Out of the strength of her own heart she awakens love in her child in true creative activity. Of course, God is not man, and his inclining in grace is therefore something different than when one human heart turns lovingly to another. Nevertheless, the analogy is of some value, particularly if the love of the mother is a pure unselfish love and, hence, draws on the power of the absolute divine store of love. The essential thing is that the child, awakened thus to love, and already endowed by another's power of love, awakens also to himself and to his true freedom, which is in fact the freedom of loving transcendence of his narrow individuality. No man reaches the core and ground of his own being, becoming free to himself and to all beings, unless love shines on him. He can do it as little as he can invent a language for himself, in which he would presume to name all things and thus be the first person to have them all for himself.[2]

This first reflection on the limits of the power of the individual and his dependence on gracious love does not take account of the separate question of guilty failure. It suggests also that man, as a biological being which emerges from the animal kingdom, does not have enough strength of spirit and reason to rise above his instincts. Further, the regulating forces of the species and of instinct, which in the animal kingdom hold the life of individuals in order, can on the human plane be replaced only by a personal free relationship to one another (which integrates the biological laws by transcending them). No single man can attain his true freedom unless he is borne by the power of men's openness to one another in love; if this is true of the sphere of the human mind, then it is naturally even truer of the man raised to loving communion with God.

Supposing this order of love were disturbed, then the idea of the second Adam, the God-man Christ, explains and reconciles the disturbance in human nature which supervened between creation and redeeming perfection. An element of guilt is involved in that essential failure in the power of the individual to offer by himself the love asked of him. An element of guilt not only weighs on him as an individual, but also and primarily on the community, which now, in the context of the family and the tribal relationships, lacks the awakening power of love. It is thus unable to raise the generation to the height of the demanded love, to the level of the freedom of the individual and the community. This failure, characteristic of the whole of humanity, does not need to be conceived of only as "punishment" for an original sin. It can also, assuming the unity of God's world plan, be interpreted as practice in and preparation for the love granted in Christ—the love of God and hence the love of men.

What is suggested here as a possibility is that this guilty disturbance in the total relation of man to God is, according to biblical-revelation reality, a disturbance which takes effect in each individual ("personal sin"). Through the interdependence of the generations, the social element embraces the individual and influences him. Otherwise, single individuals would be able to make a free decision for God which would run counter to the guilty condition of the others and, thus, be freed from this compulsion. But this freedom they do not possess. A general, guilty fault prevents them from making the personal, complete free act to which they are called as natural, social beings and especially as beings chosen for the personal love of God. The offer of God's grace and love cannot fail—God is no less ready to love us and to communicate himself lovingly to us as he was to Adam. Hence, the trouble can only lie with man's unwillingness to accept this love. Because this lack of willingness to accept is aroused for the individual within a social context, this failure to respond to love must perpetuate itself through the interdependence of the generations.

Thus, the view, widespread in the early Church, that original sin was connected with the sexual act, with sexuality altogether or still more generally with concupiscence (lust), is justified. It is a valid viewpoint inasmuch as sexuality is experienced and practiced not on the truly human level of selfless loving devotion, but on a lower level at which the objective element of self-surrender is turned into a subjective, egoistic, perverse exploitation of pleasure. This biological instinctualness is characteristic of the animal consciousness which has not advanced to the knowledge of being, but remains dully enclosed within itself and can experience instinct only as functional pleasure. It is not purified by human spirituality and raised to what alone it should be on the spiritual level—something taken into service by personal love and made to speak.

This inability to accept love results in the paralysis of the free center of the person, who, in order to become truly himself and to realize himself in freedom, must have the strength to respond fully to God and to his fellowmen. This paralysis, which does not take from man his full freedom (as Luther claimed), but hinders its full activity, its self-realization, has something demonic about it and is described by the bible as the tyranny of the devil ("the prince of this world") over humanity and the world. Such enslavement results in falsifications of values in every sphere and is only broken by the perfect loving death of Christ and removed for all who open themselves to the power of his love and draw upon it. In the loving act of Christ it is not God, turned away and no longer gracious, who is turned back to men and made gracious (this would be crude anthropomorphism). It is man, turned away and incapable of receiving grace, who is given fresh power to say "yes" to God and thus to achieve freedom.

In what sense can this inherited weakness and incapacity for full, liberating love be described as "guilt" or "sin"? A preliminary, not entirely satisfying, answer to this dark mystery might be attempted by emphasizing the ambiguity of every act of human freedom. It is always personal and social at the same time, so that whenever human freedom first comes into operation (in the "first" man), already—and archetypically—all human freedom is involved. A metaphysical point at which this human decision occurs is therefore theoretically necessary, but is not historically demonstrable. One might, however, raise the question whether this point does not exist above the whole temporal unfolding of the material cosmogonic process. In particular, does it exist above the biological development of man, which would thus be subject already and at its very heart to the law of generation and death and consequently to "vanity" (i.e., empty futility) and the "eager longing" for the revelation of the truth of being God's children, "not of its own will," as Paul says (Rom. 8, 19 ff.)?

Thus, we can move away from the idea that the Fall affecting the whole temporal condition of the cosmos took place demonstrably at one particular point in the history of the universe. We can approach the idea which some of the Church Fathers had. They connected the cosmic process with a metaphysical negative decision of man toward God. This does not have to be interpreted gnostically or in the manner of Origen (as if materiality as such were the consequence of sin), but rather in the manner of Gregory of Nyssa, according to whom God, foreseeing human sin, gave man his biological (sexual) concupiscence. This would mean that man's negative decision flowed into the process of "hominization," which preceded it in time. True freedom can never be the mere result of an unfree process; thus, human freedom must have been involved at some undemonstrable point in the decision of the Creator that man be his partner.[3]

For this view to come dangerously close to Gnosticism (and to the cabala which derives from it), the emphasis would have to be transferred to the motif of the serpent in Paradise. Stress would have to be placed on the effect, even in the "garden of innocence," of a cosmic catastrophe which had preceded the arrival of man. There would have to have been a collapse in the kingdom of the "powers," those original spiritual beings. These beings are so much part of the one cosmos that the ancient world saw them as the true moving and shaping forces of the material world (the idea crops up again, in a different form, with Schelling and Baader). The bible calls them "controllers of the world" or personal tribal spirits.

Thus, the human paradise appears already embedded in a disruptive world order, and man, called to the freedom of his decisive response to God, is exposed to demonic solicitation. Hence, the romantic psychology of Kierkegaard ("The Idea of *Angst*") would be theologically justified: when man lives childlike in innocence and grace, it is not freedom which opens up its devilish and giddy depths, but the demon himself who temptingly approaches. In this view man is brought in as an actor in a drama that has already begun, and his condition before and after the Fall is not explained just by him and his relationship to

God. There was a third element involved before him, so that
Augustine had the idea (which may have followed) that man
was created to fill the gap in the heavenly Jerusalem which the
fall of the angels had left.[4]

Anselm did not completely oppose the idea, but wanted to
preserve the independence of human, and thus cosmic, existence:
it is impossible that man was created for the sake of a drama
more important than his.[5] Eve's reference to the other power
("The serpent beguiled me") is factually true, but does not ex-
cuse her: to step out into the region of temptability was an act
of free decision, which took place between her and the Creator,
whom she should have obeyed.[6]

The former interpretation is anthropocentric, the latter cos-
mocentric. The Fathers combined both aspects and, thus, indicated the fragmentary nature of our knowledge about the fragmentariness of existence. Revelation does not offer complete
knowledge of our origins; it is only on the way toward unity that
the path leading forward begins. But that means that humanity,
centered on this solidarity in Adam, has always been borne and
sustained by the second Adam, the true God-man. He takes the
inadequate "God-manhood," as presented historically by the
dialogue relationship between God and man, and reconciles it.
The second Eve is important here (as has been shown above).
Because of her essential relation to the second Adam, she must be
free of hereditary guilt in order to bear him and subsequently to
be the fruitful womb of the Church (as "the bride without mark
or wrinkle," Eph. 5, 27) for all the brothers and members of
Jesus Christ.

Thus all the fallenness and tragedy of the sexual, which has
death in it, is already envisaged and reconciled, because there is
one who did not come into existence through the portal of sex
as a being cast out into the world and subject to fate. He, out of
freely given love, took birth and death upon himself and, thus,
gave them new value. The fateful wheel of hereditary guilt, in

which metaphysical and physical causality are intertwined, is now broken. Even before man's original decision to exist in and for himself (as temporal mortal "nature"), instead of for God and in his grace, comes God's original decision "before the foundation of the world" to love and choose us in his beloved Son, so that we may stand holy and blameless before his face forever (Eph. 1, 4–5).

Thus, man lives alienated from his real nature under the law of the first ("old") Adam. He comes to know and understand that law when he is able to pass into Christ's "perfect law of liberty" and, therefore, into his own reality. In this transition he learns that he is not only freed from an indifferent universal fate, but from a negativity that lies within his own freedom. This negativeness is an incapacity which is essentially a failure of the will, a latent or even open desire to rebel, which it is impossible for man to regard as a purely external compulsion, but must always acknowledge as an inner attitude of his own.

Man between Faith and Knowledge

From all this it is clear that man in many respects exists in a constant movement between knowledge and faith. As a created spirit he stands in a dual self-transcending relationship to fellow spirits (the *Thou*) and to the Absolute (the divine *I*). If he can only become truly himself when awakened by the love of someone else, then he will become a knowing self-comprehending and reflecting spirit insofar as he gives himself, in love and trust, i.e., in faith, to the other person. And the more profoundly he learns through this act of surrender what existence and being itself are, then the more can understanding create a new surrender, which is now a venturing forward in trust on the basis of experiential knowledge. If the first process was faith leading to understanding (*fides quaerens, inveniens intellectum*), the second process is knowledge producing new faith (*intellectus gignens fidem*).

This relationship between people is thus more than the general educative principle that whoever wants to learn must start with a faith ready to accept, so that gradually, as knowledge is acquired and connections understood from their principles, faith is left behind. A fellow human being is never a "subject of knowledge." Even if he is a lifelong partner in marriage, the depths of his unique being and his freedom could never be known except through a trusting openness of himself and the acceptance of what is freely communicated, i.e., through "revelation."

Whoever grasps this can also open himself receptively to subhuman nature and, thus, learn things from natural beings—from landscapes, plants, animals, stars—which a purely cognitive ("scientific") attitude never discovers. The depth of the significant shapes of nature, the meaning of its language, the extent of its words of revelation can only reveal themselves to one who has opened himself up receptively to them.

But while all natural beings as well as man communicate and are related to one another within a total created nature, this is no longer the case with the dialogue relationship between God and man. The absolute truth of God is different from man's finite worldly truth. Therefore, whenever God reveals himself to man, he must also give him, as well as his truth, the accessory openness and receptivity. He must bathe both the object and the receiver of his self-revelation in a common medium of divine light and establish what St. Thomas calls a connaturality between God and man. This has two names in the language of Christian theology. There is an objective one, which refers to the quality of its being—grace as a sharing in the inner reality of God: as "sanctifying" grace it gives us a share in God's being, as "helping" grace it lets us live and act out of this reality. The subjective one refers to the quality of its consciousness: divine virtue (i.e., fittingness in relation to God) as faith, hope, and charity.

This "three-in-one" signifies a single attitude with three aspects: the attitude of preferring God to everything that is one's own, because he is himself (love) and therefore is absolutely in the right, even against me (faith), and my salvation is in this (hope). These three aspects are not to be thought of as being lined up in a row; they affect one another in a circular way, they promote one another. Hope, framed by faith and love, ensures that human subjectivity is not denied in transcendence, but partakes of it, if not in itself, at least in God. This faith is, as a "living" (i.e., loving) one, the readiness, made possible by God's grace, to prefer God's truth to all truth of one's own, not only when it appears plausible to us and supplements the beginnings of our secular knowledge, but also when it seems to run counter, at least some of the time, to all our own insights. Even in this obscurity the truth of faith preserves its characteristic brightness as long as we wait in love expecting to be surpassed by God. At the same time, we know that the mysteries and distressing contradictions of the world—suffering, injustice, folly, the triumph of evil—cannot be overcome by simple formulas and easy supernatural solutions.

Faith, hope, and charity move through a fragmentary existence towards an unforeseeable perfection. Therefore, they can become only suspicious if wholeness is offered recognizably and tangibly to them in advance. In the fragmentary nature of man and the world they have a guarantee of the genuine. As a blind man feels with knowing hands the sharp edges of broken pottery, so they learn from the fragments of existence in what direction toward wholeness God points them. Such a fragment is, for groping human hands, the cross of Christ: innumerable lines of significance intersect at it, disentangle, and then entangle themselves again. A synthesis that can be grasped at a glance is all the less possible in that the synthesis that God brought about manifested itself in the ultimate shattering of all human plans, demands, and longings. Faith, love, and hope grope their way through the darkness: they believe the incredible; they love that which withdraws itself, abandoning them; they hope against hope. The darkness with its withdrawal of all available unity makes them one.

Such unity of the Christian attitude of faith, hope, and love is the ultimate basis of Christian understanding or knowledge, whose nearest analogy is the knowledge of a beloved human being. That is knowledge of quite a different kind than scientific psychological knowledge; it must stop at the moment that love cools and no longer forms the bridge between souls. Thus, there are the exultant hours in which God allows man, in a flash or in peaceful contemplation, to see whole landscapes of divine truth almost from the divine viewpoint. At such times that which is unintelligible can suddenly become amazingly clear and move into the area of the believer's experience. But the lover and believer will not long for such immediate knowledge or clamorously demand it, but rather will remain in an attitude of trusting acceptance. Being open, as he should be, he will not shut himself up in blind faith out of "humility," but will accept the understanding of faith wherever it is offered him and let himself be led into deeper love by it.

The mediator of such understanding in love is the Holy Spirit which, as the "Spirit of childhood," encourages two attitudes. The first is the immediate, open approach to all the treasures and the secrets of God; the second is the childlike spirit which does not presume to take what does not belong to it. One of the wonderful things about man's relation to God is that maturity and a childlike spirit grow in the same proportion. It is simply part of the maturity of Christian and creaturely thinking to have seen that a whole, and certainly not a divine whole, never emerges from worldly and human pieces. That is why the Pentecostal approach of the true "Spirit of the whole" always begins with the shattering of all presumptuously supposed integrations. To orderly secular reason the Spirit will appear as anarchic chaos. Love and faith "know" that and endure it.

This has its echo in the Church. The Christian comes of age

in the unity of faith and knowledge for his mission in the Church and the world. Before the world he must be able to defend and answer for that which he has known through faith and believed through knowledge. But it will also be a sign of his maturity that he always remains attentive like a child. He never separates for a moment his knowledge from his faith nor his conscience from the total Christian consciousness, which has its center only in Christ and the Church (as the immaculate and infallible bride). If before it was a matter of interpreting and explaining everything Christian and ecclesial within the fundamental relationship between God and man, then the same scheme appears again here from another direction, as the relating back of all fragmentary evidence to the comprehensiveness of the love between Christ the bridegroom and the bridal Church. Only by looking toward this end, by looking longingly up to this perfect "Jerusalem above," can anything separated and obscured in time be moved into the illuminating light of the Spirit. Christian knowledge and practice in "Church awareness," as far as they are granted to our existence in faith, love, and hope, are hence simply the same thing.

Practice in Christian Wholeness

Where man's treasure is, that is where his heart is too. Augustine loved this saying and his thinking often centered around it.

On earth bear toil, in heaven reflect upon peace: see that you act well here so that you may remain there forever. On earth there is no place where the heart can remain uninjured; if it lies about on the earth it will be destroyed. If one has anything precious, one stows it away in a high and safe place. Many men, indeed all men, when they hear of threatening war, seek a hiding place for all their valuables. . . . But what more precious thing does one have then one's heart? It is from the heart that one possesses all earthly life. Lift up your hearts (*Serm.* Morin I, 20 [504–506]).

The treasure, given and possessed in faith, is the wholeness of man, prepared in God. Faith, love, and hope are the way in which the heart, beating restlessly through time, finds a home in the eternal, together with everything that it loves here and brings with it. It is from the heart that the demand of faith comes for fidelity. This is the basis of the dialogue character, the covenant significance, of all ethics. Not mere "duty"—this is a monologue relationship of the empirical to the ideal man—but a hold, out of love, onto the love gratuitously given to one. To endure is to be faithful, through everything, in what has been once chosen and praised. This expresses a fundamental notion of New Testament ethics: endurance, more literally endurance here below—"great endurance, in afflictions, hardships, calamities, beatings, imprisonments, tumults, labors, watching, hunger; . . . in honor and dishonor, in ill repute and good repute. We are treated as imposters, and yet are true; as unknown, and yet well known; as dying, and behold we live . . ." (2 Cor. 6, 4–9). Patience, such as James recommends, is evident in the farmer who waits calmly for the rain, the Christians who should establish their hearts for the imminent coming of the Lord, the prophets who have suffered and endured (Jas. 5, 7–11).[7]

With John this enduring here below is simplified to a simple "abiding."[8] The life of persistent love does not question its own actions, does not question the Lord who lets it abide and, therefore, does not answer any puzzled question as to why it is still there: "If it is my will that he remain until I come, what is that to you?" (John 21, 22). From the Apostles' first sight of "where he was staying" and from their "staying with him" (1, 39), from the first invitation that he "stay with them and he stayed there" (4, 40), the mystery unfolds increasingly. Christ as the Son "continues forever" (8, 35) because God the Father "dwells" in him (14, 10). For the believer everything is fulfilled in his "dwelling" in Christ who "indwells," who himself with the Father and the Holy Spirit "abides" in him who "abides" in them (8, 31; 14, 17;

15, 4–10; 1 John 2:6, 10, 14, 27, 28; 3:6, 9, 14–17, 24; 4, 12–16). Whereas in the idea of "holding out" there is still a flavor of exertion so as not to be swept away by the stream of time, of habit, of opposition, in the idea of "abiding" there is no more thought of achievement. There is only the idea of the faithfulness of love to love ("abide in *my* love") which abides itself in the love of love ("as I abide in *his* love" John 15, 9–10). The love of Jesus for the Father is the same in time and eternity: in time, it transcends time. And the love of the disciples for Jesus, by being held in his love, can share in the same time which is above time.

The existence of the lover in time is, therefore, a mystery for the world, because his existence does not seem less fragmentary than any other; perhaps it seems even more fragmentary. For it makes no effort to form itself completely in time. And the love in which it is suspended apparently does not make this effort either. His treasure and his heart are somewhere else—in the eternal. There, unknown to the lover in his "earthly tent," "a house not made with hands, eternal in the heavens" is prepared, which is "a building from God." "While . . . still in this tent" he "sighs with anxiety," not for another, second, newfounded shape of being, but for that wholeness which finally gathers together fragmentariness, as a "further clothing" (2 Cor. 5, 1–4). Thus, temporal existence is an "exile," and the longing of the lover is for his home, even if love before and after death is the same. Hence, its indifference to whichever it is that conquers longing (2 Cor. 5, 8; Phil. 1, 21–23).

Love, in faith, by abiding leaves the shaping of the whole to the Lord. He himself is its wholeness. He draws to himself the best, most central, most unified elements in it, and, thus, what remains behind on earth is something definitely fragmentary, possibly even just ash, while all the fire is with the Lord. But perhaps it is a fire of unknown extent which is given back by the Lord to the world according to an unknown measure for an unknown time. What we see may be a mysterious pile of broken pieces, but it may also have the transparency of a whole, which then obviously cannot be made up of the earthly totality of *these* fragments, but comes from elsewhere. The law that operates between the fragment and the whole is one of withdrawal (in order that love may be served) and of pouring out (in the commission of love). The withdrawal can be almost vampirelike. The very best elements, the most nurtured, the most hopeful, the most necessary for progress are sucked from the fragmentary earthly form. These elements are to be used and squandered by the love of God in the economy of the "heavenly Jerusalem." The person thus deprived or anyone else who sees the deprivation or, knowingly or unknowingly, draws profit from it has no opportunity of knowing this. Thus, the wholeness implanted in fragments by the Lord can never be calculated: the strength of his cross is visible everywhere in the Church. One may think he has almost caught up with it, but this visibility does not manifest itself so much in this life as to be called an attribute of the Church (*nota ecclesiae*).

Yes, the withdrawal is more immediately related to the goal than the pouring out; for the eternal Jerusalem is to be built up out of the temporal one, not vice versa. Every new death gives not only one new member to the eternal city, but takes over with it in advance some of the hearts of those who have loved the one who has died. The validity of this law is so absolute that it cannot be questioned by any possibility of mankind developing into the future. Then, there would have to be a new horizon for man in which the death and the redeeming cross of Christ would be left behind as unimportant or superseded. But that could happen only at the cost of the existence and well-being of the individual which would be sacrificed to that of an anonymous, generically conceived humanity. Wholeness would then be humanity itself, maturing through generations as it grows out of its own fragmentary existence. Such an ideal, however, can only be envisaged by denying the basic structure of existence, as we showed at the outset. If that ideal is inculcated by education into growing human beings, it must therefore destroy their humanity at its heart.

Thus man, healed and made whole in the salvation of God, and thus in this simple basic sense holy, rests in a mysterious suspension he does not himself understand and which on that very account is strangely exhilarating. He is clearly aware of earthly imperfectibility, which does not become for him an oppressive prison. The thought of having to perfect himself at any cost does not become an obsession. Knowing of the house built up in grace for him with God, he can cheerfully inhabit his tumbledown hut and free himself through time. Assenting to his secret deprivations in favor of a beyond he cannot reach, he also assents to the secret rewards that come to him from there. He acquires strength when he thought he had none left; wings can bear him up. What is given into his hands to administer is more than he can ascribe to himself: he can therefore only distribute it as something from elsewhere which has mysteriously come into his possession.

Wholeness streams and shines through the fragments. The more uninhibited this action is, the simpler is the consciousness the fragments have of their fragmentariness. And there seems to be a strange relationship between the spirit of streaming, shining wholeness and the spirit of the abandonment of the fragment. It is as if to renounce all efforts to achieve wholeness is precisely to practice wholeness itself, as if God is nowhere nearer than in the humility and poverty of indifference, in the openness to death, in the renunciation of every hold on or attempt to make certain of God. That greater power which moves effortlessly through his renunciation—the power that works in his powerlessness—lies beyond power and impotence. And the salvation that is present in his defeat is so free that no one can prevent him from being the whole even in the fragment.

Notes

[1] Cf. Vatic. I, *Sessio* 3, ch. 1–2, and the related canons: Dz. 1782–1785, 1801–1806.

[2] Cf. Gustav Siewerth, *Metaphysik der Kindeit*, 1957, and *Philosophie der Sprache*, 1962.

[3] It is in this way that I have interpreted (in *Herrlichkeit*, II, 676–681) Soloviev's idea of the fall of the world soul (which is mankind).

[4] Augustine: *Enchiridion* c 29 (PL 40, 246), c 61 (261); Gregory the Great: *Hom. in Evang.* 21, 2, (PL 76, 1171).

[5] *Cur Deus Homo*, I, 16–18 (Schmitt, II, 74–84).

[6] For the whole question, cf. Gustav Siewerth, *Entwicklungstheorie und Offenbarung*, in *Erbe und Entscheidung*, 14th year, 1960, 1–26.

[7] Erich Przywara: *Geduld*, in *Demut, Geduld, Liebe*, 1960, 27–46.

[8] This idea is brought out more clearly in the German which uses the one word *bleiben* for the various RSV equivalents: "abide," "remain," "stay," "continue" and "dwell."—Tr. N.

4. THEOLOGICAL REFLECTIONS ON HISTORY

THE QUESTION OF THE THEOLOGICAL SIGNIFICANCE OF HISTORY

The Heart of the Question: History and the Individual

The most mysterious thing about man is that he is two things at once: a nature (i.e. an embodied mind-soul, an "individual") and a person (in incomparable, eternal uniqueness). He is both so inseparably that a human person without nature or a human nature without personality cannot be conceived.[1] So far we have considered man primarily from the point of view of his personalness: as the unique single individual who in the quest for his perfectibility cannot rest until he is certain of the resurrection from the dead, which emerges in history in connection with the message of the loving death of the Son of God. This message is strictly beyond the realms of scientific or metaphysical cosmology and anthropology.

But man is not only a race consisting of *persons;* he is also a *race* consisting of persons. The race goes on while the persons appear and then disappear, but it lasts only because it always consists of persons. Consequently, its meaning as a race, if it has one, cannot be determined independently of the meaning of the persons. This meaning, however, is not simply identical with the meaning of the single person. For he is always an individual as well and, hence, part of a totality which embraces him, even if he is always a person. Therefore, the comprehensive whole cannot be determined in its significance by simply abstracting the limited sense of the individual destiny. This brief reflection shows how difficult it is even to formulate the question of the total sense of history.

In the following paragraphs this question is not posed generally, but as a theological one. This is not to deny that the question of the perfectibility of history—or, which is the same, the significance of history—is relevant to the philosophy of history. For the man who is addressed by the theological word of God is constantly the man (as an historical nature and person) in whose being the question of self-understanding is always alive. My intention, however, is to ask the question as it is specifically relevant to the theology of man in history, if only in an abbreviated, very general form. In spite of much talk about "theology of history," the question is not asked very often these days by Catholic theology. In fact, it belongs to the *tremenda* of theology, or, rather, it is a question which, more clearly than other questions, puts the Christian face to face with the *tremendum* of the whole Christian revelation.

Let us define the question first, formally and according to its contents. Formally, we are asking about the theological significance of history, i.e., its meaning as derived from the word of God: What does Christian revelation say in scripture about history? In order to answer that question, the word of God must be understood by the man who believes it. Therefore, theology requires, and in fact already contains in its nature, a human theology. But that means more exactly that part of history is also the human self-understanding of history, however faulty and dialectic it might be. It is man who makes history, even if nature and the powers in it on the one side, and God on the other, "co-operate."

Theology cannot anticipate this human self-understanding of history; hence, it cannot attempt by itself any higher synthesis out of the human and the biblical understanding of history, as Hegel endeavored. Rather, if it is to remain true to itself, it can only place, together with history, all human historical understanding (however much that is new it may seem to discover in the course of time) under the measure of the word of God. If the human understanding of history grows, and this is apparently the case today, then that means that the interpreter of revelation cannot transfer either the traditional or the modern solutions of the theology of history automatically to the new situation. He must examine, in a fresh confrontation, with a genuine effort of the mind, history seen under the word of God.

It is much more difficult, in many respects, to define the contents of the question. First, the word of God—in the Old Testament, the Gospels, and the Acts of the Apostles—is itself history. To be sure, it is a piece of privileged history, but it cannot be so cut off from other history that one can say that at this point there broke vertically into horizontal universal history the events of divine revelation. If this were so, the biblical story in itself, in its temporal extent, would remain a quite ordinary piece of world history. Rather, it is precisely in its human actuality, in the historical shape which it forms within human actuality, in the historical shape which it forms within human history, that it is conditioned and fashioned by the Word and Spirit of God breaking in. Jewish history is messianism orientated forward in time. Likewise, the Christian community with its eschatological direction is oriented toward the future. But now this historical area, fashioned by the word of God, is opened missiologically to the whole of history. In the Old Testament this is found in the promise to Abraham that all peoples will be blessed in him, in the visions of Deutero-Isaiah of Jerusalem as the center of all kingdoms, and in Daniel's apocalyptic vision of history.[2] In the New Testament this is discovered in Christ's command to the apostles and all Christians to evangelize the whole of historical humanity.

The God of Israel and the Lord of the Church attribute to themselves in advance the power and the right over all history. This means that it is not a purely immanently unfolding history of the world which is to expect transcendental judgment. The immanent course of the world in its unfolding is subject already to the historical and redemptive power of the Lord, and with its own significance is open—through the existence of Israel and the Church—to the significance of God. Behind this perspective there stands that theological truth which is treated by Luther and Lutheran theology under the idea of the double world rule: a directing of the world to the right and to the left. And behind this again stands the Old Testament dialectic of the "glory" of God in the history and land of Israel—but equally in the history and land of all heathen peoples. Thus, the dialectic of Jew and pagan, or, put in a different way, of law and gospel, is a double dialectic which is the center of Paul's theology of history.

The description of the contents of the question is difficult because—as emphasized to begin with—the question of the significance of history can be neither equated to nor completely separated from the significance of the life of the individual, which as such is clearly and obviously claimed and seized by the kingdom of God. The individual is told what he has to do: he must repent and confess his sins, he must believe, love, hope, persist in patience, help carry the cross of Christ, be baptized into the death of Christ, and partake of the memorial meal of his suffering in order to rise with him. If only that, varied and multiplied millions of times, yet always new and always unique, were the meaning of history, then our problem would not exist. Some limit the meaning of history wherever possible to the meaning of the individual Christian life. For example, the problem of domination, of power, and of politics is equated with the psychology and ethics of the person who has power and is politically responsible—a view toward which Augustine inclines in the *Civitas Dei*. With such limitations and equations there is actually no meaning in history which is different from the meaning of the single Christian's life.

History as such, inasmuch as it is more than the sum of all individual consciousnesses, is not itself a consciousness of which one could ask a Christian attitude and to which therefore one could apply Christian norms. Empirical history cannot be baptized, nor can faith be asked of it. But, then, what kind of reality does it have, insofar as it can be envisaged from a Christian point of view? It is certainly no universal spirit which moves and acts above the heads of individuals. At the most, if one can speak of an objective spirit, it is one that is embodied in the individual consciousness, as a *universale in re*. But human consciousnesses are not atoms; humanity is not an aggregate. Rather, in spite of the immediacy of the relationship of the individual to God, these consciousnesses make up a physical and ontic whole, "a dough" (as the Fathers say), a race, which divides itself into ontic wholes such as peoples, cultures, continents, etc.

We ask now about the destiny of this whole. It has neither the existential burden (and dignity) of being born and dying with the individual, nor, therefore, the same limited horizon of the individual's relation to God and to Christ, but continues through time as continuity. To its temporal extension and—using the word with all caution and without emphasis of value—development *as such* we ascribe meaning, as for all being and events. Theologically one can say that if such a meaning did not exist, then there would be no need for a last judgment, for judgment would then be finished with the completion of all the particular judgments (on each man at the end of his life). The existence of this whole implies an integration of all single destinies in the one destiny of humanity, which as such is more than the sum of its numberless parts.

Extending the Question: Religious Time and Revelation Time

After this preliminary clarification let us approach the subject by saying that, according to Christian revelation, history as such, as well as the individual man, comes from God and goes to God. This statement, which seems banal and perhaps not even specifically biblical, questions an idea current today which sees heathen, mythical time as cyclical, returning always to its beginning, whereas revelation time runs in a straight line. If all this means is that biblical time unfolds once only, whereas time as represented in many mythical views of the world can always begin again, and thus is likened to the yearly cycle of nature and the movements of the stars (which can lead to the idea of cosmic years of tremendous length), then it is undeniable. It may be asked, however, if the unique quality of biblical time—of moving toward a goal—is not true primarily of Old Testament time, where revelation itself moves in time and history, and if the same quality of moving in a straight line can be claimed for New Testament time after the ascension of Christ. It is at least questionable if we can still speak here of events in time. Should we not rather speak of a continuance in an eternity latently present under time which flows toward and away from it? But if one wants to ascribe the Old Testament quality of moving in a straight line to the time in which the Church exists (because the Jewish is positively subsumed into the Christian)—and not only for the world's history as such, in which the Church persists— then something is said also about the theological relevance of world history from Christ to the Last Judgment.

Let us leave this problem for a moment and turn once more to the question of cyclic time. If one disregards the particular idea of repeatable time or the "eternal return," every religious idea of time is necessarily cyclical, the mythical as well as the biblical. If temporal creation came from God, then that means, for all religious thinking, that it also returns to God, that in its shape it imitates the circular shape of the Absolute.[3] The Son who becomes man combines both these circles, the "theological" (trinitarian) and the "economical," when he says, "I came from the Father and have come into the world; again, I am leaving the world and going to the Father" (John 16, 28), and thus draws the world into his own circular movement.

The cyclic time- and world-form of egress and regress which is common to all religions and does not imply in itself anything pantheistic is also the time- and world-form of the bible. Scripture agrees with most religions also in that it makes the moving out from God close to a falling away from God. It speaks of the Fall as coming immediately after the creation, and understands the return to God as a conversion, a reconciliation, and a redemption. This is the turning point in time at which time flowing out starts to flow back; this is the event, no longer mythical, but historical, which opens the way of the return home.

Herein lay, with all the profound difference, at least the possibility of a dialogue between Irenaeus and Valentine, between Origen and Celsus, between Eusebius-Augustine and Plotinus-Porphyry, and still more impressively between the biblical message of the day of the Lord with its destructive and redemptive fire and the Germanic image of the *muspilli* and the *ragnarök* myths. Maximus the Confessor consciously considers whether one should strive to reach God by endeavoring to move backward out of fallen time to Paradise or forward towards the Judgment. Both ways lead to the same goal; the road back is blocked, so we have to move forward to get back to our origin and home *Quaest. ad Thalass.* 59 (PG 60, 631 D).

This is the religious idea of time which lies behind Augustine's *Civitas Dei* and St. Thomas's *Summa*.[4] The mistaken idea of purely linear time could arise only when time was no longer conceived in a religious and theological way, but scientifically. But this lands us at once in the "antimonies of pure reason," for how could a world time which runs in one straight direction ever lead to the eternity of God?[5]

Rather, it is true that religious time is, in all the historical systems of advanced cultures, primarily vertical time: duration, which, because of the difference between divine eternity and the world separate from it, appears as "extension" (*distentio*). By the return to God and the removal of extendedness, which had been experienced as remote from salvation, this duration is reintegrated as true, saved, "eternal time."[6] This idea occurs in myth, which treats of an inner, "mystical" experience of man, which then becomes the model of political historical time. Temporal salvation lies in the conjunction between the king (as the focal point of the people) and his god (as the saving relation of the divine world to the people). This conjunction stretches from the birth and, more fully, from the enthroning of the king (as the incarnation of the god in him) to his apotheosis at his death. Political time is thus actually soul time; horizontal time has its sense and its root in a vertical time (between man and God), but this is, from its very nature, unique and comes only once and exists in the eternal now. It follows from this that an interpretation of historical time as the repetition of the (vertical) salvation cycles, even as the "eternal return of the same," no longer corresponds to the original mythical feeling of time, but represents a derivative, secularized speculation, from which the original religious life has partly vanished.

It is important here to see that biblical time, purely formally, is not basically different from this. As an act and result of creation it is duration from God to God; as sinful time and salvation time it is the same with deepened contours: duration in the turn-

ing away from God and in the turning back to God brought
about by his grace. It also is essentially soul time, personal ethical
duration, ever a superpersonal, neutral, world-historical medium.
Even where the time measures of revelation with the promise to
Abraham seem to extend beyond the limits of the single person,
it is no different; for now the God-relationship of the individual
is extended into the temporal future as the hope of salvation.
The longing to go back to God is fashioned as the longing of
Abraham, that he should "see my day. He saw it and was glad"
(John 8, 56).

The redemptive capacity of the individual to become whole,
which will be founded on the resurrection of Christ, is mediated
to itself through the capacity of the people and, ultimately, of
humanity to become whole, whereby all need of a horizontal
cycle is removed. The horizontality of revelation time as the time
of promise and of fulfillment in Christ is, as a whole, a function
of the vertical dealings between God and man. It contains the
decisive steps of God toward bringing home man who had been
alienated from him. But they are steps which, in fact, have a
shape in the longitudinal section of world time and thus give this
time extension, beyond everything which religion formerly was
able to see. They give a significance which is permanent for world
history and which makes a claim on every human being.

This was so much the case that for Jewish and early Christian
thought the history of the world was primarily and centrally
biblical salvation history, into which the history of nonbiblical
peoples entered only incidentally and was synchronized with it
as best could be. That was all the more plausible and was undertaken all the more readily as nonbiblical history was conceived
according to the same model, which could be understood as
running into the one revelation time. In addition the document
of biblical salvation (see, for example, Theophilus of Antioch)
seemed to offer the only reliable account of the early history of
humanity, which elsewhere in the folk myths was lost in ob-

scurity. Only as biblical salvation history did human history acquire a direction and a "sense" readable in time. So it remained not only until Otto von Freising, but also until Bossuet. It was Voltaire, and to a certain extent Vico, shortly before him, who abandoned this original theological sense of history in favor of the idea of universally human, secular cultural history. Here for the first time secular history becomes distinct from salvation history, but is still strongly influenced by it, because the historical direction of Christian salvation has now been widened to a general natural direction of history as the "education of the human race" or simply as secular belief in progress.

This secularization need not be mourned by theology, since the old naive equation of salvation history and secular history was an encroachment from the other side, and since that which happened in human history between "Adam" and Abraham and could be regarded as a "development," non-theological in a sense, ever more insistently required formulation. Now for the first time, as the distinction between the two "developments" emerged, the question of the theological sense of nonbiblical history could meaningfully be asked.

The old Christian conception of history had another inner limit, which we have already touched on indirectly. Revelation history, from the Christian point of view, exists in relation to Christ and continues until his death and resurrection. This "fulness of time" is, as the Gospel itself says and the Christian view of history has always confirmed, also the end of (historical) time. The early expectation of the end of the world was a correct and, in its way, plausible translation of this fact into the dimension of time. A theologically relevant development beyond the death and resurrection of Christ—if we disregard for the moment the promised conversion of Israel—was considered a contradiction in terms. With the ascension of the Son to the Father, to his throne at the right hand of God, the end is already conceived as present, and all that is still to follow can only be the making known of this end and its establishment in historical time.

That is clearly expressed in the early Christian ways of dividing up history. These all see the last age—generally the last of seven, which stretch from Adam via Noah, Abraham, Moses, and David to the prophets, etc.—as having begun with Christ. The beginning of Church time after the Ascension is also the beginning of that time for whose sake horizontal revelation time existed at all: namely, pure soul or spirit time, which formerly appeared as a vertical relation to time. In Augustine's *Civitas Dei* this vertical time—as the "pilgrimage" of the city of God far from God, but on the way home to him—is so predominant that all historical revelation time is overshadowed by it.[7] It could be said that horizontal, Old Testament time is only practice in the ultimate relation to and understanding of the time of the person Jesus Christ. Christ establishes in his earthly life the absolute norm for the world's time. He does this in his relation to the Father (which permits no inner development but is merely taken through the successive situations of a human life, fulfilling them all), and thus to the *kairos* of the Father, to the "hour" of his death and resurrection, in which the (vertical) time measure is established for all human vertical and horizontal times.[8]

It was inevitable, however, that this Church time, which prolonged itself from century to century, should finally give rise to a question posed by the theology of history, long before the eighteenth century raised the question of the philosophical and religious significance of profane secular history. The two questions are related, for, assuming that revelation reached in the death and resurrection of Christ its unsurpassable climax, which in the further course of history can only work itself out, there still remains an important question. Does secular history have only the status of the area in which this light of Christ shines, and perhaps increasingly? Or, as in modern times, does not the development of the world have its own significance philosophically and, ultimately, also theologically? The two aspects are separate and, therefore, will be discussed separately in the following.

THE THEOLOGICAL QUESTION OF THE SIGNIFICANCE OF CHURCH HISTORY

Form and Contents of Church Time

In one respect historical revelation ended with the ascension of our Lord, but not in another. For two essential facts of revelation follow it in time and are closely connected with each other: the giving of the Holy Spirit and the coming into being of the Church. Inasmuch as the giving of the Holy Spirit is an historical event and the cause of the Church's coming into being, the origin of the latter is historical also. But both can be called historical events only by analogy, for although they have an historical point of departure they have no historical end, and, strictly speaking, no historical beginning; they are the "historical" making present of something above history and yet eternal within history.

The historical beginning is more a kind of concession of the exalted Lord to temporal men. For him (and John presents this view) the Spirit is already there at Easter and given to the Church;[9] the waiting of the fifty days has already something about it of a liturgical, Church year festivity flavor and also an apologetical flavor, since the giving of the Spirit purports to be the visible sign of the Son's "arrival" at the right hand of the Father. The Church is equally realized historically with the event of Good Friday and Easter, and the charismatic filling of the assembly of the apostles with the Spirit seems almost a *demonstratio ad extra.*

Both the Christian realities which are to determine theologically subsequent Christian history are, thus, historically immanent factors whose essence transcends history. They create history without themselves being historical. But they are not less than history (i.e., mere ideas or structures); they are more than history: the presence of fulfilled eternity in time. One would use only with caution the term "eschatological" to describe them; the word is used too often and serves thus to obscure things rather than illuminate them. The word is used to describe just as much the presence of the final and eternal in time, as its temporary absence and, on the strength of that, the stretching of time toward them. But now it is important to see Church and Spirit as the dual way in which the exalted Christ, who has reached himself the historical *eschaton* and passed beyond its borders, realizes himself, according to his promise, in the middle of temporal history. "The Lord is the Spirit" (2 Cor. 3, 17); he realizes his "glory" in the "freedom" of the Spirit, so that one can also say, vice versa, the Spirit is the Lord: that which the Spirit interprets is the reality of Christ. He is reality which, for the world and for Christians, is historically past, actually present, and eschatologically prophetic: "He will take what is mine and declare it to you." "Whatever he hears he will speak, and he will declare to you the things that are to come" (John 16: 14, 13).

This interpretation of Jesus by the Spirit follows for the Church. The Spirit comes down upon the Church and not really upon the world, but this event happens with the Church in the world and for the world, for in the same context we read that the Spirit will "convince" the world. This will not come about outside or apart from the living Church of Jesus Christ, but through it and by it. This "convincing" bringing to light of the real truth through the Spirit in and by the Church will be the objective meaning of history from the ascension of Christ to his return. This is not at all a purely eschatological meaning which would remain completely hidden and be revealed only in the judgment of the Lord, but one objectively already obvious for him who has eyes to see. "He will convince the world of sin and righteousness and of judgment: of sin, because they do not believe in me; of righteousness, because I go to the Father, and you will see me no more; of judgment, because the ruler of this world is judged" (John 16, 8–11).

The universal historical significance of the confrontation between Christ and the world becomes clear within history. The

nature of sin becomes clear: nonbelief as nonacceptance of the
fact of Christ. "It is not a question . . . of the specific historical
fact of the nonbelief of the Jews, but this nonbelief has since
been the reaction against the proclaimed word, which constantly
forces it to make a decision for or against revelation. It is not that
the world once failed to recognize a noble man, but it spurned
salvation and continues to spurn it."[10] But through his resurrection and ascension Christ is shown to have been "righteousness";
he is justified before God and, hence, also before history, precisely
in that he is no longer seen. But this is the "judgment" on the
prince of this world: neither an immanent judgment on history
which would be the history of the world itself, nor a future
eschatological judgment, but one passed in history by the Spirit
which, through the Church, is present and visible above history
as objective historical truth for one who can see (the believer).
The word of the Christian gospel "and its challenge resound in
the world and the world can no longer be the same as it was
before. In the face of the gospel naive Judaism or naive paganism
can no longer exist."[11]

Time and history come from God and are on the way back to
him, in a necessary *recirculatio* from God to God, and God,
abandoned and spurned by the world, must be revealed in his
wrath at all secular history (Rom. 1, 18). The history of the
world, in which God became man, is a circular movement away
from Christ and returning to Christ. Men find their way "back"
to Christ only by living forward "toward" Christ, and hence
toward Christ with his whole history—his being rejected by the
world and his resurrection to redeem the world through the
Spirit—and toward the Church always apparent in the midst of
secular history. *Recirculatio* is the old Latin translation of
anakephalaiosis, a term Irenaeus of Lyons uses in his theology of
history. It means not just flowing backward to the beginning,
but movement forward in time as the integration of the beginning in the end, and this as the significance of the movement
forward itself, insofar as it is at once in time and above time.

At the moment, however, we are not considering world history, but Church history. The Church, as the visible community which was given its structure by the Lord himself and, at the same time, as the temple of the Holy Spirit and the living body of the risen Christ, is a polarized entity which can never be ultimately divided into two parts. The structure and the Spirit of the Church are always to be understood theologically as a unity. Inasmuch as it is a structure and an institution the Church is relatively unhistorical; inasmuch as it is the Spirit and the presence of Christ, it is eminently powerful in history. That seems at first paradoxical, for one might assume that precisely the visibility of the Church was that part of it in which it was subject to history. Church history seems to exist only because of the visible Church, whereas the presence of Christ and his Holy Spirit would appear to be the eternal and eschatological elements in that history. That is true, but it is a superficial truth. The fact that the Church as a visible institution undergoes, like all historical things, change and development, that there is a history of liturgy, a history of dogma, and a history of the papacy and of the Councils, does not determine the nature of its historicalness. It shares that with the non-Christian religions and all other Christian denominations. Its recognizability (*nota ecclesiae*) as the foundation and presence of Christ does not rest in its history, but rather in its constancy, which transcends history, as the one universal, apostolic, and holy Church. This fundamental quality is not primarily historical; it is that only secondarily and accidentally. That becomes clear if one compares it with the Synagogue, whose nature was much more subject to historical development, because revelation itself as the promise of Christ was a growing historical one.

One cannot say either that the structure of the Church *as such,* in its appearance, is remarkable for its historical potency. For its first purpose is building up inwardly the Mystical Body, and is not so much the radiation of the Church into the world and world history. Neither the sacraments nor the hierarchic shape are decoys and displays for the world; they are, rather, in their significance turned inward. One might almost say they are the *arcana* of the Church which, insofar as they are part of the structure, have no particular apologetical significance. The sacraments and the hierarchy are means; their aim, which alone has to shine out, is love. By love we know. By love the structure shows that it is filled with the Spirit. The Spirit which produces faith, hope, and charity thus shows in Christians the living presence of the triune God. The history of faith, hope, and charity in the world is the true and real history of the Church. That cannot be described, because it only half emerges into the outer historical dimension. The other and more important half remains hidden in the inwardness of the kingdom of God in souls. One sees the world-transforming impulses, but their causes cannot be scientifically established like secular causes. *One* unknown prayer, *one* hidden suffering with Christ, can have produced effects over vast visible areas. The Holy Spirit in the Church is an historical factor, but it is not something that has developed in history. It creates true history because it is its master. And it is its true master by having the freedom, not only of hovering over the waters of history, but of pouring forth from its innermost springs.

Church time as the era of the Holy Spirit is, in contrast to the Old Testament and the era of Christ, not time in which revelation grows and takes place, but time in which the unsurpassable fullness of revelation establishes and expresses itself. During the time of growing revelation significance can be derived from the dimension of its becoming—from Abraham to Christ there is something like true development and unfolding going on, and equally in the lifetime of Christ, even in his death and resurrection. However, when the attained fullness begins to be disseminated, an historical law of its dissemination cannot be established. Hence, all attempts to write a theological history of Church time which is not only phenomenal, but also noumenal, must prove unavailing. Not that this time is one of static repose or else a spiritual, charismatic chaos. But the order of the Holy Spirit is so much the order of divine freedom and infinity, that it cannot be translated into the categories of world and human history. The lines that we can draw may show divine wisdom in many ways. They may be plausible, and even obvious, in their way, but they will never show more than a fragment of the infinity of significance, which as such cannot be grasped by us.

In spite of—or, rather, because of—this profusion of meaning and dazzling radiance, we are entitled to ask the question of the theological meaning of Church time. Our basic reflections on the Spirit and the Church allow the question, but they suggest that it will be an immense answer—an answer that certainly answers positively the question of an historical sense, but *a priori* makes a periodization of this time impossible. Revelaton time was the era of the growing word of God; it stood, in a sense, under the primacy of the Second Divine Person: words need time to be spoken by human beings; sentences and sentence groups require even more time. Here we may speak also of the education of man in the hearing and understanding of the divine Logos. Now, however, that God "in these last days has spoken to us by a Son" and continues to speak (Heb. 1, 2), everything is said in all fullness in the one Word. It can no longer be a matter of learning the one thing "in many and various ways" (Heb. 1, 1), in stages of understanding, but only of seeing it in its unity and uniqueness and either of affirming or denying what we have seen.

It is certainly not the case that we moderns, with all the development of dogma, all the growing enrichment of tradition, have necessarily a deeper and more comprehensive insight into the nature of the Incarnate Word of God than, say, the Church Fathers. The manner of the historical potency of the Church, above history, is therein absolutely unique and can only be measured and affirmed from the understanding, in faith, of revelation. That means that outside the Christian faith it is necessarily misunderstood and misinterpreted, either as an institutional sclerosis of life or as something of an historical intellectual liveliness on the same plane as all other historical phenomena. But it is necessary for the Christian in the Church to have the energy to resist the temptation of these misinterpretations. He must constantly make in himself the synthesis, which already objectively exists, between the structure and the living Spirit, which is alive not only within the Church, but also proves its life in its relations with the world.

The Catholic tension between structure (as it reveals itself primarily in the hierarchic functions, which are concerned primarily with preaching and the sacraments) and the living Spirit means that the one truth may be approached more from the one side or more from the other. To approach it more from the structural side is nearer to the theological feeling and thinking of the clergy, and this thinking will seek and discover the historical development of the Church chiefly in this dimension: in the development and formulation of teaching, in the so-called development of dogma, the unfolding of liturgy, canon law, and forms of devotion, indeed even in the progressive emergence of a fixed, hierarchic structure. In contrast, the theological feeling and thinking of the laity and members of religious orders will see the elements of vital development more in the free creations of the Holy Spirit. They will discover these elements of life in everything in the Church which seems charismatic and, thus, unforeseeably enriching. From these charisms spring the foundations of the great Orders (which are not primarily of hierarchic origin, but are only secondarily brought into a canonical form by their hierarchic function), and, finally, all the holiness which is given to the Church and spontaneously grows out of it, whether it expresses itself in more traditional or newer forms.

This double dimension of growth needs further consideration before we can answer properly the subsequent question of how to judge such historical growth from the point of view of revelation.

The Development of Structure

However rich and impressive this development may be, the nature of the Church imposes clear limits upon it, which the Catholic consciousness would never think of interfering with. If all development of Christian doctrine and every new ordering of Church life—if the Church sees itself as founded by Christ—is governed by scripture and by tradition (which has always been guided by scripture), then this reverent attitude toward the Church's origins prevents the development of foreign novelty in Church history. The only thing that can possibly be new is a better, deeper, more comprehensive understanding of the old, though not by leaving out the historical connecting links, as the Protestant Reformation and many denominations have tried. The manner of progress in this is in some sense foreshadowed in what one might describe as the progress of the understanding of Christ from Mark through all the intermediate stages up to the Johannine writings: a development through meditative penetration into the *spiritus* contained in the *historia* and *littera* (for Augustine the two are one), but without losing contemporaneity with Christ. It is interesting to note that the spiritual gospel of Paul, which is almost wholly independent of the *littera* and scarcely quotes a single saying of Jesus, is part of this: Paul is contemporary with the synoptists, whereas John finally synthesizes *littera* and *spiritus* in his understanding of the *historia*.

Meditative return to the inexhaustible fullness of the beginning, of which scripture bears witness (the beginning is not this witness, but its contents, historical revelation), affects all new dogmatic and disciplinary formulations and ordinances, be they suggested by the inner logic of theology as it contemplates revelation or by changes in the Church's situation in the world.

If the former is the case, as for example in the mariological dogmatizations of recent times, which are based entirely on profound meditation on the contents of revelation and, thus, can appear to run counter to considerations of historical timeliness

—although, as directed by the Holy Spirit, they are, at a deeper level, in accord with them—we have what is perhaps the strongest feeling of development and renewal that can be expected in the Church. It is the living confirmation of the Holy Spirit in the Church, which "takes of what is mine to proclaim it to you" and, thus, truly proclaims as well its divine freedom and personality distinctly from the person of the Word. It knows no slavish cleaving to the *littera* and shows in its own freedom at the same time the vitality of the word of God itself, which from the beginning is more than the letter and, therefore, cannot be imprisoned in any book, even an inspired one (John 20, 30; 21, 25). The same Spirit, however, which reveals the inner connections of the word of revelation and by comparing the spiritual with the spiritual (*"spiritualibus spiritualia comparantes"* 1 Cor. 2, 13, for Origen the basic concern of theological investigation) produces new spirit, shows in that its freedom and inexhaustibility. Thus, the idea of a systematic survey of God's wisdom, even of his revealed wisdom, appears a rationalistic monstrosity.

Neither the succession of conciliar and papal dogmatic definitions nor the succession of theological speculations, however profound, can yield, as an historical sequence, a convincing total picture of revelation, as if the time from Christ to the Last Judgment were granted the Church above all to reduce what seems to be the somewhat confused and random words of scripture to a theological form, enriched by theological conclusions, which would be more manageable, perhaps even more or less exhaustive. A glance at the state of the relations today between exegesis and dogmatics would be enough to dispel any such theological and Gnostic illusions of progress, a situation which reveals a fundamental crisis and demands a fresh, still more careful attention to the original word of God.

This compulsion, not altogether pleasant for dogmatics, is connected with the second problem of the altered intellectual situation in the world, and bursts open almost brutally the meditation of the Church which has often considered itself as too separate from the rest of life. The Theological and spiritual contemplation are, of course, always in the service of the Church's preaching of the gospel, which must be made significant for and attuned to the ears and comprehension of men living today. If the Church as a whole—in all its members, but chiefly in its responsible hierarchy—must adapt itself in its structures (insofar as they are adaptable) to the changed historical situation, in the manner of human thinking in the sermon, in questions of the intellectual awareness of the age in the liturgy etc., then it is clear that it is primarily the world that develops and the Church only secondarily and subsequently. The latter, above history as it is, can clothe its truth in this or that particular form. Whichever one it chooses depends on the age that is to hear it.

Here too there can be reciprocal effects. An age such as ours asks, for example, that liturgical forms should be more persuasive, be more immediately transparent to their revelatory origin, than did previous ages, which laid more emphasis on the aesthetic and representative form. Every new situation, of course, requires that the Church does not make its adjustments primarily with a view to men, but wtih a view to the holy scriptures, in order, by a more complete understanding of what they mean, to be able to say and show it more comprehensibly to the men of today.   ·

In these changes it is the historicity of the world that is far more in evidence than that of the church. The particular adaptations do not alter in substance the *quod semper, quod ubique, quod ab omnibus.* And even when new aspects of faith emerge, the Church is always at pains to show that that which is gnoseologically new is something ontologically old which can be traced back in a gnoseological tradition to the origins. If that is not really the case, then that can be seen as something which was always objectively present, even if its full significance is only now subjectively realized.

This must be so, because God's evident truth, even in the form in which it appears to the world, can only be always total and absolute truth. It must even be so for the rather different revelation truth of the Old Testament, which had an inner historical dimension. This dimension was not in the form of a successive piling up of partial truths about God and his relation to the world, but a gradual revealing and making clear of the one undividable truth, which is God himself. Thus, in the promise to the chosen Abraham all are included: Moses, the judges and the kings, the prophets and the wisdom teachers, simply drew new veils off the totality which was at hand. This revelation, too, is more the education of the human race, the introduction of its growing understanding into the divine truth which remains ever the same. More precisely, it is a developing understanding of the nature of the eternally valid covenant of God with Israel, which with Noah, however, was already a covenant with humanity and with creation as a whole, rather than a "development" of this truth itself in its form in the world. This is all the more true of the New Testament, where the manifestation of God in Christ reached its unsurpassable fullness and clarity. It is less the Church that develops this manifestation in itself, in order to fit humanity for it, than humanity, which in its own development requires an adaptation of the Church to its particular stage of development. Under this aspect the problem points to the relation between secular development and the Church, which will be considered later.

But if this adaptation to the world takes place more in the form of a charismatic gift of the Holy Spirit indwelling in the Church, while it institutes, for example, a new Christian way of life, by offering a shining saint as model, an important founder of an order with an "answer from above" to the "temporal problems of below,"[12] then the theme of "structural unfolding" has passed into that of the unfolding of the Spirit, which is the next one to be treated. Both dimensions of development meet here, however, in that saints who carry conviction are able to have a profound influence on the self-understanding of the hierarchical Church and can put the stamp of their genius upon Councils or even personally found movements of reform, which are adopted by the official Church. But because the new structural form that is issued officially never proceeds without the directing Spirit, and because the intellectual and charismatic new form can never be established in the Church otherwise than in obedience to the office and with its approval, the Church appears in the course of history to be the mysterious and, to the world, incomprehensible interaction of both elements.

The Protestants are, curiously, right in both their judgments that the Catholic Church in the course of centuries becomes ever more itself, developing itself out of itself—and that in so doing it has ventured innovations, that have no biblical justification, with a freedom which, to spectators, appears doubtful and presumptuous. Both appear, viewed from the outside, contradictory, *although* both appear to be typically Catholic. The Church, people say, has not ceased elaborating its hierarchic functions, organizing and centralizing them; and when with Boniface VIII the external claim to power necessarily collapsed, it has developed this claim all the more ruthlessly in an internal sense—up to the First Vatican Council. Parallel to that it has accorded an increasing importance to canon law, made theology ever more an official occupation and an academic tool of clerical education. But how does this picture agree with the fact that today in opposition to the predominance of the Bishop of Rome the episcopate by divine law is emphasized, in opposition to the priestly office new dignity is bestowed upon the diaconate, and in opposition to the clergy the laity is called to coresponsibility for the whole Church? Further than that, side by side with the canonically structured old Orders it not only permits, but encourages, forms of community which are freer and are far harder to encompass canonically. In these and similar endeavors one may indeed praise the working of the Spirit, which does not work against the office and the structures, but through them, by showing them that they are only instruments and inspiring them to ever renewed self-correction.

Further, if the Church has been deposed from its position of power by a world making itself independent, has it not been given back to itself, and this time without the late classical cultural flavor of a flight from the world, but in a new closeness to the gospel? Is not even the material poverty of St. Francis—at any rate in certain absolutizations of his followers—something which has had a new emphasis today and has had its pure gospel significance returned to it with the "brothers and sisters of Foucauld"? And if that appears too external, too righteous, then the efforts of Catholic exegesis may show the critical eye that reform of the Church through the Spirit can go truly to the roots. Indeed, one may say that the Church becomes ever more "itself" in the course of time, but not in the ironic sense that its critics imply, but in the true and serious one that the Spirit leads it in the process of time through the cycle of its own possible forms. This process, as shown, cannot be a systematic Hegelian one, because the Church is not the world spirit which is still searching for itself; the process is, nevertheless, a temporal revealing of its own ground.

Here the question arises of whether such a progression, with all reservations, shows any qualitative character? Whether it is not simply a quantitative one of varieties and developments which are produced by a certain historical memory for advantages and disadvantages? Or whether over and above that the historical course of the Church through the ages reveals a direction in its progress? Hitherto our thinking does not seem to have gone much beyond the quantitative. On the contrary, all the Church's changes and additions reveal profoundly the axiom of history that in every gain there is also a loss. Even the most evident achievements in the Church—those of dogmatic theology —reveal clearly on closer examination this double law; greater precision is achieved at the cost of vital wholeness, greater individual knowledge at the cost of intuition, indeed most of all at the cost of a natural sense of proportion and balance. A dogma, clearly illuminated and formulated, loses just through that to the average eye the thousand threads which weave its truth into the whole. Its isolation requires (as in mariology) a rethinking of the whole—and who will undertake that?

As with technology, increasing specialization brings an increasing effect on the universal and, thus, a responsibility which perhaps no one wants to or is able to fulfill. Moreover, we are witnessing today the tug-of-war between biblical and scholastic rational modes of thought; each leads, when made into an absolute, to a notable loss of dimension. Both together would give vision in perspective; thus, the one-sided improvement of the sight of one eye would mean at the same time a decline in clarity of the total vision. In such laws of proportion the finitude and creatureliness of our powers of comprehension are demonstrated; all growth is gently and implacably forced back into a constant mobile middle.

So here there is no qualified progress. Does it exist? After all we have said, can it be expected?

The Move toward the Spirit

Again and again in the course of Church history this decisive move has been postulated and hoped for as a necessary fulfillment. Whereas the theology of history of the clergy was always predominantly a static one, that of the religious and the laity has often required an inner historical dynamism. Many see in the principle of Catholic officialdom the principle of the Church's origin—the living, dying, and resurrecting Son of God. This is a contradiction which is resolved only if the official element, if not surpassed and overcome, at least is made totally transparent and shown to be Spirit. The move from the structure, which seems

related to the obedience unto death of the Son and the hardness
of the beams of the cross, to the Spirit, which the resurrected Son
is master of and pours out in a freedom which, far from all
obedience to the will of another, has become pure possession of
the self in God: this move from death to resurrection, from mortal flesh to immortal Spirit, from the servant figure of the Second
Person to the figure of glory of the Third Person, appears then as
the only theologically justified move and progression within the
history of the Church.

The metamorphoses of this transition and its interpretation fill
the history of Christian spirituality. The anti-Gnostic Tertullian,
who had struggled so much for the incarnation of the Word,
succumbs to the seductive parallel between the "psychic" nature
of an institution and the "pneumatic" nature of the Church. The
power of the keys could be given personally only to Peter, for
such a share in divine plenitude of power could subsequently be
entrusted only to a man filled with the spirit—a "pneumatic"
man. The essence of the Church is the "pneumatic": "the Church
itself is, in its truest and most perfect sense, the spirit itself. . . .
It gathers together that Church which the Lord left at the number of three" (*De pud.* 21). It is the Montanist theology of history, in which the false claim of the institution is constantly opposed to the true claim of the "pneumatic" which goes back to
Christ. With Montanus himself the succession has taken place
at an historical moment: he personally is the incarnation of the
spiritual man.

The other great anti-Gnostic, Irenaeus, avoids this confrontation, but his theology of history, which so strongly emphasizes
the temporal flow from the Father (Old Testament) to the Son
(New Testament), does not manage either without a kind of age
of the Spirit, which here appears as the millennium. The idea of
a millennium after the resurrection follows for him from the Old
Testament promise of a final, secure inheritance, a promise
which, because Christians are still pilgrims on the earth, cor-

responding to the nomadic life of Abraham and his followers, is not yet fulfilled. Irenaeus seeks to interpret *recirculatio* and *regressus,* not Platonically, as if it was progress toward a supraterrestrial, purely spiritual home, but biblically, as the promise of an ultimate "holy land." In the Old Testament God promises his people land. This promise, throughout the Egyptian and Babylonian exile (wherein as a punishment of the people the land was never to be free of unbelievers), always points toward a homeland which is finally owned, and is earthly and holy at the same time. Israel today lives in this spirit, and according to Irenaeus the Church also, as the new Israel, must inherit it.

Since humanity went out not only from God, but also from an earthly Paradise, its ultimate perfection must be found not only in a new heaven, but in a new earth: *"nihil allegorizari potest* [in eschatology] *sed omnia firma et vera"* (*C. Haer.,* 2, 426, Harvey). The characteristic point about this view of the last things is that it is at the same time the completion of the horizontal march of history from the Old to the New Testament: it is the complete incarnation of God, who now in the final world-Jerusalem is seen everywhere face to face (*C. Haer.,* 424, 428). And it is transcendental perfection, since the millennium comes only after the resurrection. These are motifs which, without our being able or even desiring to identify their historical origin, would confirm the qualitative directional flow of New Testament time also and not allow us to dismiss too readily either the literal, earthly messianism of the Jews up to the present—in its biblical, Palestinian, and secular communistic form—or else cosmic evolutionism (as is today represented in the Church by Teilhard de Chardin).

Both the different eschatologies of Tertullian and Irenaeus, which come at the beginning of the history of theology, give way to a more unhistorical conception, held by the greatest and most influential patristic theologians, Origen and Augustine. Both are dominated by the cosmological world-plan of the Fall and the

return, not only of the individual soul, but also of the Church
as the heavenly bride of the Word: the Church as the *civitas dei*
does not exist only "since Abel"; it is, "before the foundation of
the world," the "community gathered together from the beginning," as the psalmist says. It is the "great mystery," for which
a man leaves his father and mother, for which Christ leaves his
heavenly father and the heavenly Jerusalem, in order to retrieve
his sinful bride, who had fallen onto the earth, to wash her in
the sacrifice of his flesh, and to bring her home: "for how could
he have loved her if she did not exist?" (Origen, *Comm. in Cant.*
2; Baehr. 8, 157–158).

Here the Irenaeus aspect disappears entirely, and the Tertullian aspect achieves its orthodox form. There can be only two
"times" of salvation history: that of the coming down of the
Word in promise and in the incarnation up to the death on the
cross, and that of his rising again in his spiritualizing resurrection and ascension, in which he takes his bride with him, now
in spe, one day *in re.* The *in spe* is characterized by what Tertullian calls *disciplina,* the order of the Church, an institution as
essential for Origen as for Augustine. Yet through the *spes* the
res must become ever more transparent, and through the institution truth, spirit, and the love, which is the central significance
of all sacraments and Church forms, have ever more to shine.

For both Church Fathers there is a certain unreality about
"mere" officialism and sacramentality. Rather, they do not exist
in the New Covenant as "mere" at all—to understand them like
that is a misunderstanding of the "psychic" man or the *hap-
lousteros (rudis)*—because in the New Covenant, through the
incarnation of the Word, each *littera* has become *spiritus.*[13]
Whether full transparency of the letter in the comprehending
spirit *(gnosis)* is possible on this earth—as Origen was inclined
to assume, and as his followers strove for in their partly anti-
institutional exaggerations, i.e. whether the institutional Church,
without being completely canceled out, can be illuminated

through to its very core and shown to be what it "truly" is and what it was intended to be by its founder—or whether this remains unattainable here below because of sin, weighing down even the best in the Church, the basic idea is the same. In contrast to the more Gnostic Augustine of the youthful years, the aging bishop of Hippo saw ever more clearly this fundamental idea: living in the Church is the daily renewed progress from the letter to the spirit, from the wrapping to the essential meaning, from the law to the gospel, from the Old to the New Testament, from the "mere" institution and sacramentality to the "naked word" and the "naked love." That Christians do that is the only possible apology for Christianity, which becomes credible only when form shows and justifies itself as content.

Seen in this light an evolution of the Church in time becomes an irrelevant and quite improbable idea: why should a later generation be more able than we are today to achieve the movement from the earth to heaven, eternally asked of it and to be daily accomplished, the movement from the mere transient "flesh" to the resurrected spirit-flesh? This move from the "second" to the "third" realm is the purely qualitative, in the face of which all historical variations must remain quantitative only. Hence, Origen and Augustine necessarily rejected every form of millennialism. This remained, like Montanism, thenceforth outside the purview of the Church—until Joachim and the Franciscans.

If one wishes to understand Joachim's expectation that in Church time after the kingdom of the Son (and of the Church institution), there would come a third kingdom of the Holy Spirit (beyond the institutional), one must not see him as a renewal of Tertullian and Montanus. He is not a fierce opponent, like them, of the hierarchy, but seeks to impart an historical shape in terms of monasticism to the inner heightening of form, the filling of form with content. The starting point of his interpretation of history is not the linear overtaking of the Old Testament by the New, but the symbolic mirroring of one in the other. This type of exegesis has been characteristic of theology from the beginning. He describes his insight thus: "When I awoke at daybreak, I pondered the revelation of St. John. Then, the eyes of my spirit were suddenly dazzled by the brightness of knowledge, and the fulfillment of this book and the agreement of the Old with the New Testament were revealed to me." It is as if one opens a book and from the correspondence between the right and left pages the spirit and meaning leap out as the quintessence of the whole.

The triadic, trinitarian scheme, which Joachim develops out of the diptych of the Testaments, by adding the kingdom of the Spirit as a third one in the time plane, does not fundamentally agree with this traditional starting point. Yet, on that account, this is the consequence that had to be drawn, because the correspondences between the Old and the New Testament were understood literally and therefore temporarily: this event in the New Testament corresponds to that event in the Old Testament. Thus, an idea of correspondence is introduced into the diptych which presumes a homogeneous time dimension of revelation and excludes it from the analogy relationship of *littera-spiritus*. In other words, since the second age of the Son is not seen as essentially spiritual, the age of the Spirit has to be added in succession to the other two. The new "pneumatic" millennialism is based on an underestimation of the spiritual power in the institution of the Church and thus projects, secretly but effectively, the chronological presuppositions of the Old Testament not only into the second, but also into the third age. The apparently superspiritual nature of his conception proves, on closer acquaintance, to be subspiritual.

Yet Joachim is not far from the truth, as the institutional and sacramental elements in the New Testament demand to be interpreted spiritually (i.e., "existentially," according to the usage of the New Testament): not as an abstract event *ex opere operato*, but as a lived life of faith in Christ, as it emerged shortly afterwards in the "Christ-man" with the stigmata and the charismatic plenitude, Francis of Assisi. It was unfortunate that Joachim's slight distortion set the interpretation of the phenomenon of St. Francis on the wrong track. Properly understood, it could have had a far greater influence, not only in the field of spiritual but also of dogmatic theology. The significance of everything institutional and sacramental could have been read by means of the "model" of St. Francis and given a better and more comprehensible theological setting. The theological impulse, which should have worked itself out within the Church, was largely dissipated in para-ecclesiastical directions, which soon became secularized and led by strange subterranean ways to the "enlightened" modern idea of progress in the religious field and, ultimately, in the intellectual and cultural ones.[14]

The third kingdom of Joachim is an eschatological estate of religious orders (following the estate of marriage in the first kingdom and the estate of the priesthood in the second) and in this is a typical piece of monastic metaphysics of history. This "monastic" theorizing continues through the Fraticelli and Cola di Rienzo, the secret orders behind Hieronymus Bosch, and the spiritual brothers of the Renaissance. It flourished among the Rosicrucians, the Freemasons of the Enlightenment and the nineteenth century, and was to be found in the confraternities of George or Guénons, in Derleth's project for an order, and in the Nazi *"Ordensburgen."* All through this blows an apocalyptic wind, but in the direction of a final kingdom within history.

There is a strange connection with the theology of history of Bonaventure, as Joseph Ratzinger recently showed clearly for the first time.[15] Bonaventure follows the basic idea of Joachim that the (seven) ages of the Old Testament correspond to the (likewise seven) ages of the New Testament. But he avoids the triadic interpretation by seeing the expected age of the Spirit, not as a third age after the New Testament, but as the last one within Church time. His view is close to the millennialism of Irenaeus, who, from his theological understanding of the Church, likewise does not expect something beyond the visible (institutional) Church on this earth. There is a difference between the two men: for Irenaeus the "spirit age" is after the general resurrection, for Bonaventure it is before this and within Church time.

The latter, as the general of the Franciscan order, developed his view of history in an intense struggle with the Franciscan theology of the "spiritual men," whose fundamental intuition "became for him an axiom of the theology of history which possessed unimpugnable certainty."[16] The prophecy of Joachim that the order of the end would follow the Sermon on the Mount *"sine glossa"* encountered too clearly the prohibition by St. Francis of glossing the gospel and the rule. But it is a very minor concession to the spiritualists if Bonaventure saw in the existing order only the germ of the contemplative final one which was to come—this one would realize Origen's *gnosis*, the full understanding of faith in the Holy Spirit—and not its fully present reality.

Bonaventure supported the idea of a qualitative revelation time, which was present only implicitly in Joachim, by a philosophical and theological speculation about time which did away with the ancient, Aristotelean, purely quantitative conception (which made it also potentially infinite and admitted of a *creatio ab aeterno*) and made time the measure of the finite creation which goes out from and returns to God (*"non tantum dicit mensuram durationis, sed etiam egressionis"*).[17] He followed here Augustine's idea of time which would be finite, without entering upon the problem of *distentio* (between creation time and sinful time). Even if the newfound biblical qualitative idea of time had not of itself required shaping and dividing into ages in the fashion of Joachim and Bonaventure, it may nevertheless be said that Joachim's concept, and particularly the Franciscan development, despite its overrational, and to us naive, historical prophecy, was responsible for making men aware of the underlying category of qualitative theological time in its different layers—creation time, sinful time, revelation time, and Church time. These four aspects of theological time are not homogeneous, but agree only by analogy. It is not possible simply to construct New Testament time according to the pattern of Old Testament time. These facts do not mean that New Testament time, however "eschatological" it may appear, is not still to b﹣ regarded as true creation time, as time which is fulfilled by being time.

Ratzinger is right when he vindicates this idea of Bonaventure for theology. He is also correct when he sees the basic difference between Bonaventure and Joachim as lying in the christocentric position of the former, for Christ (as the axis of world history, at which alienated sinful time becomes "returning" salvation time) is the Lord of all times, and especially of the final title of history, which is to reveal his sovereignty most clearly. Insofar as such revelation is thought of as the shining through of the glory of the Spirit through the veil of the letter and the flesh of lowliness, it can be thought of as the "age" of the Holy Spirit and as the era of the end. On that account, it does not have to be regarded as a third age following the sovereignty of Christ in the visible Church founded by him. Putting it in psychological terms, the spiritualists, following Joachim, reform out of a secret resentment against the hierarchic institution, as Tertullian and Montanus had already done. Bonaventure, on the other hand, reforms out of childlike obedience to the Church, in which he sees no rigid, separate institution, but the living Body of the incarnate Christ.

Bonaventure's essay has never been followed up by official theology. The question of the appropriateness and the limits of a theologically important development of Church time was not satisfactorily answered, as is very clear with the problem of the conversion of Israel, which we shall be dealing with. It could be followed up from scripture, this time without the burden of a world-historical interpretation of biblical salvation history. More precisely, the salvation story as the historical revelation of God would have to be distinguished from the general history of mankind, in order, at a second stage, to be confronted with it. The Middle Ages showed that the developmental dynamic of the biblical salvation story (which was seen as world history itself) can be extended and transferred beyond its original setting: the development in the Old Testament toward Jesus Christ. Thus, one can see, in fact, the modern idea of the development in world history since the age of the Enlightenment as a "secularization" of the original biblical one.

The question remains, however, whether this transference to world history, now understood "secularly," is really nothing more than secularization, or whether it has not been stimulated and justified by definite new knowledge. If this were the case, then things could, in fact, be the other way round. The idea of development could be originally a category of world history and only secondarily one of salvation history, insofar as a development in salvation history is growth chiefly because it depends on historical, cultural development in order to reach its goal in Christ. This possibility can be discussed only when we come to consider the secular aspect in full. But first let us try to make plain or deny significance in the historical stretch of time, i.e., a qualitative view of Church time.

Invisible Growth

In what the New Testament says about development one has to distinguish carefully between the affirmation of the fact and its recognizability, which is not necessarily implied.

The parables of the Lord which speak of an organic, gradual process, "the sower" in Matthew 13, 3–9, 18–23, "the growing seed" in Mark 4, 26–29, "the weeds" in Matthew 13, 24–30, 36–43, "the mustard seed" in Matthew 13, 31–32, and "the leaven" in Matthew 13, 33 are clearly introductory. They describe an event

which has now begun quietly and in secret but will be fully revealed in its world-embracing magnitude only at the Last Judgment. This position of the parables—at least in Matthew—will
suggest caution if one tries to set them against the motif of early
expectation, which emerges later in the gospel, and to use them
as evidence of a long historical development in time of the kingdom of God. This "growth" of the kingdom is not primarily an
historical process, but the inner encounter of the world as it is
("the field is the world") with the Word of God: the world is
touched, penetrated, and transformed by the event. Of course,
it is the world in its universality that is meant, not simply Israel
or the Church.

This is in accord with the comprehensive view of the beginning, with its goal of the world harvest whose reapers are the
angels. The event of the beginning is the slightest, the event of
the end is the most momentous, from which nothing is excluded.
Thus, the movement from the slightest to the most momentous
can appear only as "growth," and thus must happen through a
stretch of time. The period of this growth is clearly distinguished
from that of the harvest, particularly with the "weeds" and the
"growing seed." There is a time of waiting for the sower, but also
of patience for his servants, who would rather root out the weeds.
There is a time of letting the "mustard seed" do its own work,
infallibly and automatically.

This is all that is said, to start with. We still do not know that
the Word of God which is sowed in the world is Jesus Christ
himself, and that it is he, dying for the world, who is the seed
which falls into the earth and bears much fruit (John 12, 24),
that he himself is the vine without which the branches cannot
bear any fruit (John 15, 1 ff.). Therefore, the time of waiting and
letting grow, the time of the Church after the Ascension and
until the Last Judgment, will also be a time of growth for he who
waits.

This becomes apparent later in Paul, where both things are

emphasized together: that which was performed once and for all
—the Incarnation and the Redemption on the cross—and its
inner working out through time. There is a "waiting" of Christ
"until his enemies should be made a stool for his feet" (Heb. 10,
13), which links up with the waiting in the growth parables and
should not be weakened by any ideas of an historical growth. That
this waiting is also a "reigning" of Christ is stated by the same
quotation from the Psalm: "For he must reign until he has put
all his enemies under his feet" (1 Cor. 15, 25).

The Apocalypse finally describes this waiting and reigning as
an eschatological struggle, the result of which is proclaimed in
advance by the angel in the sun (Apoc. 19, 11–21). This battle,
which also calls out the heavenly hosts, is ultimately a struggle
for heaven itself (Apoc. 12, 7). It concerns above all the working
out in history of the victory of Christ: a fight against those powers
which were roused from sleep by the arrival of Christ and come
from heaven and earth, from the depths of the sea and the depths
of the earth, into the world in order to fight for their dominion
that has been challenged (Apoc. 12 and 13; Eph. 6, 12). For us,
it is won in advance by Christ, so that the believer can trust in
him and his "armor" in order to be sure of victory.

The growth of the victory of Christ, that is, the cause of Christ
himself in the world, is described by Paul in terms of growth. He
does not speak of it so much in the dimension of the individual
life which longs for its perfection, as of the Church, which the
risen and ascended Lord makes capable of this growth from above
and which he organizes throughout its members. Or rather, as
the individual, only as a "helping member" of the Church, can
fulfill his own task through "speaking the truth in love" (Eph.
4, 15), that is, through living the gospel in lived love, the Church
itself is built up and, through the growth of the Church, the
world itself, the universe, as the great and real Body of Christ, is
led toward its perfection.

Everything that God the Father founded and made possible

through his will in heaven and on earth is to be gathered together in Christ as the Head (Eph. 1, 10). What Christ introduced through his death and resurrection (Eph. 2, 13 ff.), what grows with the growing structure of the Church in the Holy Spirit acting from within (Eph. 2, 20–22), has ultimately a cosmic dimension.

In this sense there is a real process and progress in the universe, which continues unceasingly in time. It is a progress which cannot be calculated in any way statistically or psychologically, progress which takes place "within" and yet constitutes the movement of the whole history of the universe, which continues as long as history. On the "day of redemption" this "progress," whose true nature has been hidden, the hidden, but real growth of the universe toward Christ, is over and the Church is finished, and its result—that the universe has its Head in Christ and its Body with Christ—will emerge.[18]

The cyclic nature of this growth is everywhere apparent, without on that account hindering it. "For we are his workmanship, created in Christ Jesus for good works, which God prepared beforehand, that we should walk in them" (Eph. 2, 10), so that, if we truly progress, it must be with the "growth from God," from God, toward God, and through God (Col. 2, 19).

The "fullness" of Christ, toward which the whole Body strives, is already reached in the Head and thus is already presumed in the growth of the Body (Eph. 4, 13). A further important point is that *the law of cosmic progress is to be sought nowhere outside the law of personal progress and yet is to be regarded as true progress within the history of the world.*[19] It is not that only the individual can consummate the meaning of Christianity within his mortal existence—the dying and the rising with Christ (Rom. 6, 3 ff.; Gal. 2, 19 ff.; 3, 26–29)—while total history, deathlessly surviving the individual, would have no further Christian events in it. It is that *the law of life in each individual member of Christ exists as such only within the*

Church, which knows no other law than to strive to resemble its Head. But since the Church has dimensions in time which transcend the individual, its law can apply to world history as a whole.

If one looks back from this point at the growth parables, their world-historical dimensions seem confirmed and explained. They open up a real range of historical growth from the sowing of the seed by the Son of Man (Matt. 13, 37) to the world harvest of the angels. In this time

the independent seed of life is at work, through which the Church of Christ is to advance and develop until the time of the harvest. What the different stages of this development are, which are enumerated in the parable of the sowing (Mark 4, 26–29), is beyond our understanding. . . . But the nature of the image and the basic idea require that there must be true growth in the kingdom of God on earth, without ceasing and without check until the day of perfection.[20]

Thus, we have the fact of progress without being able to verify it. Hence, one is not able to relate automatically the growth of the tiny mustard seed beyond all other garden plants to the outer growth of the Church. But when we read of the weeds appearing after some time, "when the plants came up and bore grain" (Matt. 13, 26), the concern of the servants indicates that here something, at least something symptomatic, is made manifest; it is something whose calming explanation is simply that it is a secret work of the devil.

The hiding of the leaven (Matt. 13, 33) in the dough does not run counter to this idea of visibility. Rather, both images refer to the particular kind of visibility which is characteristic of God's kingdom. Even the "treasure hidden in a field" is "found," and then "covered up" again by the finder (Matt. 13, 44); and all the parables of the kingdom are concerned with the "uttering of what has been hidden" (Matt. 13, 35), with "understanding and not understanding" (Matt. 13, 11–17). It is utterance which can give offense, which is therefore never a neutral confirmation of the kingdom's being "here or there." "The kingdom of God is not coming with signs to be observed" (Luke 17, 20); it is "within you" (Luke 17, 21), because it is acceptance itself by the believer. Therefore, "Whoever does not receive the kingdom of God like a child shall not enter it" (Luke 18, 17).

Thus, if it were possible to write a theological history of the kingdom of Christ which would be more than a piece of world history, which would tell of the visible Church as an institution with its limitations, its aspirations, its power, its excellences, and its shortcomings, it could only be for believers. They "knowing all things" would find only an interpretation of their own experience of faith. As believers they would find nothing else, nothing new; they would discover only an obvious, visible confirmation of their faith, and in addition—because the historical account is the account of the word of God—a new call to them of the word.

Charismatic and Apocalyptic Prophecy

Such an understanding of world history is made clear by the "parable of the fig tree," in whose branches the sap rises and which puts forth its leaves; the sign of approaching summer is here the sign of the nearness of the kingdom (Matt. 24, 32 ff.). Although the *logion* has moved into the context of eschatological discourse, its sense is not essentially different from the answer to the Jews who asked for a sign. "When it is evening you say, 'It will be fair weather; for the sky is red.' And in the morning, 'It will be stormy today, for the sky is red and threatening.' You know how to interpret the appearance of the sky, but you cannot interpret the signs of the times" (Matt. 16, 2–3). The sign of Jonah which alone Jesus promises them is also to be the only one for the history of the Church and eschatologically: it is *his* sign. And just as the former apocalyptic sign means not only the imminent end of the world, but also the situation of the kingdom of God under the sword of the end—by implying at the same time the approaching destruction of Jerusalem—all that Jesus says has this appeal to the situation. Not in the pallid sense of a hellenized Christian morality (as an appeal to the individual conscience to decide what ought to be done now), nor in the even more pallid way in which modern situation ethics understands it (which practically only considers the individual in his temporality), but in the way that the prophets of Israel spoke: from a time for a time. That calls for a salvation history situation of the People among all the people; the People that is now addressed in this situation by the word of God, and at this intersection point of the horizon and vertical, can and must know what it has to do.

This specifically Jewish challenge to man—which, particularly with Mark, begins with the act of faith, which one must "be able to make" and on the basis of which one will then "be able to do" everything—reaches its climax in Jesus, and, thus, goes into the whole of Church time. Gentile Christians often fail to see this, thinking that this kind of time sequence is Old Testament in style, because it implied a growing revelation. On the other hand, a complete revelation, which rests, finished, in the *depositum fidei Ecclesiae* and is administered by it, would dispense one from such an historical vigilance of faith. But just this kind of "sleep of the man with possessions" (Luke 12, 19) offends against the ever more urgent command of the gospel to watch through the ages, and so not to miss the final arrival of the Lord and bridegroom. If the history of the Church is largely a "war of missed opportunities," which cannot be won by subsequent dogmatizations and canonizations, then it is because of the Gentile Christian misunderstanding of this Jewish theological element in the New Testament.

This amount of knowledge about the significance of salvation history must suffice for us. It assigns a qualitative meaning to

the historical course of time—more than the mere summation of
the results of all individual existences before God—but at the
same time precludes any other knowledge of this significance
apart from the sensing in faith of the signs of the time. Because
a fully alive and determined commitment in faith of one's existence is asked of him so that his time may move within the Holy
Spirit, we may call this knowledge charismatic and existential. It
cannot be converted into neutral knowability. We may call it,
more simply and more biblically, prophetic knowledge, which,
divinely inspired, knows about the importance of the hour. In
the Old Testament it was a single man to whom was given to
proclaim what hour it was by the divine clock; the others had
to believe him. Through their belief they were able to share in
the open knowability of the time of divine favor. In the New
Testament there is another, a Church mode of open knowability,
which can be expressed in words in certain particular given
formulations, but is fundamentally imparted to all believers by
the giving of the Spirit. "And in the last days it shall be, God
declares, that I will pour out my Spirit upon all flesh, and your
sons and daughters shall prophesy, and your young men shall
see visions, and your old men shall dream dreams" (Acts 2, 17).
"The testimony of Jesus is the spirit of prophecy" (Apoc. 19, 10).

What is the relation of apocalyptic prophecy to this charismatic
prophecy? Does it not go one step beyond charismatic prophecy
by filling out from the viewpoint of God the qualitative direction
of time, which we know from the extraordinary growth of the
Church and the universe, toward the full figure of Christ, and
present it in overwhelming images? Assuming that we were unable to fit this succession of pictures to an historical chronology,
that we could not even say definitely whether there is anything
like a chronological relation between the (total or partial) sequence of visions in heaven and the temporal historical sequence
of events on earth: would not even then our knowledge of the
significance of salvation history be wonderfully enriched?

With the reservations already made we may say that it is. The apocalyptic view of things offers the assurance that history as history (and not only as the sum of individual lives) has before God a completely clear and overwhelmingly magnificent sense. The translation of this sense into an aesthetic or symbolic view is the best way in which man, still struggling within history, can share in this vision. The image and the sequence of images reveal a richly pregnant, full-to-bursting load of meaning, without it being possible to separate out intellectually the sense from the image and give it a form in which it can be apprehended in an ordinary earthly way. No other ending to the Old and New Testaments was to be expected than a final surpassing of the form of Old and New Testament prophecy, whose nature is something quite different than a technique of knowing future events in advance. If the interpretation of the state of the times, which the gospel demands of the man who truly believes, is to be opened up to for the last time and shown to be true of the whole of Church time, indeed the whole of creation time, then this could be done only in "mirror and riddle." It can be accomplished only in images which do not have as their content the reporting of decisions, but are themselves, in their form, like the parables of the gospel, images of decisions: images, which from their latent presence, demand a *yes* or a *no*.

The temptation to develop this sequence of images in terms of world history has understandably beset Christians, particularly since Joachim. But, quite apart from all self-refutations in the calculation of the end or of the single stages, the temptation has always brought an uncomfortable feeling with it. By attaching one of the symbols to a circumscribed historical situation, the symbol exchanges its divine fullness of meaning for an earthly mundaneness; it loses its inherent theological dimensions. On the other hand, the historical situation in time appears vested with an aura of meaning which grotesquely distorts it.

What can one say of the attempt of Féret[21] "to divide the teachings of the book into two groups"? One group is "without an immediate connection with the concrete course of time" (general "elements of a theology of history"). The other group contains "prophecies in the narrower sense," which are recognizable by their connection with the historical situation of the author (his struggle with the Rome of Domitian which, with its cult of the emperor, demanded adoration), which he then expands to embrace the whole of world history.[22] Anticipating the general "categories" of the history of the seven seals, the four riders, the trumpets, the vessels of wrath, etc., the book, according to Féret, moves from the animals on ever closer to concrete prophecy and reaches it in Apocalypse 17, 1 and 20, 15.

But if the woman who sits on the animal (the power of the world) and on the "seven hills" (Apoc. 17, 9) is really supposed to be contemporary Rome ("without question"),[23] and her "fall" the collapse of its heathen power; if we are supposed to be living now in the following age of the "ten kings," to be followed by a third age (the millennium), where after a long struggle the Christian structures and institutions will have established themselves even in the worldly sphere:[24] what a devaluation of the tremendous picture of the whore of Babylon filling the history of the world! What a devaluation of the lament at her downfall which resounds through all eternity, and which takes up and surpasses all the laments of the Old Testament, the lament for the fall of the king of Tyre and the dirge for the fall into hell of Pharaoh! "This prophecy concerning the Roman Empire," says Féret, "is of little consequence to us today, for the event is very remote from us. But we can easily understand the effect which it must have had on the disturbed and troubled Christian community."[25]

No, this approach is impossible. On the basis of the three historical victories of Christ—first over the woman Rome, then over the ten kings (?), then over Satan, bound for a thousand years—we can as little ascribe to ourselves the "optimism" of an unbounded progress,[26] if only in relation to an interpenetration with the leaven of Christendom of the historical, social structures of humanity. The abolition of slavery, on which the Roman state was based, and the rejection of serfdom also, which still "compromised the free, proud unions of the Middle Ages," by the "properly understood liberalism" of modern times seem to recommend this optimism to the author, even though he knows that this is not to prejudge the decision of the individual. Later, when we deal with progress in the secular sphere, we shall return to this thesis and show its genuine contribution; but on no account is it to be supported by or burdened with the images of the Apocalypse.

The images say as much as they want to. They open the dimension between heaven—where the universal Lord of history sits on the throne with the slaughtered Lamb and all the terrible things of the temporal drama change into pure praise—and the earthly events, which the angels mediate, judging and preserving, sealing and unsealing. A relationship is established which cannot be simply limited to the bare philosophical relationship between changeable time and constant eternity. Rather, it is one in which eternity, i.e., the triune God together with the whole heavenly Church, continues living and acting beside temporal history and, in fact, by constant action holds onto it. The events and turning points of this simultaneous controlling movement give rise to the succession of images, without our being able to say whether they are longitudinal or latitudinal sections through historical time. Perhaps from the point of view of eternity it does not much matter.

Féret has an eye for the inner reciprocal relationship between heaven and earth. He also correctly sees that the saint, who at every moment follows the Lamb in heaven, can still be someone who lives very much on earth. On the other hand, someone at home in heaven, because he has died on earth, can still be active here. He even interprets the "first resurrection" for the millennium in this fashion,

The saints and martyrs, inseparably connected with Christ, direct the progress of the truth of the gospel here on earth; and the final victory of this truth in the total life of humanity is at the same time the beginning of its invisible dominion on earth and among the peoples. . . . St. John, moreover, emphasizes particularly that only the martyrs and the saints "become alive again," like Christ and with him, and live on in history until the thousand years are completed. The other dead . . . do not awake to life again before the Last Judgment and hence cannot perform any more evil deeds in history, as the saints are able to perform their good deeds. Under these circumstances it is not surprising that the good must one day triumph.[27]

Although Féret's basic idea seems to be correct, his quantifying interpretation does not appear justified. Moreover, the devil is let loose once more afterward for the last time, in order to be cast again, and finally, into the burning pit. The statements of the Apocalypse are all concerned with the vertical connection between heaven and earth and cannot be transferred to the horizontal. In the vertical they comprise the significance of temporal horizontal history. Therefore, one is able to say that even the final intensification, which the Apocalypse of John shares with the other eschatological pronouncements of the New Testament (Matt. 24 ff., 2 Thess., 2 Pet., 1 John, Jude), is an expression of the threatening character of the end forcing its way into time and of time moving toward the end. This is true even if one cannot deny a horizontal intensification of the contrast between Christ and the powers (whose rage is all the greater the less time they have left, Apoc. 12, 12) as something lying in the nature of a significant account of time and its "drama."

Church Time and the Conversion of Israel

The words about the Antichrist in Paul and John (2 Thess. 2, 7; 1 John 4, 3) also refer to the intensification of that which is already present. There is one future event which it does not seem possible to fit into this category: the final conversion of Israel, which Paul envisages in Romans 11, 26 and to which the mysterious words of Christ in Matthew 23, 39 refer. But as Jesus leaves the time of this conversion unstated—does it occur in history and thus influence its subsequent course, or does it refer to the end of history and the introduction to the transcendent judgment of the world?[28]—so Paul's words also leave it vague. He describes the event as a *mysterion* (Rom. 11, 25), a word he also applies to the secret of the Antichrist (2 Thess. 2, 7) and the general resurrection (1 Cor. 15, 51), the one imminent in history, the other transcendent. The interpretation of it within history might be indicated by the fact that the salvation of "all Israel" is a taking up of the Old Testament promise, as the whole context of Romans 9–11 shows. But is this promise itself imminent in history? The way it is understood in the Old Testament and later Jewish exegesis is not sufficient justification for it.

The quotation from Isaiah in Romans 11, 26–27, concerning the deliverer from Zion, who will banish ungodliness from Jacob, is to be interpreted, in view of Acts 3, 19–20, transcendentally in terms of the return of Christ. And yet, the context undoubtedly speaks of Church history in time; what matters is the dialectic of the one who is chosen and then rejected. There is no immediate connection with the Last Judgment of Christ, nor with heaven and hell. So we must reject this idea. The relation between Israel and the Church, in the Pauline context, has nothing to do with the separation of the sheep and the goats in the parable of the judgment. It was an error of Augustine's, fraught with consequences, to relate the text of Romans—which, when discussing the election of Jacob and the "rejection" of Esau, is concerned with the theology of history—to the predestination of individuals to eternal salvation or damnation. What Paul states is a basic law, perhaps even *the* basic law of the whole Christian theology of history: Israel fallen in history will be raised again in history. How could this text be understood other than historically?

And yet before the abyss of this *mysterion* theology hesitates. Is not the *yes* and *no* of God, his having mercy and his hardening the heart (Rom. 9, 18), simply the basic rhythm of salvation history from the beginning? Has not this *yes* and *no* found its final form in the dialectic of the cross, where the chosen one is rejected and the rejected ones chosen? Must one not inevitably see this mystery of the cross as represented in the history of the world by "both peoples," those on the right and those on the left, those in the light and those in the shadow? Must not, therefore, Christ's resurrection, and, thus, the total recognition of Christ by Jews and Gentiles, be related to his return in glory as the Lord of the whole of history?

Gaston Fessard,[29] following the ideas of P. Huby, has argued strongly against Maritain, Journet, and Féret. He holds that the eschatological interpretation is the only one—and the only traditional one—which is acceptable for the theology of history. The New Covenant is founded in the agonizing, crucifying, and rising above Israel according to the flesh. And if it is true that the man on the cross "has broken down the dividing wall of hostility [between Jews and Gentiles] . . . in his flesh, . . . that he might create in himself one new man in place of the two" (Eph. 2, 14–15), "then one has only to place this text beside Romans 11 to see that the difference between Gentile and Jew can be removed only on the day that the new man has attained his full measure (Eph. 4, 13) and fully and finally unites both peoples in his total Mystical Body."

If we agree that Israel's conversion takes place within history, what, after that, could be unbelief and hardening of the heart? Both the evangelical and the Pauline perspective would be superseded by the evolution of mankind; the fundamental biblical pronouncements would be historically relativized. The statement of Paul would have less importance than the Old Testament prophecies, which retain eschatological value over and above this historical event. No, the basic New Testament statements concerning the theology of history are ontological in nature: with the dialectic between Jew and Gentile stands or falls the whole structure of the New Covenant. Apart from Fessard, this has been seen most radically by Karl Barth.[30]

This is also clear from the existential situation of the (Gentile) Church, which, grafted onto the tree of Israel, must beware, because it does not stand rooted in itself, but "against nature" in something strange: "It is not you that supports the root, but the root that supports you" (Rom. 11, 18). Or is it the fact that Israel has been broken off, which causes the Apostle "unceasing anguish"? Is not the collapse of all its prerogatives (Rom. 9, 2-5) something which deeply affects the Church of Christ as well? While the original social promise remains unfulfilled, can this Church be the pleroma in the true sense? Has the mystery of the reconciliation of the "near" and the "far" in the flesh of the crucified one (Eph. 2, 11 ff.) really been performed as long as the near ones, for the sake of those who were once far, remain far themselves? And does not this open up the possibility of a place where something theologically historical, which as yet does not exist, can take place for and with the Church?

Of course, one can say that Israel has basically found her salvation in the "holy remnant," the few in Israel who embraced the Messiah in order to found the nucleus of the Church and one day judge the twelve tribes (Matt. 19, 28), so that the Church of Christ is now already a Church of Jews and heathen, and the eschatological event will only make this more apparent through the influx of the Jews. But that is only half the truth which does not illuminate the other half: the "rejection" and "hardening of the heart" so emphasized by Paul; the "being left" by the Messiah and by the apostles all through the Acts. This ordinance can be removed only by an act of salvation history which cannot be replaced and forgotten by, e.g., an increased number of conversions from Jewry. One cannot see how single conversions could make an adequate contribution, hitherto withheld, by Israel to the

Church (which remains, in the main, a Gentile one), let alone have done so in the past.

It is rather to be feared that a particular forced Judaizing, which is becoming fashionable these days in biblical theology, is somehow only mimicry and cannot replace an original contribution of Israel. The clearly visible Gentile flavor which theology, and hence also the gospel, had from the beginning, cannot be removed by any countertendency now. It is not enough to "imagine" how Jews experience and understand certain things; one must also be able to have the same experience within himself. That is true, in spite of the fact that the wild olive branches were grafted onto the holy tree, that the original cell of the Church was Jewish and the whole of sacred scripture is Jewish. Thus, although the universal Church of Christ contains fundamentally both, it is still not simply the last synthesis of both until "the whole of Israel is saved."

Israel's hardness of heart is the eternal proof of the fact that the earthly Church remains essentially in a condition of pilgrimage, as long as it does not eternisize itself and rob itself of its true temporality, and let its Gentile-Greek heritage think and speak rather than its Christian soul. On the other hand, it is outstripped and outshone by an Israel, which is far more expert in worldly and temporal matters, and is almost forced back into its humiliating role of patient waiting. The positive shaping of the world which it writes on its banners is done far more effectively by the others, and it is only unwillingly that it submits to the will of the true Lord of the Church, who lets the hidden world harvest be more helped by their suffering, their failure, and their carrying of the cross than by the endeavors of the Christians which are naively well-meant and naively flee the cross. To be on the cross, for the Church, does not mean to celebrate the cross as a past event or possess it as a principle which it administrates, but to be forced to stand in an historically irremovable conflict.

If this gulf between Israel and the Church cannot be over-

come by approximations (as, for example, that between Protestant and Catholic would have to be), then one must assume that
the fissure created by the gospel of Christ can only be closed in a
transcendent, eschatological way. It is such a saving event that it
cannot split temporal Church history into two halves. But in that
case one of the fundamental characteristics of Church time is that
it is the time of Israel's "hardness of heart," the time of a
proclamation of salvation which has no effect where it ought to,
a time in which all effect on the "peoples" is still an incomplete
fulfillment of God's promise. According to Ezechiel 16, Sodom
and Samaria are justified before Jerusalem, but they in no way
supplant the unfaithful bride, for whom the promise was really
intended, before the judgment of God.

The profoundest drama of Church time is not that between
"Church" and "world": for the world of the peoples has been allotted to the Church as a mission field, and it achieves many suc-
cesses there. It is that between Israel and the Church: where Jesus
and his cross seemed to fail; where the prophet was without honor
in his own country, his representative is not likely to be more successful. "A disciple is not above his teacher . . . it is enough for
the disciple to be like his teacher" (Matt. 10, 24–25). As there is
something provisional about the cross until the "irreversible
promises of God" are finally fulfilled in his own truly chosen
one, the whole of Church time itself is characterized by this provisional quality. It is significant that the "ecumenical movement"
either almost forgets Jewry or—no less mistakenly—treats it as
just another sect to be converted. There is a certain fundamental
unconvertability which the disciples of Christ do not care to
regard too closely, and in which Israel simply represents mankind
defying God. With all the possible partial success one might have,
this unconvertability stamps this particular missionary and ecumenical activity with the sign of the vain, useless cross.[31]

As for the theological insight into the significance of the history of the Church *as* extended through time, in spite of our

knowledge, through faith, that it has significance, there still remains the impossibility of obtaining it in this life.

Notes

1 This is said primarily philosophically, but it is also true theologically, since in christology the element of human personality is not excluded as something that can be dispensed with; the man Jesus possesses, beyond all uniqueness in time, his own absolute uniqueness as the incomparable "only" Son of God.

2 Cf. Josef Schreiner: *Sion-Jerusalem, Theologie der heiligrn Stadt im Alten Testament*, 1962.

3 Georges Poulet: *Les Métamorphoses du Cercle*, 1961.

4 Chenu: *Introduction à S. Thomas d'Aquin*, 1950, 270.

5 One must reread at this point Kant's delightful essay, *"Das Ende aller Dinge"* (The End of All Things): "That is where the reflective man turns to mysticism (because reason . . . likes to dabble in the transcendental, it too has its secrets), when reason does not understand itself and what it is trying to do . . . and all thinking itself has an end." (Insel, 1921, VI, 647).

6 Cf. above, Chapter 1.

7 Cf. above, Chapter 1 and my introduction to a selection from the *Civitas Dei* in the Fischer Bücherei.

8 This is the point of my "Theology of History" (Sheed & Ward, 1963) which sought to offer just the bare essentials of a Christian conception of time and history.

9 Insofar as Christ is the kingdom of God come near to us, the Spirit hovers over him since his baptism in the Jordan; insofar as he is secretly the Spirit of the kingdom that is coming, he overshadows the Virgin Mary; insofar as the kingdom is promised in the prophets, the Spirit is present and working in them. Only in the Holy Spirit could Abraham believe.

10 Rudolph Bultmann: *Johannes*, 14th ed., 434.

11 *Ibid.*, 436.

12 Walter Dirks: *Die Antwort der Mönche*, 1952.

13 Cf. my *Parole et Mystère chez Origène*, 1957.

14 Cf. Karl Lowith: *Meaning in History: The theological implications of the philosophy of history*, University of Chicago, 1957.

15 *Die Geschichtstheologie des hl. Bonaventura*, 1959.

16 *Ibid.*, 37.

17 2 *Sent.* d. 2 p. 1 a. 2 q. 3 c. Cf. Ratzinger, 143.

18 Heinrich Schlier: *Der Brief an die Epheser*, 1957, 207.

19 Cf. the patristic theologumenon of the correspondence of world history and individual personal history (Ratzinger: *Volk und Haus Gottes in*

Augustins Lehre von der Kirche, 1954, 197–218). J. Guitton has strongly criticised this view (*Le Temps et l'Eternité etc.*, 3rd ed., 1959, 370 ff.), without, however, completely understanding the problem.

20 Leopold Fonck: *Die Parabeln des Herrn*, 1909, 120.

21 H. M. Féret O.P.: *Die Geheime Offenbarung des hl. Johannes, eine christliche Schau der Geschichte*, 1955.

22 *Ibid.*, 38 ff.

23 *Ibid.*, 218.

24 *Ibid.*, 230–234.

25 *Ibid.*, 223–224.

26 *Ibid.*, 234.

27 *Ibid.*, 230–231.

28 When compared with Matthew 26, 64 ("Hereafter you will see the Son of man . . . coming on the clouds of heaven.") and the rejoinder in Apoc. 1, 7, the transcendental interpretation seems more likely.

29 *Théologie et Histoire.* In: *De l'Actualité historique*, 1959, I, 95–119, 215–241, 243–291; II, 27–71.

30 *Church Dogmatics*, II, *Doctrine of God*, pt. 2, *Election and Command of God*, Allenson, 1957.

31 H. Schlier: *Das Mysterium Israels*, in *Die Zeit der Kirche*, 1956, 244.

5. MAN IN SACRED AND SECULAR HISTORY

Is there a theological meaning in world history? This new question can only be posed where some kind of distinction is made between the Logos and salvation history, and a mutual relation is established between them. Such a distinction for the sake of establishing the relation can be made in varying degrees of clarity and intensity. There can and should not be a complete division between them, either from the point of view of theology or the philosophy of history, if the unity of historical man also implies an ultimate unity in his history. For it is only out of such unity that history can be conceived theologically or philosophically.

155

HOW THE BIBLE ASKS THE QUESTION

Does the bible present an image of the history of the world which
can be distinguished from salvation history? To seek it in the
modern sense as universal history would be an anachronism. The
only thing that we can expect to find, in terms of the history of
civilization and theology, is a distinction between salvation history as history, which as such is particular, and its claim on the
history of the world.

Light from Protology

One of the first places where this relationship must emerge is
protology, that late and very speculative construction of the
priestly circles, which follows history before the calling of Abraham back to Adam, in order to place it in the light of the coming
election of Israel. This emerges from the condition of the Gentile
world like the particular out of the universal, and also like being
out of nonbeing.

The universal was from Adam and Eve and from Cain and
Abel, the expulsion from Paradise and the ever deeper and
broader forgetting of God. And yet throughout the whole there
lives a promise of salvation (see the proto-evangelium) and a
provision of salvation of which we see the contours when individual luminous figures emerge from the mass of sinners:
Enoch and other "primeval saints."[1] This promise is further
revealed in the choosing of Noah and in the covenant God makes
with him which almost competes with the covenant with Abraham. For in Noah (who is neither Jew nor Gentile, as the difference did not then exist) a divine covenant is made with the whole
of mankind and the whole of creation, a covenant which stands in
a relation to the covenant with Abraham as the all-embracing universal to the particular. This particular, on the basis of the covenant with Noah, must have a dynamic openness to the universal.

It is not in Abraham, but in Noah, that all peoples are openly
blessed for the first time. They already had been blessed im-

plicitly since Adam and the promise of salvation made to him. This is one of those elements introduced into the biblical theology of history by the Jewish priestly circles—in that late period which Jaspers calls the pivotal age of world history (800–200)—which relativizes and places in perspective the next stage in salvation history: the blessing of all peoples in Abraham and the promise to him. The two motifs are not resolved even in the New Testament. On the one hand, the Abraham tradition is the main one in the synoptics and John (8, 35–58) and completely so in Paul. On the other hand, the story of Noah is quoted by Christ himself as a type of saving election (Matt. 24, 37–38). Paul compares the faith of Noah, like that of Abel and Enoch, with that of Abraham (Heb. 11, 7). Both Petrine letters (1 Pet. 3, 20–21; 2 Pet. 2, 5) take Noah as a peg on which to hang a typological soteriology in relation to the whole cosmos. Thus, in the bible a salvation sealed by Noah for the whole cosmos stands in the background of the salvation for all peoples which comes by Abraham. The sign of this covenant is the rainbow; even the animals are brought into it.

From the foregoing, one can conclude that when the covenant made with Abraham is considered, there is no salvation for the "Gentiles." However, when the covenant made with Noah is looked at—as well as the whole of early biblical history—salvation, latent and at certain points even visible, presents itself as available for all men. Hence, the "wisdom of the Egyptians" and of the other surrounding peoples is not simply condemned, however exclusively and jealously Israel is bound to its God and covenant of salvation. Thus, the editors of Genesis do not have to destroy anxiously all traces of an exchange between polytheism and the religion of the patriarchs. On the contrary, they can use with a certain liberality the traditional general store of legends in order to stylize them and place them within the ethnological context.

But apart from this, the area outside Israel and the Church is virtually ignored in both the Old and the New Testament;

nowhere is there manifest any interest in an historical logos proper to the "peoples" as such.[2] This negative is, from the point of view of eschatological salvation, provisional only, and in the course of the Old Testament it reveals itself ever more as such. Its end is almost visible during the time of the Babylonian captivity. And yet there are no approximations or liberal introductions of foreign logoi into the stern line of the Logos of Israel. Only the Yahweh's claim to power over the Gentiles is understood ever more profoundly and spiritually from the judgment of conquest, through the divine right of judgment which God passes whenever Israel remains faithful, even to the positively making use of the Gentiles and their kings (Cyrus) in order to direct the salvation fortunes of Israel.

Also in the New Testament any other meaning of the "peoples," as the approach of those who were distant, receiving a share in the promise and its fulfillment in the fullness of Christ, cannot be conceived. To search for a creation Logos of history which would be different from that does not come within the purview of the revelation of salvation, as little as a creation Logos of nature and of men as natural beings, which would be applicable to everything, is its concern. Deutero-Isaiah, it is true, shows the eschatological homage of the Gentiles to messianic Jerusalem and the procession of their kings with presents, *aurum et thus*. But these are not further discussed; they receive their basic value in saving history through this approach in homage, just as in the Apocalypse the meaning and value of the crowns of the twenty-four are that they are thrown before the throne of God.

Light from Eschatology

Thus, from biblical protology we have moved to biblical eschatology, particularly as it is developed in the prophetic and apocalyptic ages. The attempt has been made to derive the whole Christian theology of history from the beginning in Daniel's apocalyptic visions and his world kingdoms.[3] These have largely influenced the periodization of history from the Christian view, because Daniel clothed contemporary events (the persecution under Antiochus Epiphanes in Dan. 11) in prophetic forms, and thus invited his contemporaries and those coming after to interpret the actual prophecies of Chapters 7 through 10 and 12 (and, later, the Apocalypse of John) equally in terms of world history. Then there is the dream of Nebuchadnezzar about the great statue (Dan. 2), which Daniel is able to relate and interpret, and the other one of the great tree (Dan. 4), which the king tells himself and which Daniel also interprets for him. Like the signs of Belshazzar (Dan. 5), these dreams relate to imminent events that turn out to be true. Thus, the kingdom story of the "peoples" is subject to the same law of significance as that of the Jews, and what distinguishes Jewish prophecy from the powerless Gentile prophecy (since the wise men of Babylon are not able to interpret, just as the wise men of Pharaoh could not compete with the prophetic spirit of Moses) is Daniel's power of interpretation:

> Blessed be the name of God for ever and ever,
>   to whom belong wisdom and might.
> He changes times and seasons;
>   he removes kings and sets up kings. . . .
> He reveals deep and mysterious things. . . .
>   and the light dwells with him. (Dan. 2, 20–22)

Then there is the theology of the intermediate beings. As angels of the peoples they direct the fortunes of nations: Israel's angel Michael (Dan. 10: 13, 21; 12, 1) is now one of the angels of the people. Also, they fight out the decisive battles of history in a higher, heavenly sphere. Finally, they interpret the prophetic visions, like Gabriel (Dan. 9, 21–27) and the unnamed angels of the final vision (Dan. 12, 5–12).

Here world history unquestionably has become a theological event; the whole of time is stirred up in relation to the final time;

the whole area between earth and heaven is drawn into the decisions involved. The "Son of Man" is in sight as an event both within history and at the end of history; Christ will not resolve this dual relation, but confirm it frequently (cf. Elias, the baptizer). Thus, the Apocalypse will hold open both horizontal and vertical areas of time and people them with beings and events which show and preserve the consciousness of the relevance of secular history for salvation history.

At the end of the Old Testament a secular universalism, which places the uniquely special history of Israel within a total pattern of saving events, corresponds to the protological universalism, as represented by the equally late priestly theology. It is, therefore, not enough to describe Israel as the possessor of the salvation promise and of the salvation fulfillment to come one day and the Gentiles as partaking of this salvation in the messianic age. There is visible beyond that a working of God through the whole of history, which in the sense of the bible certainly cannot be described as a "natural providence" (if those words have any meaning). God works and guides events in relation to ultimate salvation, which has its center in Israel, but concerns the whole world.

THE EXTENSION OF THE QUESTION IN THE COURSE OF THE HISTORY OF THEOLOGY

The Beginnings

One cannot blame the Christian apologists from the second century on for starting to elaborate their doctrine of the *logos spermatikos* as the first Christian philosophy (or theology) of history in connection with biblical revelation. Although Stoic elements may have influenced them, they sought to keep the basic scheme biblical, and it is. It is biblical precisely in the curious alternation between two contradictory motifs. The first is a logos in the nonbiblical peoples, which has in it the seeds of the whole, which ripen toward the fullness of the Incarnate Logos in the gospel. The second is a logos with the same peoples, which can be explained only by borrowings of pagan wisdom from the chronologically older Hebrews, i.e., by a debased revelation truth. Both motifs are found side by side, not only in the more naive apologists, but also in the best such as Clement, Origen, and Augustine. This apparent uncertainty is in fact theological conscientiousness, which does not seek to decide how God disposes of his revelation outside the sphere of the bible. The borrowing theory is closer to the obedience of faith which refuses to relativize the bible in the manner of liberalism. The theory of a logos which is of the Gentiles leaves God the freedom of assigning them one in relation to total salvation.

This theory, also, may be regarded as the expression of a true obedience to faith, if the divine Logos, which became flesh in Christ, is taken as the one which is the ground of the universe. If all things are "for him" (Col. 1, 16), then so is the history of the Gentiles. The obscuring of the logos with the Gentiles is not, then, to be ascribed to the lack of divine light, but to the inexcusable darkening of their own minds (Rom. 1, 18 ff.). If that is the case, then the spiritual *spoliatio Aegyptiorum*, as primarily Origen advocates, i.e., the adoption and Christianization of pagan wisdom, cannot be a profanation of divine wisdom, but only the harvesting of what belonged originally to the true Logos and could be understood only from it and the bringing of it back home. The philosophy, mythology, and poetry of the pagans belong rightfully to Christ and, after the necessary total crisis (1 Thess. 5, 21), to the people of Christ also.

The Church and the Religions of the World

This harvesting tendency, which has an Old Testament flavor, is contrasted with the Christian missionary tendency of spreading abroad; here lies the fruitful germ of a theology of secular history.

The gospel message which the apostle of Christ takes out then appears as the totality and fullness of what the peoples already possess as their own in fragments and obscure forms. That this fullness of light appears as an historical event—the death and resurrection of Christ—is the difficulty of preaching; thus, the preacher will be all the more anxious to present the factualness of this salvation event, not as something strange and different, but as that which is the necessary inner fulfillment. Paul took this line in the Areopagus, and still did not belie himself as an apostle of Christ; the "unknown god" which the Athenians worshipped was not for them what Paul makes of him, i.e., the absence of the true and living God. This interpretation of their consciousness is drawn out of its own corruption and obscurity into a light which shows the Athenians for the first time what in truth they lack.

Indeed, the true handling of the "theology of the point of contact" demands a gift of discretion which even in the best men is often lacking, especially when missionary zeal makes the differences appear less than they are. The combining of different elements in the late Middle Ages makes this question emerge with great urgency. Through the light of theology, to which Augustine had subordinated all the light of philosophy, the primordial philosophy breaks through in a new and powerful way. The illumination doctrine of Augustine could always be interpreted backward to Plotinus and Plato, and accordingly the concrete unity of the Logos in the trinitarian and Incarnate Son could be traced back to the unity of the Stoic-Platonic, even Parmenidean, God. One could keep the former before his eyes and talk in the language of the latter.

Then there was the medieval longing to move from the letter to the spirit, from the institution and the sacrament to the *intellectus* within them, as we have already seen with Joachim and Bonaventure. At that period there was a growing awareness that the "peoples" could only take from the Church (and its mission) its "form" if they found in the form that *intellectus* which would impart to it, beyond its naked factualness, an inner necessity of salvation history. The Christian missionary conscience moves in the same direction. Beyond all conquests with the tools of power, all baptisms by force and crusades against Islam, seeing that these are all highly inappropriate, because un-Christian, means of preaching the gospel, it seeks an intellectual encounter with other religions. For even where missionaries have gone out unarmed to preach Christ—as in the mission Gregory the Great sent to England, in the evangelizing of Ireland, in the mission to the East of Otto of Bamberg—they went chiefly to uncivilized peoples.

But now one had to adopt the weapons of the spirit, like Thomas Aquinas against Islam and the philosophizing Jews. It was a matter of penetrating even further into the enemy camp, as St. Francis tried and Raymond Lully succeeded in doing. Roger Bacon called for a Christian theology which knows itself face to face with the history of religion. One had to know and to have studied Judaism, pagan philosophy, Islam, Buddhism, and Brahmanism, to grasp the central idea of each world religion. Through such study he then could see the nature of that religious fullness which is what Christianity is internally and should also be externally.[4]

In an even more pressing intellectual crisis Nicholas of Cusa wrote his *De Pace Fidei,* a work so daring that one can only wonder that it was never put on the Index. "If we proceed according to the instruction of Christ," he told John of Segovia, "we shall not go wrong. Rather will his Spirit speak in us, which none of the enemies of Christ will be able to resist. But if we choose invasion with the sword, then we must fear that we who have drawn the sword shall also perish by the sword."[5] In the heavenly council of all religions which he, "rapt in an ecstatic light of the wind," sees in session, over which the Logos presides, and which seeks the one truth, both ways are tried: to show the dogmas about God and the Incarnation as the inner depth of the highest philosophies (without being able to speak, in Cusa's sense, of an actual deduction) and then to take the positive Church institutions, such as the sacraments, and make their spiritual meaning transparent.

This is not the place to discuss the manifold ways derived from this council of ideals via the Platonism of the Renaissance, via Vitoria and Las Casas, to Leibniz and Böhme, to Schelling and Hegel. That they exist is obvious. Even in Cusa one can see the reason: the Christ of the last book of the *Docta Ignorantia,* in his whole personal concreteness and historicity, is simply world reason. Thus, the opponent who has really thought through and understood Proclus has also, by implication, thought through and understood Christ. He can be shown that God, who has dismissed the unequal from himself, must be the unity of unity, correspondence (*aequalitas*), and identity (between unity and correspondence), which is the scheme of the Trinity. Hence, one only needs to enlighten the pagan about what he knows already without knowing that he knows it. But in order to be able to enlighten him in that way, the Christian himself must be enlightened, that is, be a "pneumatic" and a contemplative.

These theories of the *logos spermatikos,* even where, as with Roger Bacon, they demand an historical empiricism, still remain within the framework of theology. Only when the necessary empiricism becomes emphasized and the logos of the Gentiles is made the subject of scientific investigation, does there arise that dialogue between the theology of man in history and the philosophy of man in history which the present work intends. Voltaire, and Vico before him, was the first to make this clear. History no longer as salvation history, but as the dimension of man as man, history as the product of man (though under the guiding providence of God), is now contrasted with a history whose significance is primarily implanted by God into the chaos of time.

THE RELATION OF THEOLOGY AND THE PHILOSOPHY OF HISTORY TODAY

Where They Meet

Modern philosophy of history has three main concerns. The first treats the description of peoples and their cultures, particularly those which, as belonging to "history," are already complete and thus can be studied in full. One could examine their political history, but also their inner spiritual history in which their cultural achievements and their philosophy were the expression of their self-knowledge. There is inevitably a tendency, in such a description, of seeing civilized cultures as unities. One could see them as somehow cyclic, and thus organic and morphological, compared with which their sequence—like pearls on a chain— and the question of a "total development" became a secondary, additional one.

The second concern deals with the idea of a development in salvation history, which, however, was in the bones of the European. Thus, it was all the more natural to use it as the guiding thread, in that the Christian theology of history had already conceived the developmental idea in the revelation of salvation in terms of world history, and medieval theology had made many attempts to extend this framework of development eschatologically and interculturally. Over and above this, however, there was a third element, which could not appear as a separate one on its own, but strongly influenced the first two elements and emerged as independent in the twentieth century. It can be called the "Jaspers" idea of "axial time." This idea has been employed by many modern philosophers of history under different names. It represents the movement of humanity "from *mythos* to *logos*" (E. Cassirer, W. Nestle, B. Snell), the "discovery of the spirit" and hence of suprasymbolic universality.

Of these three concerns one may call the first the demand for an empirical science of history, the second a hypothesis which comes in the first place from theology, the third a fact which can be interpreted in different ways. The various combinations of these three elements will provide the major varieties of the modern philosophy of history.

One can emphasize the description of cultures in their finitude, against a biological, an aesthetic, or a skeptical, pessimistic background. Voltaire's optimism was sadly shattered. Vico saw a dialectic of history that was stronger than the intentions of men and which converted their hubris each time into a *ricorso* to barbarous beginnings, from which a new fruitful beginning was possible. Herder, religious and a believer in development, saw in history chiefly the individual culture and its cycle. Ranke, Danilevski, and Burckhardt, each for different reasons, did not move away from the individual culture either. Spengler showed the cycles as tragically closed within themselves.

On the other hand, it is possible, particularly in a rationalistic-minded theology, to regard the messianic education of Israel simply as a general education of the human race, as do Lessing and Mendelssohn. In this fashion the biblical salvation story is placed in a wider, more comprehensive historical scheme and, thus, either makes the Christian element the most important, as Hegel does (for whom the incarnation of God in Christ is the central point), or else smooths out the Christian element into the rest of the philosophy of religion, as does all liberal Christian, half-theological, half-philosophical history writing. We find the combination of the first and second elements in Toynbee: cyclic cultures which nevertheless show a spiral movement.

The third element, that of "axial time" operates throughout in the background and emerges with Comte, who sees the move from *mythos* to *logos* as the true progress of humanity and makes it, secondarily, the dynamic force of every individual culture. When Comte describes this move in terms of a triad—from the theological to the metaphysical, then to the scientific age—that does not matter, for it is not a Hegelian dialectic, but a rectilinear increase of knowledge. That Comte gave the recognized historical phenomenon such a specific valuation shows how deeply theological even he remained in his thinking. The same move from the *mythos* to the *logos* can also be seen in a different light: as the loss of the sacred origins, of the nourishing roots—thus, in Rousseau, in the *Sturm und Drang* movement, in the Romantic philosophers and poets, up to Bergson, Klages, and Theodor Lessing.

Today the waves of this dispute appear to be subsiding; the fact of this movement, however, is emerging ever more clearly as the dominant motif of history. It can be welcomed as the raising of man's mind out of the mists of animality and of the mythical dreams of prehistory. It can be regretted as the loss of man's connection with maternal nature and his passing into the realm of abstract intellect and, therefore, inevitably and irreversibly into a technical age dominated by a technical image of the world in which man is the master of nature. One can hope and fear and will be right to do both.

The fact stands and cannot be altered that man, in a loneliness he has never experienced before, has to take over the responsibility for the one world. That is what happened with the "breakthrough to the *logos*" and is so tremendously important that for us today the first and the second motifs are less important. It is no longer possible to hold a purely cyclic theory of culture. To cry "progress" at this development of the world—either for an atheistic Marxist or a Christian—is naive. At least the ambivalence of the situation must be apparent, as with Nietzsche, Eduard von Hartmann, Scheler[6] (influenced by von Hartmann), Erwin Reisner,[7] Jakob Klatzkin,[8] Theodor Lessing.[9] One does not have to fall into the opposite excess of regarding all spirit as sickness of life (Thomas Mann), as the fall and at the same time the blind alley of being, which technology makes ever more shut in.

These two extreme valuations show how easy it is to interpret the historical movement of humanity in these terms. One can interpret it in an evolutionistic way, by subordinating unproved theses and theories to the historical growth of nature and the spirit.[10] Or, he can arrogantly underestimate, from similar prejudices, the intellectuality of primitive, early and golden age cultures. Or, lastly, he can fail to see the constant corporeal ties of man and of all culture—hence the limitation of image and fantasy—and fall into utopian rationalism. If we took this essential limitation of human imagery seriously, man would find his optimum state in the eternal reciprocal relationship between body and soul, instinct and spirit, image and idea, art and philosophy. Then the whole move from the *mythos* to the *logos* would be a one-sided distortion which would be a profound threat to man, and we would have most urgently to reconsider our historical position—if there were still time. If the mind is rooted in the image depths of nature, that means that it is rooted in the unconscious and the undisposable, which the technical intellect cannot get at. Technical self-forming of man, thus interpreted, would therefore be a contradiction in terms.

But all these serious reflections do not remove the fact that the movement has taken place and is fraught with consequences. Let it be noted for the moment here in all its naked factuality and, together with the two other motives, brought into a relation with the theology of history, after this has lost its burden of secular history.

In fact, there is a true encounter here. It is not at all the case, as the evolutionists thought, that in view of the "fact" of a universal evolution[11] Christianity with its absolute claim is inevitably relativized and thus can be dismissed. Nor, on the other hand, is it true, as Christians sometimes claim, in an oversimplification, that the idea of evolution is nothing but secularized theology, and therefore there is no need for any dialogue with it. Nor is it sufficient to dismiss such a theology by pointing to human nature which is still the same in its sinfulness, which still needs the same salvation—which from a Christian point of view is undisputable

—and by declaring every human advance in history *a priori* as unimportant from a Christian point of view. Only when these simplifications, on both sides, are cleared out of the way can the real problems emerge. There are actually two problems: one is concerned mainly with the Old Testament, toward the end of which comes the "axial time." The other is concerned with the New Testament, or more exactly Church time, in its relation to the self-understanding of humanity as it works itself out.

One may ask at the outset to what branch of knowledge this particular investigation belongs. Are these theological or philosophical statements? Insofar as facts of biblical revelation are confronted with facts of general history which do not come out of the bible, but out of empirical history, and insofar as the latter are not used in order to understand better the former, and insofar as we, on the contrary, are making statements about world history, we are not making theological statements in the true sense. We are not dealing with things that can be known from revelation as such, even if one can ask whether such a confrontation does not illumine also elements of revelation, which then could be considered a theological process. One can, however, assign the statements we are about to venture (this is true particularly of the second group of statements) to fundamental theology or to a general Christian science of history, which establishes itself as a third science at the point at which the two perspectives overlap and a "supernatural" light falls on the "natural."

The Old Testament and Axial Time

"Axial time" has been contrasted polemically with the "fulness of time," which indicates a total misunderstanding of the latter. For this fullness is not something that can be established in terms of the philosophy of history; the return of the world to the Father, reconciled by the blood of Christ, is not an empirical fact. The proof of it lies in the fact that every sinner is "con-

temporaneous" with his Redeemer. Nevertheless, Jesus Christ
with his mission—not only divine, but also earthly—is, as a true
man, a man of his time and environment, and is determined
"horoscopically" by the coordinates of historical space and time.

The "fulness" which he brings vertically (Col. 2, 9) must stand
in relation to this web of horizontal relations in human history,
even if we can never observe, from our earthly viewpoint, such a
"fulness of time." The horizontal web concerns, above all, salvation history in the narrower sense, the history of Israel, which has
reached an inner maturity that not only means the vertical
descent of the Messiah from God but also the fulfillment of his
human constellation. In his relations with his mother Mary, with
his cousins Zacharias and Elizabeth and their son John, and with
the whole surrounding world of people and politics in which he
was able to choose his apostles and his friends and bring them to
a specific human understanding of his mission (for the grace of
faith does not simply replace nature), Christ realized fully the
web of interpersonal and environmental relationships. The history of Israel, viewed from the point at which the fullness of time
is reached, becomes ordered and intelligible.

From stage to stage the connections and the necessary conditions become clearer, not merely the "advances," but above all
the punishments, catastrophes, purifications, sufferings, and priva-
tions. The necessity, e.g., of the long prophetless age after the
exile—on the whole a very dialectical way in which the *no* grows
together with the *yes,* in which together with understanding there
is the growing danger of misunderstanding (e.g., of the old
promises as a "static wisdom")—is evident. Christian contemplation has the right to admire the harmonies of biblical revelation
in all its dimensions and to demonstrate the "necessariness" of
this freest of acts. An analogy can be made to the aesthetic sphere
in which one can observe in a freely created work of art such an
appropriateness of every part to the whole that the alteration of
a single spot of color in the painting or of a single note in the
symphony would impair or even ruin the whole.

But now the Israel of the bible itself is involved in a particular interplay of historical forces. It lies geographically between Egypt and Mesopotamia, with Syria and Asia Minor to the north; in a wider context it lies on the border between Asia and Europe. It also stands in time at the turning point of world history. With its roots fully in mythical times it moves through, in its own way and without any basic help from the other cultures on their way to their logos, to its own Logos: the Living Son of the Father. Yet the total breakthrough of the advanced cultures from image thinking to intellectual thinking, from a politico-religious *mythos* to an individual, personal (mystic) religion and philosophy and thus to a secularization of nature and the state, from which all the magical has been removed, is simply the natural condition for the universal preaching of a supranational and nonsyncretistic religion.

Certainly, something analogous happened with all the great religions which developed during the axial period. Buddhism, in particular, benefited from this in its expansion eastward, as did later eclectic hellenistic culture. This fact neither supports nor injures the claim of Christianity which has to justify itself on its own grounds, but it offers the natural historical basis for its expansion. From this it is evident that the axial period had to precede the gospel as a *praeparatio evangelica*—and not just as one particular preparation, but, apart from the inner and far deeper preparation of Israel, as the one absolutely necessary prerequisite. The theological Logos, Jesus Christ in person, meets the philosophical logos, which makes possible his inner acceptance by all mankind and the culture of the world. Again, there is no question here of any value judgment about the event. Whatever it is, it is a development, inas.nuch as that which was hidden is uncovered. that which existed in a childlike, dreamlike half-conscious state emerges into tne bright radiance of reason, whether one welcomes it or not.

More important is the question of how far the process of the breakthrough flows beneath and supports the events of the Old

Testament. The answer to this would require many separate investigations in order to be sufficiently differentiated. But it is certain that there is a relationship. The "development" of revelation moves with the general course of civilization, but it uses civilization for its own, quite different purposes. There is the one aspect of salvation history that revelation seems as it were to stand still and wait until man's growing powers of understanding have caught up with the depths and consequences of that which has been already given. There is the other aspect—and it is perhaps the more important—in which the more profoundly understood presence of the living God himself appears.

Both events, the philosophical and the theological, are unique. The axial period cannot return. Israel's religion is part of history and, thus, bound to that time (even in its supernatural aspect). An Israel after Christ is not only a theological contradiction; it is also a historico-philosophical one. In order to continue to exist it must somehow detemporalize itself: around the "letter" of the law or the "spirit" of wisdom or enlightened Gnosticism. Its institutions, its temple cult, and its priesthood together with its sacrifices are bound by time and cannot return (even in today's state of Israel): thus it can replace its former institutions only by secularized ones. In the Qumrân the end is already visible.

Yet Israel goes on, ambiguously, without any possible inner development, since on the one hand, it is a "branch broken off" next to the living Church (Rom. 11, 17), and on the other, it is the "holy root" (Rom. 11, 16) on which the Church is grafted. It is as if frozen in this ambiguity and, thus, apparently shares in the lack of development of the Church. But the time form is different: it is determined by the messianic historical development of the Old Testament, but at the same time by the missing out on the messianic Christian message. Hence, Israel will be through all ages the fount of inner-historical (and hence anti-Christian) messianisms. It will be a principle of dynamic utopian movements, inspired by a transcending, absolute belief in the inner perfectibility of man and the world, a belief which will always reproach Christianity for having betrayed man and the world to the beyond. In the contrary accusation of having betrayed the faith of the bible is completed the theological mystery of the mutual "jealousy" between Jews and Gentiles, the responsibility for which is assigned to God (Rom. 10, 19). For the Church cannot achieve its ultimtae fullness, its return from exile, before "all Israel is saved."

The New Testament and Secular History

The second statement is concerned with the relationship between Christianity and secular history. The message of Christ, in contrast to the Jewish one, is not conditioned by time. The fullness of the divine Logos which has appeared is essentially for all times, and in his filling the Church (as the fullness of his fullness: Eph. 1, 23) he is incapable of being surpassed. If the Old Testament was theologically the drawing of the Jews out of the cradle of the mythical religions to a life with the living, holy God, then the goal is reached theologically forever with the Church of Christ: the Church as the Church cannot develop.

What is possible and is the theological significance of Church time is the working out of the presence of Christ in the Church in world history. This working out cannot, strictly speaking, be called a development, either for the Church or for the world. A merely geographical extension of the Church over the whole world is not in itself a theological event or criterion, even if Augustine sometimes seemed to think that this was an argument against heresy. A quantitative preponderance is no testimony to a "little flock." The universality of the missionary command of Matthew 28, 18–20 lies elsewhere and deeper: it refers to the inner ordering of the world and its history toward the magnetic center of the Son of God. This can and must and will always happen ever anew as a decision, as a *yes* or *no*, thus as a growing *yes* and a growing *no,* in which the important thing is not the preponderance of the *yes* over the *no,* but the inevitability of the choice.

The myths are fading. If they are artificially renewed, then they do not last or become clearly anti-Christian, daemonic forces. But ideologies relate themselves, consciously or unconsciously, in assent or dissent, to the "program" of Christ. The transitional field between life within the Church, to which the gospel and its proclamation belong, and the life of the historical world outside the Church is filled with an ambiguous process of exchange which precisely in its dual character manifests the basic law. On the one hand it is part of the intention of the Christian kerygma that the "spirit" of Christ is taken over into secular situations and is "incarnated" there: e.g., the spirit of brotherly love in a factory, between the management and the employees, and among the workers themselves. This radiating of Christ through the Church into the world is part of the illuminating mission of Christ which he passes on to the apostles. But this illumination means a certain spiritualization, a living out of what is spiritually important; it requires action and not just words, (as the parable of the two brothers shows in Matthew 21).

This kind of practical realization was Cusa's intention in his attempt to reconcile the religions. But the realization in the world happens outside the realm of the Church and "detracts" consciously or unconsciously, in good or bad faith, from the origin, which is Christ. Thus, Chesterton is right when he says that the world is full of Christian ideas gone mad. The Gospels and the Church are plundered like a fruit tree, but the fruit when separated from the tree goes rotten and cannot be used. The "ideas" of Christ cannot be separated from him, and hence they are of no value to the world unless they are fought for by Christians who believe in Christ or at least by men who are unconsciously open to him within themselves and are dominated by him. Radiation is only possible if the radiating center remains constantly active and alive. Here there is no question of stars that have long become extinct continuing to shine.

The separating of the Christian ideas connected with Christ and those which have become cut off from him cannot be carried out empirically within world history; it is reserved for Christ at the end of time (Matt. 7, 15–23; 1 Cor. 3, 10–15). But that this separating process is going on, that in this respect the parable of the seed, which grows together with the weeds, fulfills itself before our eyes, can be empirically observed. To be able to see this is part of the ability to read the signs of the times and is also a comfort for the waiting Church. It is a certain kind of progress which is not the progress men desire to see. It is almost more the progress of the weeds, by which one is able, however, to gauge the growth of the corn. It is the progress of ambiguity, and thus of seductability, from which a "divine growth" can be seen (Col. 2, 19).

The question of where the natural development of man can and will lead can be asked, but not answered. If it were to lead historically to a situation which with Christ would be even more urgent than it appears to mankind today, it could not lead to a general lessening of the distance between the believer and the contents of belief, to a progressive inner assimilation and absorption of the message, the challenge, the deed of Christ. Is this stated sufficiently unambiguously in the program of Teilhard de Chardin? There is no spiritual and moral cross which can be separated from the real crucifixion on Golgotha.

The cross, however, means, and will always mean, powerlessness unto death in the darkness. The way in which the omnipotence of Christ will work itself out in history until the end of the world can never be separated from or supersede this powerlessness. Paul and John knew that, and the Church of all ages must know it. It is not thus that it is distinguished from the Synagogue, as the two statues in Strasbourg cathedral suggest. The Church has fundamentally the deeper insight into the cross—and the insight

comes from the grace of the Resurrection. But does that insight
not also embrace the deeper experience of the darkness, the inevitability, and the God-forsakenness of the cross? The Church is
fundamentally the place of the legacy of sin. But does that legacy
not also embrace the responsibility for carrying a heavier burden
of the world's sin, without wanting or being able to distinguish
between what is *my* and what is *your* sin? The Church has a
clearer vision of the approaching end. But does that vision not
also embrace a more inward enduring together with Christ under
the threat of the hour which "no one knows, not even the angels
in heaven, nor the Son, but only the Father" (Mark 13, 32)?

Notes

1 Jean Daniélou: *Holy Pagans of the Old Testament*, Helicon, 1957.

2 The placing of the different peoples under the tutelage of "people's
angels" does not emerge as a leading motif in protology. In terms of literature
and the history of tradition it is combined with the motif of the confusion
of tongues at the tower of Babel; the nationalizing of mankind appears here
pessimistically linked with the Fall as a falling away from original unity;
a separate destiny is granted to the people by their angelic *archontes* and
their separate language, but it is not described in detail. As (in Paul) Christ
will break the power of the *archontes* forever, in order to be the sole ruler
of history, the Pentecostal Spirit will transcend the multiplicity of tongues,
so that throughout the differences which remain (as everyone hears his
own language) there is a basic spiritual and eschatological language which
goes through all of them. Cf., for a discussion of these points, E. Peterson:
Der Monotheismus als politisches Problem, *Theologische Traktate*, 1951, 49–
147; J. Daniélou: *La Division des Langues* in *Essai sur le Mystère de
l'Histoire*, 1935, 49–60. Cf. also his *Origene*, 1948, 222–233, and Martin Buber:
Pointing the Way, Harper, 1957.

3 Cf., e.g., Hans Eibl: *Metaphysik und Geschichte*, 1913.

4 E. Heck: *Roger Bacon. Ein mittelalterlicher Versuch einer historischen
und systematischen Religionswissenschaft*, *Abhandlungen zur Philosophie und
Pädagogik* 13, 1957.

5 *Opp.* VII, 1959, 97.

6 *Die Stellung des Menschen im Kosmos*, 1928; *Mensch und Geschichte*,
Neue Schweizerische Rundschau, 1929.

7 *Die Geschichte als Sundenfall und Weg zum Gericht*, 1929.

8 *Der Erkenntnistrieb als Lebens– und Todesprinzip*, 1935.

9 *Europa und Asien, Der Untergang der Erde am Geiste,* 2nd ed., 1923.

10 Cf. the constant warnings of Adolf Portmann and his attitude to Teilhard de Chardin.

11 As evolution one may consider more generally the development in time and space of the one world logos in the different world cultures, a qualitative fanning out (as e.g., Herder demonstrates with his "ideas"), which does not necessarily involve a higher development through time and, thus, places evolutionism in a narrower sense in a wider intellectual context.

6. THE DIALECTIC OF HISTORY

Beyond the tremendous question concerning the possibility that history has a theological meaning, there is little more to say. Whatever can be said with any theological validity, i.e., interpretative of revelation, can be said only *sotto voce*. To endure with Christ under the threat of the hour means at any rate to renounce any attempt to bring secular history and salvation history clearly into one focus. Nothing in the growth of secular history is a clear sign, unmistakable to a neutral intelligence, that we stand at a particular point of salvation history. Nothing permits us—to take over the ideas of Paul Schütz which he opposes to those of Teilhard de Chardin[1]—to turn "prophecy" into "prognosis" or to regard both as the two sides "of a single, complete act of knowledge."[2] If they are the two eyes with which man looks at the end of history and whereby he obtains a plastic image in perspective of the events leading up to the end, then it is unavoidable that each eye—that of knowledge and that of faith—assists the other with its sight, so that a philosophical and theological total science of the sense of history may be undertaken. The hubris of this has already been indicated earlier.

The Christian understanding of history cannot embark on such an undertaking, which would emulate the great idealist or biologistic monisms of the nineteenth century. Teilhard's attractive synthesis of both elements rests on the idea of the irreversibility of secular history, which, as the way of unconscious nature to human consciousness, and of human pluralist consciousness to its integrating unity, must involve an ever more profound self-reflection and self-understanding. Since, however, revelation shows that the ultimate goal of total cosmological and historical integration is the God-man, toward which all history runs, into which it grows as a mystical total body, the synthesis of the philosophy and the theology of history no longer seems a distant and daring postulate, but a *fait accompli*. Irreversibility leads inevitably to the total reflection of the "noosphere" in a kind of higher total consciousness, and this, perspectible only in outline from below, can be made apparent by theology from above.

That fits extraordinarily well. So well, that the deep gulf seems closed, and one steps from one plane to the other without any difficulty. In fact, if the divine total consciousness has already become visible, one cannot understand why the philosophy of history had not already stumbled upon it. Total reflection of the noosphere: if this were possible, why should it not be the attaining of the divine consciousness? Have we not here gone back from Marx and Feuerbach to Hegel, and from Hegel to an understanding of the bible appropriate to his age?

Even if we must reject this modernly got-up christosophy as an illusion—because man possesses God in it all too clearly; the "image and likeness" identifies itself dynamically with the unattainable original—even then the questions which arise with the convergence of the philosophy of history and the theology of history remain unanswerable. But is not convergence which cannot end in identity better described as concurrence? Is not the course of history in relation to an immanent image of unity, which is set beside the Christian and prophetic image of unity, superimposed on that image and does it not outshine the image in radiance and power? For spiritual insight means invariably also increased power. The question can, thus, be divided in two: that of the unity of the spirit as world reason, and the question of the unity of the spirit as world power.

But in both questions there lies a common connecting element —freedom. The more the spirit belongs to itself, the freer it is in itself and in relation to the world. But who is this spirit? Is it the spirit of each individual, as it reveals itself in mutual revelation and in exchange of persons open to each other? Certainly, it is this also, for no integration of a total human spirit can or should be allowed to overshadow the freedom of the person in Marxist, Hegelian fashion, and demand from the individual the sacrifice of his freedom for a total consciousness for which he is not responsible. Is it the spirit of the theological "total consciousness" which ultimately remains the spirit of one particular being, the Redeemer and Judge of all? But then the freedom of the consciousness of this God-man is much less available to the individual men who are supposed to be integrated by him. Christ's whole freedom and, hence, also his whole power remain in his own hands, and no increasing growing together of the historical spirit of mankind and the historical power of mankind could ever from below even approach the sovereignty of the free spirit-power of Christ.

In the sequel each of the aspects—human spirit and Christian spirit, human power and Christian power—will be considered separately, in order finally, with the question of freedom, to be seen together.

THE QUESTION OF THE SPIRIT

The Openness and the Exclusivity of Reason

If in the question of the spirit the freedom of the individual is not to be overshadowed by an anonymous world judgment, then integration can be conceived and sought only in the way that Jaspers calls "open reason" and "communication."[3] It might, however, be assumed that the growing assimilation of cultures and, as a result, of world-views and religions, on the basis of the ever-growing technical mastery of space-time dimensions, poses a problem. The problem is that the individual is, thereby, placed in a more imperative need of human spirit-unity and, therefore, of a more serious demand for integrated communication. Such a world-culture would not favor personal and so to speak particularized world-views imposed by a totalitarian philosophy but, on the contrary, would resist all absolutizing of particular systems which would oppose a basically open reason with a basically closed one and would reject the universal communication of human knowledge.

However, this "open reason" is only "limited" by its formal object, "Being as such" (*Sein als Sein*), as compared to its "adequate" object: the seeming being of the worldly, sensible, etc., that is, the philosophical intelligence and its openness to the no longer adequately intelligible nature of being. The nature of being only mysteriously appears in formulas that oppose all rational grasp. This is the reason for keeping all serious philosophizing open. On this level, "revelation" can only mean the concern of the philosophical intelligence with this or that formula, and nothing would stand in the way of an unending conversation which would begin with communication among the philosophers and would continue among all those who are concerned with the matter. The participants of these conversations would then involve not only all philosophical systems among themselves—in the unity of their questioning and the examination of their object—in an unending fruitful exchange which has already begun and will continue into the future, but also all religions as well, insofar as the source of the religious "understanding" of man as a natural and historic being can be recovered.

This would also hold true when the form of the transmission of the revelation could be explained as "supernatural," in which case the content of the revelation would be beyond the grasp of the intelligent questioner, as for instance is the case with Islam, even leaving aside what it borrowed from the bible. If all religions were so conceived, revelation would then be as Lessing describes it: a help by God in things which mankind could and ought to have discovered by itself, so that it may become "more easily and quickly" aware of itself in its historical development. All "enlightened" and liberal theology leaves it at that and, thus, by understanding revelation, within the framework of religious philosophy, as open reason, has an easy time of it. The dialogue between world-views and religions remains then a dialogue among men about God.

The situation is different[4] when the theology of biblical revelation fundamentally and clearly goes beyond this frontier and claims to have heard the word of God and to be able to interpret it. A word that is, by definition, the word of a totally different consciousness than that of any man, and which, as the word of an absolute consciousness which expresses itself in it—for of what else should it speak to men?—will say things that man would be unable to discover by himself. Things not primarily about man, but about God. Things which, however, affect man because God affects him. Such a word from the ONE God cannot, without a catastrophic upheaval in the order of creation, respond simultaneously in the countless millions of individual human consciousnesses so that—by a kind of preestablished harmony of innumerable "private revelations"—they would be informed of it in dialogue and communication *a priori,* as is the case with human reason.

As the word of the ONE it can only be given at ONE place in time and space, in the total difference of a human being who as such proclaims the total difference of God, manifests it, and represents it for all men. That is the true theological fact which divides it off from the area of open philosophical reason, closes the openness of the latter, commits it to one point, and thus seems to be an absolute stumbling block for reason. If Christ is the one whom the (Catholic) Church considers him to be, if the (Catholic) teaching office is that which it claims to be, then no discussion is possible with either, for both stand on a different level from "open reason."

It is of no advantage to include parenthetically and "provisionally" the question of the absolute claim of the bible in human dialogue, because the discussion can reach no conclusion so long as this parenthesis remains. Thus, the only alternative for a Christian[5] is either to include his faith parenthetically for others, and be a kind, loving man among other men, or, asserting his faith, to work apostolically for his faith. In the former case he may hope by his humanity to exercise indirect propaganda for his faith, since the tree is known by its fruits; in the latter, he must accept, when it comes to the point, putting a limit to "open reason" and demanding of it obedience to the word of Christ. Whether this is a valid alternative is for a Christian, as for everyone who has to do with him, of fundamental, practical importance. It must, therefore, be seriously considered.

In the communication of open reason there is the suggestion that the other, with whom I am engaged in an exchange of questions and answers, understands me on the basis of a similarly structured reason, but also that he is another being. One might say that I and the other are two "samples" of an identical reason, like copies from the same stamp, in which the nuances of being different fall away in mutual understanding. For a spiritual dialogue the common reason would require only the empty, abstract category of being different, which is necessary and adequate. The otherness of the other would be unimportant, and in the exchange of communications and mutual knowledge it could be reduced asymptotically to a minimum. The nuances would, indeed, be unimportant if reason was a generic idea and the other could be subsumed under it as an individual.

If, however, the other is conceived as an eternal spiritual being, unalterably different, corresponding to a unique idea of the one God, then the dialogue between the two persons as such could no longer proceed within the medium of a generically conceived reason. Such a dialogue can take place only in the supranatural (which does not mean "supernatural" but "supracategorical"[6]) region of being, where no kind of "abstraction" is any longer possible. What in spiritual persons can be abstracted and subsumed under a common idea must always exclude the essential element, namely, that which is unique. But if one wanted to apply the idea of "uniqueness" to all, then one would have deceived oneself and achieved nothing.

With personal uniqueness philosophical thinking reaches its limits. It cannot be removed by assigning the unique to the sphere of the senses (conceiving the idea, as the spiritual element, essentially as "general" and "formal"), for the unique is not the sensuous element, but the very core of the person. Nor can one nominalistically deny the general idea ontological validity, for it is not primarily a problem of epistemology, but of being itself. Thomas Aquinas ascribes to pure spirits ("angels") this qualitative uniqueness (though not to men) and then sees their mutual knowledge of one another arising logically from inborn ideas (as a sharing in the original creative idea that God has of every unique spiritual being). It is difficult to supply such a theory of knowledge to the relation between men—assuming that they too are unique spiritual beings.

How can we resolve this most burning of all philosophical questions? If it is not approached and solved in full consciousness, we are left *practically* with an ancient scholastic *"individuum ratione materiae."* And, hence, logically with a Kantian formalism of knowledge. And, hence, with the Hegelian world spirit in whose process individuals are simply absorbed together with their qualitative difference. And, hence, ultimately with the Marxist or biological evolutionistic system, in which everything that does not obey the general, anonymous law becomes non-existent and, if it still persists in asserting itself, must be exterminated. But how can one avoid these questions when the human reason is so constructed that it can think only by abstraction (from the only essential thing!)? *Abstrahe et impera:* find in the individual case what makes it subsumable under a law known to you, and then you have it within your intellectual domination—thinking is essentially power.

Does this terrifying conclusion offer us a sign? To follow it up, let us once more look at the other aspect of the spiritual person: one has not only "reason," he has also "freedom." Now, as there is in reason the abstract neutrality of the general idea, so in freedom there is the abstract neutrality of the empty indifference to everything. If I am free, then I can choose this or that, what is of value and what is without value, good or bad. But is that really freedom? Rather, is it not merely a deficient mode of freedom, at the most a built-in part of its total working? Admittedly, it is true that a single spiritual person is qualitatively infinite and that another spiritual person can choose in true spiritual love this person as the object of his reverence and devotion—as happens or can happen in a Christian marriage. Then, does not this choice fill the emptiness of indifferent freedom? Does this choice ever need, for the sake of a more embracing totality, to be reconsidered, or even just relativized? Why *only* Beatrice? Are there not countless other women? But if really only Beatrice, is Dante, therefore, now without any "open reason"? Is elective love a prejudice, on which the philosopher of history smiles? Or, rather, does not he who, beyond elective love, talks of "open reason" and of "communication" and of the "catholicity of reason" show that he has remained caught in the formalism of Kant?

In elective love there is obviously a possibility of overcoming the indifference of freedom and, hence, abstracting reason. Let us leave it to the epistemologists to explain the fact that love can give an intuition of the uniqueness of the loved one. It is a possibility which approximately corresponds to the original "paradisal" man, but is no longer given to him who has fallen away into the indifference between good and evil and into the sphere of abstracting exclusion for the sake of control. Eve sufficed for Adam, whereas the whole mass of animals known, named, and dominated by him, did not suffice for him. The *one* is qualitatively infinite, whereas the *many*, in their quantitative infinity, do not attain the required quality.

The strange thing is that men who have chosen in love (for example, married men) live in a truer and deeper and, hence, less talkative communication than those who, living in the unfulfilled openness of neutral freedom and neutral reason, vaunt this openness. That choosing freedom is more liberal, i.e., more giving and more devoted, than that freedom that does not choose and considers itself liberal in its self-preservation and looks down on those who have "committed themselves." Kierkegaard treated once and for all in his *Either/or* the aesthetic existence of Don Juan and the ethical possibility of marriage, and behind it and through it, the religious and the Christian possibility. That with Kierkegaard marriage mediates between the aesthetic and the religious is important. He chooses Regina Olsen in order to bend his roving freedom under the yoke of serious, elective love. But he dissolves his engagement with Regina in order to enter an even deeper, still more ultimate, elective relationship to Christ.

Exclusivity and Openness of the Covenant

This mediation overcomes the dilemma we envisaged, at the beginning, between "open reason" and Christianity. Open reason, in the sense in which it is generally suggested, is already fallen, sinful reason. In any event, it is an immature reason. Those who are married or who have wedded themselves, in a higher love choice, to God (in Jesus Christ) revere the love choice of others, which they know from their own experience as that which brings fulfillment. They do not, therefore, ask of others that they acknowledge one's own "immortal beloved" as their own. That does not follow automatically, by any means, if we are speaking, not on the level of biology and of individuals (where marriages exclude one another only for practical reasons), but on the level of spiritual beings. Here it is a choice of the qualitative uniqueness of the beloved *thou,* a choice which, as the uniting of the chooser and the chosen, is itself qualitatively unique and cannot by any means be relativized.

Historically, this absolute election of a single spiritual person takes place only within the sphere of biblical revelation. For within this sphere God himself appears as the infinite and free spiritual being, who alone, in his freedom, can create uniquely the ideas of spiritual persons who precisely in their uniqueness, and also in their freedom, are likenesses of the equally unique and free God. Everywhere else the sphere of reason must dominate the sphere of love. Only from the free uniqueness of God can an "exclusive" love between persons justify itself before the universal reason: as a decision which is not provisional, but final and irrevocable.

The model of such a final and free choice must have been put into the world by God himself. This happened necessarily when God, in an indivisible act, revealed himself as a free being and showed himself freely as the one revealing himself. If God is not apparent as free and personal, then he is not, in the full sense, apparent, but remains hidden behind the symbols of a world-ground, and then there does not appear to be any eternal significance in a created human being. But if God is apparent as a free, personal being, then his appearance is in the manner of a free election, scandalous for all-leveling world-reason. In the center of the divine self-revelation stands Yahweh's covenant with Israel: here, abstracting man is trained in the fulfilling exclusivity of the relationship to God.

This exclusivity, suggested again and again by the image of a marriage between God and his people, is not removed in the New Testament, although now all the "peoples" are admitted to the covenant. The covenant also, as the new and eternal covenant, is something absolutely concrete and, hence, in the inclusion of all "peoples" inevitably "exclusive." The catholicity of the covenant of God with humanity has nothing of the character of liberal reason which excludes by abstraction and then discusses the concrete. It could only have the deceptive appearance of "open reason" in virtue of the fact that God is the one who originally chooses sovereignly in love. He preserves the manner of the inclusion of all "peoples" (and, hence, of all philosophies and religions) in his exclusive covenant as his love secret. "If it is my will that he (John, who embodies choosing love) remain until I come, what is that to you (Peter, who embodies and represents the exclusively chosen community)? Follow me!" (John 21, 22). Inclusion remains uncertain for Peter (and, hence, for all in the visible Church and Christendom).

It is undoubtedly true for the Christian, however, that the relation of God to mankind possesses a concrete, sacramental covenant nature in the personal relationship between Christ and the Church, the "bride without spot or wrinkle" (Eph. 5, 27), which finds its personal concrete embodiment in the immaculately conceived mother-bride, Mary. In distinction to the horizontally coordinated unique love relationships between men (such as Dante and Beatrice), the love of the absolute, unique God for humanity as his bride is such that this love relationship can of its nature be only unique and totally resists any abstract categorizing. Thus, the uniqueness of all love (between man and man, but also between man and God) is to be seen as an image and likeness of the absolute uniqueness of the love of God in Christ for mankind; indeed it receives the seal of absolute uniqueness (as in the indissolubility of marriage, and so on) from that. The secret of Christianity, which is no longer open to "open reason," is the secret of the integration of all qualitatively infinite love in the uniqueness of the love of God for the world in Christ.

This secret can be understood by regarding the Christian image of God: Christ is for God the Father from eternity the "only beloved," the "only-begotten" in the unity of the Holy Spirit. Absolute love in God is itself three-in-one and "exclusive," and in this "choice" God chooses to create and to love the world. This uniqueness is disseminated through the infinities of qualitatively unique love in the world in order to remain eternally united in the trinitarian choice and to be gathered in again. The secret becomes apparent in the way that the Church is at the same time open to all and "a garden locked, a fountain sealed." The secrets of the Church's love are essentially public, and yet secret (because they are visible and intelligent only to lovers). Here there corresponds to the communication of "open reason" the quite different "communication of lovers" (*communio sanctorum*), who—within the sphere of the concrete love of God in the Church for the world and for all men—are connected like communicating conduits from uniqueness to uniqueness.

We must, therefore, say (in the language of Hegel): In the sphere of the Church there is no "objective spirit" which is not at the same time subjective spirit. The subjective spirit is the Holy Spirit of the personal God. His is the presence of the living God in his covenant; in the actuality of the covenant is the presence of the living God. Inasmuch as this most concrete act of love is the normative model and the enabling reality for every personal love within the Church and the world, this subjective spirit is at the same time objective spirit. But it is that in this manner, and not as general reason, however open. The Holy Spirit is primal in God himself; he is the God-person which proceeds from the Father and the Son, uniting both, and by means of this double origin it possesses also a double character. It is "breathed," not "begotten" like the Son. Whereas the "begetting" is the sphere of the Logos, the Spirit "beyond" the Logos is in the sphere of love. And it is this as the union and oneness of those two divine persons which in their personal being represent absolute mutually different being. Since the three persons are not abstractly, but concretely, identical as God, each is the other of each, as with human persons; the "other" of the Spirt, however, is the union in love of the other and the other.

That is the secret background without which Christian life in the world cannot be made comprehensible. For this life cannot be open to everything on that level at which Kant's or Hegel's or Jaspers' liberal reason seeks to be open. This kind of openness is an expression of the lack of absoluteness of all human, even philosophical reason; it manifests the relativity, variableness, and incompleteness of all points of view which do not go beyond the world (*veritas intellectus nostri mutabilis est: Summa*, I q 16 a 8). It appears even more questionable if one considers that it sinfully strives to put its abstract and empty openness, with which it avidly tries to gain power over the concrete, in place of the true openness of love which is grounded in God's self-communication: *eritis sicut dei*. The openness of reason is a necessary creaturely substructure for the highest act of reason necessary within the grace covenant with God, just as the indifference of freedom is a necessary creaturely substructure for the free answer of man to the God who incomprehensibly chooses him.

The Christian existence can be open on the level of the Holy Spirit, i.e., of love, which, without raising itself in abstraction above the poles it understands and looking down tolerantly on them from above, takes place as the encounter between the two beings that are different—and, in fact, more takes place than is understood. The event of the Holy Spirit in redeemed creation is its incomprehensible capacity of entering into each single, limited, inchoate subjectivity which does not, perhaps, even sigh for a wider spirit. It sinks itself in the depths of immured hearts and their narrow, fearfully limited horizons in order to burst them open "in groans too deep to be uttered" to light and to the warmth of love. That is the *charis* of God at work. The *charisma* of Christians is to be permitted to share in a unique way that cannot be systematized in this grace of divine love and, thus, to mediate between the uniqueness of every spiritual being and the uniqueness of the love of God for the world in Christ.

The Inevitability of the Apocalypse

This very mediation, however, becomes the more difficult, the more strongly the secular openness of reason—in the "reflection of the noosphere about itself" and, thus, in the necessary attempt to reach an integration of all partial positions in a total human combination of thinking—realizes itself, and, hence, is in opposition to the unity of the covenant with God which relativizes it all. Here the significance of the question for the theology of man in history emerges. Here we see the truth of the theological statement that it must become ever more difficult to be a Christian in a world which is becoming unified.[7] It is not because Christians themselves have difficulties in taking part in cultural work or in being at the level of dialogic reason in just as open and understanding intercourse as non-Christians. Rather, it is because secular reason as it links up cannot be other than tolerantly relativizing, and from its point of view must expect Christianity to understand itself as relatively as it is necessarily understood by others who are non-Christians. At this point the Christian's testimony to truth is a testimony of life and blood (*martyrion*).

This law of the theology of history is supported by the apocalyptic statements of the bible. However much one "demythologizes" these statements, showing their images to be conditioned in detail by their age and conditioned by the human in the whole, the core of the statements cannot be avoided: world history will be increasingly a struggle between two spirits, and the more power the spirit of the world gains, the more difficult the situation in the world will be for the Spirit of God. The love of the many will grow cold. There will be more and more substitutes for true Christianity.

The third animal that rises from the earth will resemble the Lamb and yet will speak as the dragon and so seduce the inhabitants of the earth that everyone will be slain who does not adore the image of the animal. "It causes all, both small and great, both rich and poor, both free and slave, to be marked on the right hand or the forehead, so that no one can buy or sell unless he has the mark" (Apoc. 13, 16). The world spirit, in closing its ranks, becomes a world power which makes existence on the earth impossible to everyone who resists this process. The universal world spirit, as "open reason," excommunicates everyone who understands communion in a way different from it. It triumphs precisely as reason, since he who is excommunicated by reason excommunicates himself, and, thus, proves himself to be unreasonable.

If God introduces himself as the one who incomprehensibly chooses into humanity, and if his choices are "without regret," then it is impossible that world history develop other than in a tremendous and increasing dramatic tension. Whoever takes the idea of the development of the spirit seriously—which cannot be anything other than increasing integration—as Vladimir Soloviev does, following Schelling and Hegel, must, if he is to go on thinking in a Christian way, reach the increasing apocalyptic alternative, which the "story of the Antichrist" presents symbolically. The Christian fact within history is, through its existence, the cause of the fact that the "noosphere closing itself" expressly places itself under the sign of "anti."

The profundity of Christ's words becomes clear when he says that when called by God a man is placed in an either–or situation. Revelation has called him not only from the enfolding maternal womb of nature—men of the axial period had left this behind them already—but from the enfolding anonymity of the symbols of the ground of the world. He can no longer place himself under these signs without saying *no* to God's sign, Christ. And if he has spoken this *no*, then he must, whether he wants to or not, go through the exposure into which God's covenantal election has called him, without the enfolding covenantal love. He is alone in his exposed position, and so the "closing of the no-osphere" does not only become a triumphant taking possession of oneself, but also a gesture of self-defense and of anxiety in which all the demonisms of a freedom which does not comprehend itself are let loose. The depths of this exposure open up fully when we consider the other side of integration: the question of power.

THE PROBLEM OF POWER

Power in the Order of Nature, Grace, and Redemption

Everything that exists has power because of its being and its nature; it asserts itself against nothingness and against the other. It functions in its environment and the world as that which it is. The more inward its shape, the more powerfully it can work outwardly. Where life becomes spirit and attains freedom, the existent being controls with a new strength its possibilities until it raises itself above the whole world, eye to eye with the unconditional. The free encounter between men makes all the registers of power resound; even pure self-revelation in the medium of language is power, and all the other modes of communication, which may be quite contrary to one another, are that in countless variations.[8]

Among creatures and among men this exercise of power is linked with a medium that is receptive of power, whether this submission is a willing one (and, inasmuch, itself powerful), or unwilling (and, therein, impotent, lacking the power of self-defense), or, finally, willingly accepting the fate of having to submit. The more that life rises toward spirit and freedom, the more that the state of being, overcome purely physically (the self-assertion of the strongest animal in the herd and hypnotic domination is part of this), *can* be transformed into a free mental acceptance of inferiority and impotence, where formerly there was only quiet resignation to the ineluctable decrees of nature and of destiny.

The affirmation of impotence of which the spirit is capable raises the question of the power-relation between life and spirit, *bios* and *logos*, "instinct" and "reason." There are three possible answers, all of which have found their defenders. Spirit is a qualitatively higher stage of life; hence, it is more powerful. Spirit and body overlap like two spheres of power in which the higher, stronger one dominates the lesser one. Or, one assigns the true power to the spirit and sees in the body and in instinct the area appropriate for the passively obedient carrying out of its orders. Or, finally, one sees spirit and life as so opposed that one assigns power to instinct and surveillance and biological impotence to the spirit, so that the spirit has to put the alien forces of life into action in order to reach its goals.

This arrangement (systematized by the later Scheler[9]) is totally opposed to the second one (which is Platonic). The first one offers a balance between the two, but under condition that both spheres are acknowledged as having only a relative power and, hence, a mutual creaturely dependence. Spirit can exercise maximum power over life, but also vice versa. Impotence reigns in both spheres because the whole spiritual-corporeal creature does not draw on an original power, but on power lent only by the one absolutely powerful God. Hence, in relation to his creature the creature is ultimately wholly impotent, even if forms of cooperative power, often of the highest kind, are imparted to it by God.[10]

Here we must raise the theological question, and, hence, the question of the theology of man in history. The creation account

culminates in the investing of spirit-endowed man with the royal
sovereignty over the whole natural world (Gen. 1, 26–29), but
with the conscious dependence of this free authority on the one
absolutely powerful God (Gen. 2: 9, 17–16). Thus man, as a pure
creature, presses toward the maximum exercise of his own power,
as given him positively and actively by God. On the other hand,
man, as a "partner" in the covenant with God, as someone called
in grace to intimacy with God—as Adam and Eve were—is placed
in another relationship to power. In the covenant of grace man is
first and foremost he before whom, for whom, and with whom
God's incomprehensible omnïpotence of love manifests itself. By
letting this omnipotent love reveal itself to him and by acknowl-
edging it, he is placed, through this recognized loving openness to
this event, in a new, incomprehensive cooperative power with the
grace-power of God. If man in the order of creation is chiefly
masculine (as the dominator of the world), in the order of grace
he is chiefly feminine (as the receptive womb for the marvels of
the power of God).

But what happens when sin disturbs the power relationships?
Sin is the usurping of divine power. It expresses itself in the
natural order as titanism toward the world, in the order of grace
as the loveless denial by receptive love of almighty love. How can
this double disturbance in God's redeeming love be removed
without the true freedom of man being affected, without his free
love being ravished? The whole biblical revelation is the answer
to it. It is a highly differentiated answer which unfolds in the
history of salvation all aspects of power. To treat the problem
fully we should have to speak of the power of God which de-
termines, limits, and deploys that of man. We should have to
speak of the power and authority of those commissioned by God
—the judges, kings, and prophets—of the power and impotence
of Israel, of the *exousia* of the Son of God, of the power of his
teaching, his miracles, death, and resurrection, of the power of
the apostles, the whole Church, the priest, the layman. We should

also have to speak of the power of man in his original state, in the state of original sin, in grace, and in glory; similarly, we should speak about the power of the snake, the adversary, the Antichrist, and the "world powers" (*exousiai*).

Only a few leading ideas can be followed up here, chiefly in order to make distinctions between the problem of power, actually a problem of the theology of history, and those questions, such as psychological and sociological ones, which are only concerned with the philosophy of history and, hence, are not discussed here. In order to make this distinction which is of fundamental importance, it is essential to start somewhat further afield.

The bible possesses a wide terminology for all aspects of power: there are nouns expressing the capacity of acting out of oneself, actual ability and performance, physical and spiritual power, and power in the sense of authority, rightful domination, superiority. Then, there are the verbs which express similar concepts, not forgetting those which denote the misuse of power and its violent misapplication.

With reference to the latter let us remember the words of Jesus in Mark 10, 42: "You know that those who are supposed to rule over the Gentiles lord it over them, and their great men exercise authority over them." Luke 22, 25, adds bitterly, and they "are called benefactors. But not so with you. . . ." The element of violence in the worldly exercise of power does not need to be excluded when Paul (Rom. 13, 1–7) recommends Christians to submit to the worldly *exousia* because all *exousiai* come from God. These worldly powers are even ordered by God, and those are the servants of God who perform his commissions. This secular power is there chiefly in order to frighten those that are evil (Rom. 13, 3–4). The law is not set up for the just, but for the unjust (1 Tim. 1, 9), for it "does not bear the sword in vain;" submission to it is so necessary that one should obey "not only to avoid God's wrath but also for the sake of conscience" (Rom.

13, 5). Peter's instructions to the slaves—"be submissive to your masters with all respect, not only to the kind and gentle but also to the overbearing" (1 Pet. 2, 18)—is an echo of the words of Jesus and of Paul. Peter and Paul support this command theologically by referring to the attitude of Christ, who suffered wrong (1 Pet. 2, 21 ff.). One ultimately looks to Christ in obedience (Eph. 5, 6–7; Col. 3, 24); in him the secular order is so transcended that any immanent questioning of power relationships is unnecessary (1 Cor. 7, 20–24).

On the basis of these texts we can make some fundamental distinctions, according to which the following ideas are arranged.

The purpose of biblical revelation was not to change or question the power relationships in the order of creation. *Gratia supponit naturam.* The bible assumes the creaturely power created by God, the individual (physical and spiritual) as well as the social (in family and state). This power can be misused through original sin and the actual guilt of men, but it is, nonetheless, a good creation of God. We can also give a subjective turn to this idea: *fides supponit rationem* or *revelatio (theologia) supponit philosophiam*—a theology of power presumes a philosophy of power. It is part of the reverence of God before his creature that he does not replace or forestall what his creature can discover and perform by his own powers (like a father who does his son's homework). Rather, he reveals to man what, in the depth of the heart of God, man is essentially incapable of seeing and understanding by himself. That this light which breaks forth out of the depths of God is, nevertheless, a tremendous gift for creation and reason and an aid in all the spheres of nature (*Vatic.* I, sess. III, c. 2) does not contradict what we have said.

The formal object of biblical revelation remains—apart from the power lent by God to his creatures in the order of creation— the unique divine power of grace, as it appeared ultimately in Jesus Christ, and hence once more in man. It is the God-man, who as the "Son of Man," as the brother of all and as the head of

all the "members," makes the new divine power immanent in
humanity. All understanding of the Christian theology of power
depends on seeing this self-revealing divine power (in Christ, in
the Church, in the cosmos) truly and exclusively as the power of
grace (grace as opposed to law, John 1, 17), the power of the one
God which goes as far as lending men the power to receive this
power (John 1, 12).

In the concrete man and his concrete history the power of
creation and the power of grace must collide (according to the
idea that *non destruit, sed supponit, elevat, perficit)*, and from
this collision the most difficult questions of human ethics will
arise. This is all the more true because the power of creation
always includes cosmic powers with all their mysterious, neutral,
good, dangerous, and bad elements. Thus, man, at the center of
the collision, is caught in a huge struggle between the divine
omnipotence and the powers and princes of the cosmos, a
struggle, on the side of God, "against the principalities, against
the powers, against the world rulers of the present darkness." For
this conflict he needs the whole armor of God, the armor of the
God of grace, and none other than this (Eph. 6, 12 ff.). Thus Paul
writes at the end of the biblical revelation.

Nevertheless the bible is not to be called "pacifist" on the basis
of such texts no more than, because of other Old Testament ones,
it can be said to favor (civil or holy) war. Here again revelation
does not seek to remove or question the existing order of creation, even where, as a result of original sin, the original ordering
of power has become confused. That there is violence—between
individuals and between states—is simply noted and accepted.
And only the manner in which God's new power of grace is
combined with this confused order of creation power—the way it
uses it, implants itself in it, submits to it, and overcomes it from
within—is different, according to the historical stage of the
approach to the ultimate Word of God, which is Christ.

The development of revelation can make it possible for later stages to include an immanent criticism of earlier ones. But they do not simply substitute themselves for them, like truth replacing error. Old Testament revelation offers provisional ideologies which are transcended in profounder, truer types of the Christ to come. Yahweh starts by entering the contest with national gods in order to prove himself, through battles, conquests, and annihilations, as the stronger, the truer, and ultimately, as the only true God. The earlier conceptions of God in the bible are not criticized as wrong, but as incomplete. The return of Elijah to the mountain of God where Moses received the covenant teaches him that God does not reveal himself in fire and storm, but in a "gentle rustling." The civilization and religious consciousness of Israel pass through their sociologically normal stages, as do the literary forms in which they are expressed. The songs of the heroic age have their laws of amplification and glorification of power, and later ages will look back reproachfully and anxiously ask if God has abandoned his old ideals of powerful and miraculous deeds (Ps. 89).

But however much the cultural and sociological forms change —and the divine power incarnate in each one also changes its phenomenal contour—this succession of images, nevertheless, remains the ever clearer revelation of a single entelechy which remains true to itself. This is so true, that it is precisely the later reflections of Israel's self-understanding and the later version of its holy books that offer the lasting meaning of the earlier stages and impart that meaning to the bible. One should read the bible backwards, i.e., from the prophets to the kings and judges and back to the beginnings. In its ultimate significant form that is really the way the bible is written; it comprises in its end all the undeveloped theological ideas which are ultimately seen as essential historical stages of a process which can be interpreted only historically.

Thus, for the Old Testament it is above all important to observe the way the word of God always raises itself above every stage in which it is incarnated and to which it speaks its word of being. To take an important example, when the prophets casti-gate the social conditions in Israel in the name of God—where the just man is robbed and ravished and the unjust rich man triumphs as ruler—this stage of revelation which is incorporated in the sphere of social justice has ultimate value within this sphere, but it does not contain the last word of revelation on the problem of power. The "poor man of God" who is ravished is justified and given power in Jesus Christ, through the power of God, in a way that transcends the vision of the prophets and could not have been predicted by them. And all biblical revela-tion took place in order to serve this power of God as it ulti-mately appeared in Christ in all the historical stages which were necessary for the incarnation of God and thus for man's under-standing of God. For what value would a revelation of the inner power of God's love have had for man if belief in it had not also brought with it an inner understanding?

But such an understanding is rooted in creation and in the knowledge of God as the *principium et finis mundi,* inseparable from the human spirit. All revelation in grace of God's power will build on this primary understanding, and thus also assume a proportionality between God and man, deepen it, broaden it, transcend it, stretch it to breaking point, but never destroy it. We shall see this in the section to come. Further, we shall have to show how all the power shown in revelation is only the power of love of the triune God.

Proportionality of Power

God's omnipotence is, for scripture, obvious. It is that quality which bursts forth most radiantly from the Old Testament, to-gether with his holiness and his goodness. It is not surprising that it is often named together with his "glory," i.e., with the unique divinity of God in its manifestation (Is. 2: 10, 19, 21).

This is a connection which the New Testament retains (Mark 13, 26; 2 Thess. 1, 9; Col. 1, 11). Paul names the eternal power and divinity together to designate that which man had always discerned of God through the framework of the world (Rom. 1, 20). But the quotation from Colossians 1, 11 shows also that the revelation of the eternal power of God is not a kind of spectacle which God provides for his creation. His omnipotent power neither overwhelms nor crushes the little power of the creature. On the contrary, it is a communication, a sharing, a powerful strengthening of man, which corresponds as such to a particular power of God. Not only before man, but also in him, God's strength is to become open and apparent. The reaction of man, responding with power to the power of God, is made possible by this divine power. It is an answer that man truly gives as created nature, but he is empowered to give it through the love and grace of God's power. We must illustrate this proportionality by a few examples.

Jesus talks to the people in parables, and this mode of address represents, among other things, an adaptation to their powers of understanding (Mark 4, 33). It is the same adaptation which is expressed surprisingly in the talent of the parable: each receives according to his own capacity (Matt. 25, 15). At the Last Supper also, where the Word of God goes "to the end" (John 13, 1), and speaks openly and no longer in parables (John 16, 29), he restrains himself so as not to overtax the disciples' powers of comprehension: "I have yet many things to say to you, but you *cannot* bear them now" (John 16, 12). We find the same economy in Paul: "I fed you with milk, not solid food; for you were not ready for it" (1 Cor. 3, 2). Further, in the same letter he writes even more strongly, that because there is no reproach in it God "will not let you be tempted beyond your strength, but with the temptation will also provide the way of escape, that you may be able to endure it" (1 Cor. 10, 13).

This relation between the "capacity" of man and the grace

given him (as word, as strength, but also as temptation) can, from a human point of view, be dislocated to a maximum of God and a minimum of man, so that the demands of the grace-power of God appear as beyond the strength of human nature. Paul labors under a burden by which he was "utterly, *unbearably* crushed," a burden which robs the Apostle of all joy in life. His life seems to have lost its value and importance by being overtaxed in this way (2 Cor. 1, 8). But precisely this dislocation is seen as a training in trusting faith, not in oneself, but in God, who raises the dead (2 Cor. 1, 9), through which Paul becomes the example of the community. It is following him who in the Garden of Gethsemane "is strengthened," not so as to fight in his own strength the suffering laid upon him, but so as to endure in human powerlessness under the overtaxing omnipotence of God.

That God's power orders itself in proportionality toward man's power is seen in that the words of Jesus represent for his hearers, and especially his enemies, a human intellectual force which challenges them to a response. When the Jews "*could* not reply to this" (Luke 14, 6), then an incapacity in the hearers is pointed out which arises, not through being externally overcome, but as the result of an honest inner dialogue between mental force and mental force. The Jews enter on this contest: they try, but "they were not able in the presence of the people to catch him by what he said . . . [and] they were silent" (Luke 20, 26). And again with Stephen: "They could not withstand the wisdom and the Spirit with which he spoke" (Acts 6, 10).

The central act of faith, as an act of acknowledgement of the superiority of God in knowledge and capacity, must be a human act in which the intellect is involved, in analogy with the way in which, in (undisturbed) creation, human power relationships presuppose in the receiver a free acceptance of the event, a self-forgetting openness. Thus, in the sexual sphere the procreative "power" of the man is nothing without the woman's giving of herself, which allows the man to be "powerful" in her. Similarly (as Pestalozzi saw) the paedagogic power of the teacher is greater, the more readily and deeply it is accepted and absorbed by the mind of the child. And even the political ruler, in order to ensure the continued exercise of power, must make himself loved by the people.

All natural religion which possesses inner truth and vitality depends on an analogous human openness, devotion, readiness, transparency to the power of God. Where no spontaneous divine revelation is recognized as present and effective, then religious "technique" must endeavor to produce by human agency this transparency, for which the classical example is Zen-Buddhism. It cannot be otherwise than that Christ, the new "great prophet (who) has arisen among us" (Luke 7, 16), begins by showing men's hearts that trusting transparency to God and teaching it to them. He fulfills the role of a helper, mediator, and strengthener, like a yogi with his pupils. The words "if you can do anything" of the desperate father (Mark 9, 22) express total reliance on the power that Jesus may have. But Jesus takes up the words "If you can" as though to ask, "What do you mean? That only I can do anything and you nothing?" "All things are possible to him who believes" (Mark 9, 23). Who is this believer? Neither the man without Christ, nor Christ without the man. But here is already—in the sense of Paul's doctrine of faith—the man who trusts in Christ, the man who in the grace of faith in Jesus (Rom. 3: 22, 26; Gal. 2: 16, 20; 3, 22; Eph. 3, 12; Phil. 3, 9) is able to make his human act of faith.[11]

Precisely in this sense Christ does not tell his disciples that they can do nothing, but that they can do nothing without him: "Apart from me you can do nothing" (John 15, 5). This saying, then, has its victorious counterpart in the Pauline cry "I can do all things in him who strengthens me" (Phil. 4, 13)—to take one more human example, just as a woman would say to her husband, "Without me you can do nothing, but with me everything," and "I can do everything through you, who gives me the power."

However immeasurably the power of God is above all creaturely power in its sovereign independence, God still seeks to preserve in the working of his grace the covenant mystery of mutualness, as he laid down in his creation and as he reveals as his inner trinitarian secret.

Paul's cry "I can do all things" is, thus, not to be seen as a pious exaggeration, but as the expression of his sharing in the belief in the divine omnipotence—insofar as the latter deigns to communicate itself to the creature according to the divine will and wisdom in the economy of salvation. It presupposes that man enters into the attitude of Jesus Christ, into the obedience of him who had at his disposal the entire saving will of the Father. Hence, "Whatever you ask in my name, I will do it" (John 14, 13), and "If you have faith as a grain of mustard seed . . . nothing will be impossible to you" (Matt. 17, 20). This faith as complete child-like devotion—in contrast to the schizophrenic "doubt" of the epistle of James, taken up by Pastor Hermas and, in the Middle Ages, by Wolfram's Parsifal—as simplicity of sight turned directly to God (Matt. 6, 22), is the condition and result of union with God, in which the power of God is imparted to the creature that is open to God.

This reciprocity, which does not merge the will of the creature in the absolute will of God, as happens in the mysticism of the Gentiles, but preserves its identity, is such a profound mystery that only the trinitarian mystery offers an adequate framework for it. Only because the Son, who is obediently subject to the power of the Father in all things and yet has total power over the heart of the Father, shares the power of his love with us, can we understand the words in John's prologue (1, 12): "he gave [them] power to become children of God." Through these words we see that the children of God are not simply dealt with over their heads, but that they themselves possess the power to become the children of God. It is a power given to them, it is true, but given to them as their very own. Thus, they are able to claim from the

Father their rights as children. These rights are by no means simply legal, but are a part of their being, for they are "born . . . of God" (John 1, 13).

The Power of Love and the Self-limitation of Freedom

Now that we have shown how the divine power of grace manifests itself in the natural power of the creature, we must consider the specific nature of the power of God as it emerges in biblical revelation. It is exclusively the power of divine love which works itself out as redemptive for man, and through him for the world, by the justification and sanctification of man.

Before its inner nature is treated, let us discuss its necessity for man alienated from God. Original sin, as the loss of the original reciprocity of the love relationship between God and man, involves for man the loss of that "power to become a child of God," without his therefore losing, or wanting to lose, the will to be God's child. For by virtue of his call and destiny to share (supernaturally) in the divine life man cannot renounce the privilege he possesses *de jure.* He lost this privilege *de facto,* when he sought to have power over God, which he could have only through God and in God; but he wanted it to be his own power, without God. Thus the sin, once committed, necessarily continues, since man has to strive to win again his lost privilege by his own power— which was precisely the first sin. There is the same law in the relation to God that exists analogously in the relationship between two people who love each other: the one who gives offense cannot demand forgiveness from the one offended. The more he tries to force it through pressure in his actions, the more he infringes the laws of mutual love.

The sinner is utterly dependent on the free initiative of God's love which comes to meet him (*gratia praeveniens*), not only in order to find God, but also to find himself in God. In God he wins back his own ultimate inner freedom, without which he is unable to rise to that integration of himself, to that polarization of all his psychic, physiological, and physical capacities which permits the full incarnation of his spirit in the world (through his body). In humanity there is no such thing as an individual who is closed and shut off. Rather, there is a reciprocity of human centers of consciousness, and not only *ratione materiae (communis)*, but also *ratione spiritus,* because the true image of God lies in the reciprocity of man and woman (Gen. 1, 27). Thus, it is clear that the disturbance of the original love relationship with God and the dialectic between impotence and violence which follows from this disturbance (as Augustine has shown) must be translated into a similar dialectical relationship within the world. This is true in the individual (and in the relations between the sexes) between "spirit" and "flesh;" further, it also holds true in the social and political and economic spheres in many forms of the disturbance of the balance and in the attempts to remove such disturbance by force.

From the *Civitas Dei* of Augustine (with its theories of original sin as the disturbance of the relationship between soul and God and between soul and body, as well as the violence of earthly power relationships, according to the pattern Assur—Babylon—Rome), via Luther, Jansenius, and Pascal the lines run to the *Epistle to the Romans* of Karl Barth, in order to show this irremovable dialectic of religion and ethics within the framework of original sin. Physical and spiritual power is left to man who cannot cease to make religious attempts to establish, by himself, a harmonious total order in the world, in which God would also be recognized in his place. But man, because of human power, refuses to acknowledge his total impotence to reestablish his relationship with God outside the free movement of God's grace.

The Church expressed this essential element of the truth in the Council of Orange in the spirit and terminology of Augustine: man's freedom and nature have become so impotent through original sin that without God's grace he now only has the "strength of desire."[12] Anselm of Canterbury in his doctrine of freedom (*De Libertate Arbitrii, De Casu Diaboli, De Concordia ... Gratiae Dei cum Libero Arbitrio*) has shown how to reconcile the seriousness of the Augustinian doctrine with the rights of nature. These rights of nature were later defined by St. Thomas (and Trent against Protestantism). Fallen nature, which preserves its capacity for freedom as well as its reason, still has these rights. But it cannot make the ultimate act of freedom asked of it by its unique supernatural goal and thus for its final self-liberation and self-conquest. Canon seven of Orange said that it is impossible for human nature by itself to think of or choose whatever pertains to salvation. One needs the light and strength of the Holy Spirit to gain eternal life (Dz 180). After Augustine and Prosper (who inspired these canons) the Church later emphasized more the universal effect of the redemption of Christ and the offer of his grace for all men of good will, even if outside the Church and Christendom. But whenever man's power does rise freely to itself out of all his corrupt involvements, whenever he does gain power over himself and in that power orders his relation to God and to the world in freedom, this happens only because of the gracious self-revelation of the inner life of God.

This self-revelation of the inner life of God is redemptive love; and whatever of divine power is manifested in his self-revelation is the power and glory of his love. That is the gospel for St. Paul: the "balance" between the fear of sin and hope of faith, between the threat of judgment and the promise of redemption, is removed since the death of Christ, is overcome in favor of a still greater victory of grace (Rom. 5, 15–21; 8, 28–39). "For the Son of God, Jesus Christ, whom we preached among you . . . was not Yes and No; but in him it is always Yes" (2 Cor. 1, 19). But this *yes* is the deed and decision of God; it cannot therefore be performed and made one's own in a theoretical, contemplative way, but only in deed and decision. The prophetic, existential language of the bible invites one to do it, resisting as it does a "systematic" interpretation of eschatology. Only in this way does it become clear that it is in the New Testament, where the total *yes* of God's decision on the world resounds, that the message of hell as the eternal loss of God's grace also resounds. Hell, like purgatory, could have had no place in the religious view of the world in the Old Testament. God's loving deed in Christ on the cross (and in Christ's descent into abandonment by God and into the darkness of death) is so precious and exposed that it cannot be presented to man, with his understanding dulled by sin, in any other way than against that background.

If all the power that appeared in Christ is the power of God's love, then it is impossible that in the whole cosmos of grace, thus in the Church also, any other form of power should become manifest. Even the powers imparted to the Church can only be the bringing near (re-presentations) of the love of God. Hence, however much there may be a sphere of "justice," "injustice" can agree only by analogy with the law of (fallen) nature, because all membership of the Church is absolutely voluntary and thus excludes all compulsion in the exercise of power. This is true because the norm for the individual lies necessarily *above* him, namely in the normative love relationship between God and man in the person of Christ himself, and through Christ in the normative relationship between him as the bridegroom and the immaculate and perfect bride, the Church (Mary). Church authority has power over the individual only inasmuch as he confesses his faith and, thus, grants to the Church and its representatives power over him to lead him, even against his own evil will, according to his own better will.

The way in which Paul uses his official authority shows clearly that he always asks it to be seen as an expression and outflow of the love of God in Christ. Its naked emergence is a limiting idea which is approached according as the faithful move away from the living center of the reality of faith and strive toward the border of a life without faith (as defiance of God and the Church) (2 Cor. 13). Christ himself, as we have seen, had always appealed to men's faith, i.e., to an initial movement of love. "Do you believe that I am able to do this?" he asks the blind man in Matthew 9, 28. "He *could* do no mighty work there," (Mark 6, 5) where there was no faith. Lack of faith is the guilty inability to accept the words of Christ: "Why do you not understand what I say?" (John 8, 43). All the authority of the Church—to preach, to administer sacraments, and to perform pastoral work—is the power of love over those who are willing and ready to believe. This willingness, expressed for the child by the godfather, is a prerequisite of baptism, which the first entry into the Church manifests.

The original decision of God to reveal his power as love means something like a *self-restriction* of his absolute power. It is as if divine justice ties its hands toward sinners through the saving event of the cross. This self-restriction of God has its manifestation in the obedience of the Son to the salvation will of the Father which was given as a law: "The Son can do nothing of his own accord" (John 5, 19); "I can do nothing on my own authority" (John 5, 30). Because of this incapacity he cannot defend himself against the secular, ravishing power of the Jews and Gentiles. And his disciples do not fight because his kingdom is not of this world (John 18, 36).

On the other hand, in this self-limitation of divine power in love there lies the absolute removal of limits and, thus, the revelation of the divine omnipotence before the world (Eph. 1, 19). The large number of expressions for "power" which Paul uses in speaking of the wakening of the man Jesus, powerless in death, for the sake of our resurrection, shows that the extreme of divine power is manifest. Hence, one must say that the self-limitation of the *potentia absoluta* of God for love is therefore itself omnipotence, because it is compelled by nothing outside God—as, for example, is his punishing justice by sin, i.e., the necessity of restoring the world order. Rather, his absolute power is pure inner self-determination and, therefore, corresponding to the divine inner being, proves to be absolute freedom of self-giving, humility, and loving selflessness.

Hence, the mystery of the weakness of God, that appears in the life and suffering of Jesus (and accordingly in the Mystical Body of Christ, the Church), is actually the mystery of his manifested omnipotence. This mystery, which is not a "paradox" in the dialectical sense, can be made familiar to the understanding of the believer in three stages, without losing its essential quality of mystery. For every attempt to arrive at a rational explanation by human reason must inevitably fail when the profound depths of an absolute divine freedom are involved, a freedom which as such is one with the eternal Logos. In one's reverent search for the *intellectus fidei,* however, he can say the following things.

God's (loving) power appears the more absolutely if it is not tied to any creaturely power (of secular laws), more sovereignly if it appears in weakness. It is within the authority of him who is eternal life to be life even in the mode of death. He can, as it were, allow himself to die, and to die even in impotence and shame, and to "taste death for every one" (Heb. 2, 9) and to experience the eternal darkness of being abandoned by the Father. "I have the power of laying down my life"—and this "laying down" is total and final because he has the (same!) power "of taking it again" (John 10, 18). Such completeness of power beyond the most extreme creaturely antithesis (of life and death, abandonment and self-ownership) is expressed in the central words of Paul: "It pleased God [in the highest, free power of decision] through the folly of what we preach to save those who believe . . . the weakness of God is stronger than men. . . . God chose what is weak in the world to show the strong" (1 Cor. 1, 21–28).

Seen from the point of view of man this loving decision of

God to take the way of weakness means the appearance of the major *dissimilitudo divina* as opposed to all the similarity between worldly and divine power, however great: this transcendence makes all confusion between the two impossible. That is why the Christian faith, as the passing beyond all one's own real or imagined strength into the mystery of the weakness of Christ, in whom all the power of God is "hid" (Col. 2, 3), is a reverent openness to God to let him perform these mysteries of weakness in man, because only in this mystery does the power of God break through: "My grace is sufficient for you, for my power is made perfect in weakness" (2 Cor. 12, 9). To perform this act of reverent openness in weakness is to follow Christ to the cross, where he showed the full obedience of love to the Father. Paul goes as far as to say, "For the sake of Christ, then, I am content with weaknesses, insults, hardships, persecutions, and calamities; for when I am weak, then I am *strong*" (2 Cor. 12, 10).

The second point is already included in what we have just said: the weak man offers less resistance to the power of God's love. Finding no more strength in the world and in himself, he is, as it were, forced to depend on God and becomes the special property of God. This aspect is the particular Old Testament contribution to the mystery of redemption; it represents the tradition of *anawim* Yahweh, which is the particular Amos-Jeremiah-Psalms tradition[13] and, in a further sense, the whole Asian tradition of rising above all creaturely power to the lack of resistance to the spirit which is given over to God. The "poor and little ones" of the Old Testament are those who are called blessed in the first beatitude of the Sermon on the Mount, because they offer empty room for the Holy Spirit, just as Mary, who was empty for God, praises in her song of praise the "lowly ones" whom God raised, while he put down the mighty from their seats.

The "evangelical counsels" are to be seen in the line of this Old Testament tradition which is fulfilled in Jesus and Mary:

virginity as foregoing sexual power (not only by a man, but also by a woman, for the sake of unique fruitfulness through God in the poverty of one's own power); poverty as a total, bodily and spiritual attitude of renunciation toward all means of power of one's own in order to be someone who is solely at the disposal of God and in his name; obedience as not anticipating truth and decision, but remaining totally transparent for the divine truth and decision in the realm of Christ and the Church. The "renunciation of violence," enjoined by the Sermon on the Mount (Matt. 5, 39 ff.), belongs here. It raises Indian passivity to a higher level. Also, in the context belongs "taking no thought" for the morrow (Matt. 6, 25–34) and the desire to be dependent alone on the preserving and bestowing power of God's love.

In the weakness of the poverty of the cross (in all its forms), there appears finally the Spirit of God, as the original in the copy; the Spirit of absolute love, which in its freest self-limitation exists beyond strength and weakness, dominion and humility. Here theologies are developed which see in the Son's weakness on the cross not only the (utilitaristic) element of satisfaction, but a self-presentation of the innermost secret of the Trinity. Thus, for St. Francis, and later for Tauler, the poverty of Christ is the manifestation of one of the tenderest of God's qualities, which one may describe as "divine poverty." In the blood of Christ there appears for Catherine of Siena an expression of the nature of the heart of God which could not be expressed in any other way. Thus must one interpret for a Platonic thinker such as Origen the surprising words that even the Father (as the "supreme God") is perhaps not free of suffering. In Paul himself we have the kenosis of the Son of God (the result of his refusal to cling to his divinity) appearing as an adequate expression of his divine attitude of love, and, hence, of divine being itself.

Accordingly, the Holy Spirit is described as groaning within groaning creation; it is weakened together with the weak, limited together with the finite spirits caught in their clouded subjectivity, frightened and lashing out around them. It flows together with the whole process of the world which struggles for the manifestation of its sonship of God. The Christian is the point of intersection of this dual groaning of the creaturely spirit and the divine Spirit: "we ourselves, who have the first fruits of the Spirit, groan inwardly as we wait for adoption as sons" (Rom. 8, 23). The creature is no longer just a vessel for the presence of divine power, nor is he now only the occasion for the epiphany of the sovereign majesty of God, but is united directly in his impotent self-giving with the absolute self-giving of the triune, absolute ground of all being.

The Dialectic of the Theology of History

The interaction of power and love cannot be estimated, even within an unfallen creation, unless it is in fact a mysterious process whereby the very acceptance of the operation of the power of the beloved is at the same time a delightful authorization by the beloved to accept him: again, the sexual analogy is here the most revealing. But the first innocent couple were set into a world which—at least in the wider context—had already been disturbed, a natural environment in which there were the most bitter, merciless, and mortal struggles for life, food, and coupling with or leadership of the herd. Man, who has declared his solidarity with this disturbed world, is forced by the necessities of life to this tough fight for survival. He fights for his place in the sun, fights for his wife, for his friends, fights with a God whom he experiences in prayer as an adversary. His life is drudgery; it is, as Job says, the craft of war. It makes him hard, perhaps rebellious, perhaps definitely submissive.

If, like the old Faust, he is able to wrest a stretch of coast from the sea, if, gathered with his own kind, he is able to wrest a piece of life from fate and make it livable, then he is pleased, builds the cyclopean wall a little higher, becomes intoxicated by the

progress of his domination of matter and by his dreams of evolution. No one robs him of his Titan's dream, as little as one can
prevent the ant from building up again and again its destroyed
dwelling place. No one rids him of the idea that this determined
will to reach the top is the best, perhaps even the most divine
quality he has. He loves the quality so much that it does not
matter to him that he has to sacrifice his own limited individuality, as long as the mighty building of power that he is helping
to build can eventually be completed. With the same serenity
with which he sees millions of other lives that are stunted, that
fail, and that are swallowed up, he contemplates in thought his
own death.

As world technology integrates more and more the work of the
individual and relates it effectively to the total power goals of
humanity, the deep satisfaction of him who has conquered someone else becomes a universal feeling: we will manage it. Through
us the world progresses. We break out of the prison of nature
into the freedom that is worthy of man. We even utilize the
negative forces of nature; poisons are used to heal. Why, one day
we might even master death. And if it is true that a god once
died for us on the cross, then does not that death serve more
powerful living? Have we not the right to interpret its effect in
this way, to draw more living power, more strength of freedom
for ourselves, to consider ourselves therefore capable of new,
undiscovered resurrections? Did he not come in order to help us
from within to break into the realm of freedom? Do we not show
him the greatest honor by now seeing ourselves as capable of this
freedom—no longer as Titans fighting God, but as authorized,
mature sons of God, even in our earthly work which the fatherly
Creator has entrusted to his children? *Gratia perficit naturam!*
Christ wants the Christian who is open to the world. Why should
the children of darkness always be more clever than the children
of light? We must beat them in their own field and dedicate the
forces of the world to God, not by renouncing them, but by using
them. We must let them bear fruit for the kingdom of God, thus

assisting the will of God to realize itself, not only in heaven, but also on earth.

This program of Christian progressivism is curiously close to that of its opponent, Christian integralism. Whereas the latter seeks to occupy the positions of earthly power in order to proclaim from them the teachings of the Sermon on the Mount and the cross, the former makes the positions of the Sermon on the Mount and the cross the inner dynamic for progress in earthly power. Both, ultimately, have reduced the problem of power between God and the world, between grace and nature, to a monastic form which is easy to handle and can be managed by men.

At the beginning of this section, however, we rejected those unifying formulas which—as with Tolstoy or Gandhi—transfer the gospel rejection of power to the earthly political sphere. A similar unifying formula justified—since Constantine, Justinian and Charlemagne—the use of worldly power for the purposes of the kingdom of God. Today we are aware of how mistaken this latter solution is, but less aware of its modern variant, which takes technological means of power and the so-called "reflection of the noosphere," which those means made possible, and seeks to interpret and exploit them in a direct christological way. Is the cross an energy factor for the evolution of the world? The cross of Christ means to have the will to complete impotence, to the fear of the Mount of Olives, to the most extreme shame and bitterness, to being betrayed, denied, abandoned, to a death as a bankruptcy. The cross signifies relinquishing all hope which one has experienced and which has strengthened one, all the faith in which one has lived, all the love one has felt. The will to all that is the direct purpose of the life of the Redeemer. Whoever wants to follow this life must at least wait in patient expectancy to see whether God will not ask the same of him. On no account can he hope to use the mortal suffering of his master to his earthly advantage.

Such an acceptance of divinely ordained suffering, however, is

totally opposed to the aims of the technical progress of civilization. The latter is concerned with the overcoming of suffering,
whatever the cost. Battle is joined with every kind of suffering
—physical and mental. The sick, the dying, even those giving
birth, are no longer allowed to suffer. Not even if man thereby
loses a greatness and a depth, a purity and a radiance, that he
can gain through pain alone. Of course, the means of suffering
are more than ever in the hands of humanity, in case someone
does not agree with the doctrine of the increasing conquest of
suffering.

The power of the world, which becomes more concentrated
the more the world becomes unified, cannot remain neutral to
the gospel of Christ, if only because it can establish no connection with the gospel. Christ's kingdom "is not of this world"; it
is at once impotent and omnipotent in its relation to the world.
If the concentrated power of the world were to offer it its aid, it
would not know what to do with it, for "the kingdom of God is
not coming with signs to be observed" (Luke 17, 20). If the world
sought to oppose the kingdom, then this has long been regarded
as the normal situation which need not surprise or disturb any
Christian. In it we have the promise of God's powerful, invisible
help. The more that the power of the world becomes conscious
of and realizes itself, the more the kingdom of God slips from its
grasp, because as a whole it is the area of God's power. And it is
by no means the technical man who "christifies" matter, for the
Eucharist remains the freest self-realization of the crucified and
resurrected God-man.

As with the spirit, which tries secularly (as "open reason") to
bend over backward and close itself where God's Spirit keeps the
covenant open as a love choice, the encounter could lead increasingly only into the apocalyptic. So, also, with power which
must increasingly strive in an earthly way to get rid of the
impotence of the cross or else incorporate it in itself and utilize
it. It will attain the throne of omnipotence only beyond the im-

potence of death and the underworld. But the way in which positive values of created power are drawn into and made to serve the world-redeeming power of God remains, to the annoyance of worldly powers, forever hidden from it.

According to Paul the powerful rulers of the world, the *archontes*, are partially "put out of action" by the working of God's power in Christ; in what way they may still be used is not stated. Insofar as they are worldly powers opposed to God, they are thrown after the apocalypse into the burning pits to devour themselves. But this will not happen until after the realm of power, closing its ranks, has "surrounded the camp of the saints and the beloved city" and besieged it (Apoc. 20, 9). Then, the Antichrist "by the activity of Satan will be with all power and with pretended signs and wonders, and with all wicked deception" and do his work upon those "who did not believe the truth but had pleasure in unrighteousness" (2 Thess. 2, 9 ff.).

Notes

1 *Parusia. Hoffnung und Prophetie,* L. Schneider, Heidelberg, 1960, 445–464. Schütz also quotes the words of Adolf Portmann's, "I draw the sharpest line against what Teilhard de Chardin says when in prophetic vision he presents that which is to come as a clear consequence of knowledge."

2 Teilhard de Chardin: *The Phenomenon of Man,* Harper, 1959.

3 Karl Jaspers: *Der philosophische Glaube,* 1948; *Der philosophische Glaube angesichts der Offenbarung,* 1962.

4 Concerning the conflict between both universalisms, cf., especially, Wilhelm Kamlah: *Christentum und Geschichtlichkeit,* 1951.

5 In the following we are taking him as the representative of the revelation religion of the bible. The same would be true for the orthodox Jew. For the problems of the relations between the Jewish faith and "open reason," see my work on Martin Buber, *Martin Buber and Christianity: A dialogue between Israel and the Church,* tr. by Alexander Dru, Macmillan, 1962.

6 Cf. above, Chapter 2, "The Perfectibility of Man."

7 H. Schlier: *Jesus Christus und die Geschichte nach der Offenbarung Johannes',* in *Einsichten, Festschrift Gerh. Krüger, 1962,* 316–333.

8 Richard Hauser: *Die Macht nach katholischer Ethik,* in *Von der Macht,* 1962, 187–204. Cf. also *Macht,* by the same author in *Handbuch theologischer Grundbegriffe,* II, 1963, with a bibliography.

9 But Aeschylus' *Prometheus* already assumes it: the "old" gods and Titans, the representatives of power, are subjugated by the new Olympian gods under Zeus, and the Titan Prometheus has fought on the side of Zeus (because the spirit needs force in order to attain power), but is now nailed to the rock by the servants of Zeus' Kratos and Bia (violence and compulsion). The revolt of power against the spirit shown in the first play of the trilogy, the only one to be preserved, would have, in the two following ones, led to a reconciliation of both realms. But Aeschylus shows what abysses the problem of power and spirit open up.

10 Erich Przywara: *Analogio Entis*, 2nd ed., 1962, 127–141; he discusses the advance from negative to positive to active potentiality in the creature, but the basis of the whole is in the relation to God of mutual otherness.

11 Cf. my essay *Fides Christi* in *Sponsa Verbi*, 1961, 45–79.

12 Cf. Council of Orange, can, 8, Dz. 181, can. 13, Dz. 186 *(infirmatur)*; Dz. 199 *(inclinatum et attenuatum)*; can. 1, Dz. 174 *(laesum)*; can. 21, Dz. 194 *(perditum)*.

13 Albert Gelin: *Les pauvres de Yahwé*, 1953.

7. THE WORD AND HISTORY

THE EXPANSION OF THE WORD

Man has his essential word, and history has its essential word: both meet and penetrate each other in a comprehensive word and direct us back, from a higher vantage point, to the first thoughts of our study. That man and history are commensurate with each other—that man has a historical shape and a human history—has already been indicated more than once. Man exists in a transcending extension beyond himself, not only toward some things and his environment, but toward the world, toward being in general. Wherever being is illuminated, however obscurely, there is his humanity, and he becomes illuminated to himself as spirit. There he exists in the freedom which has not only arrived at the real, but also been able to distance itself from every individual piece of reality. This paradoxical unity of oneness and

219

distance is the miracle of language.[1] In it the power of the living has become spirit, for in language man possesses things in their origin, their being, and, thus, has the quasi-divine power of being able to let them exist. Even where he does not himself live immediately—and in the past and future, also—even there he has ceased to be present as a finite being himself.

The expressive power of his words is what gives man dominion over nature and raises him like a king above all the beasts (Gen. 1, 26–29), because he is able to name them in such a way that they really are called what he calls them (Gen. 2, 19–20). By themselves they are unnamed, as they are incapable of raising themselves into the light of self-comprehension; but the word of man knows and names them from the height of his light, and, thus, he dominates them in their innermost being from a higher point than they can themselves. And yet, man can be open to being only by unconditionally renouncing in advance the holding fast to any particular. He can know it only by letting it go, in the power of letting it be, which can mean for him—the speaker— powerlessness, death, self-extinction. Through such surrender to the superior power of being, all great spiritual power is bought on earth. This becomes sublimely and tragically clear where the world appears, in its comprehensive temporality, as history. For, on the one hand, man's word of power reaches beyond his personal mortal existence into history, shaping and constructing. On the other hand, this transcendence can take place only if there is a submissive recognition of the omnipotence of death and fate.

A king by his words as ruler shapes his era and, hence, creates a lasting, continuously active piece of history. The prophet reads the future in the present, and vice versa, and incorporates his age in a more comprehensive order. Poets, above all, and teachers of wisdom have created words which will have effects in history after they are dead. But they dominate the future only by having taken the risk of self-abandonment: their witness, their testament, and their tradition may last, but they may also fail. Then we see the powerless side of their words, which are swept away by the tides of later generations.

This historical reaching out of the human creative power in the word occupied the minds of the biblical teachers of wisdom at an important and effective juncture between the ancient peoples' understanding of man and history and the understanding, still unknown, of the new people grouped around the Incarnate Word of God. Jesus Sirach speaks not only for Israel, but for all peoples;[2] he speaks not only of mere physical generation (which as such is not a word), nor of physical power, but of the phenomenon of "fame," in which God glorifies man in his human words before history:

Rulers of the earth by their authority, men of renown for their might, or counselors in their wisdom, or seers of all things in prophecy; resolute governors of peoples, or judges with discretion; authors skilled in composition, or poets with collected proverbs; composers of melodious psalms, or discoursers on lyric themes; stalwart men, solidly established and at peace in their own estates—all these were glorious in their time, each illustrious in his day. Some of them have left behind a name that is remembered to their praise; but of others there is no memory, for it perished when they perished, and they are as though they had never lived, they and their children after them (Sirach, 44, 2–9).*

He goes on to praise those who are not forgotten, whose descendants are their rich legacy, whose grandsons "remain true to the command of their word" so that "their memory lasts forever and their fame does not fade."

These famous men, however, go beyond the law of ordinary historical life. Their word is mysteriously included in a greater, eternal word of power which is spoken from the highest height, a word that is implanted through them in history and soon will pass into the full mortality of a human life, in order, in

* Holy Bible, Confraternity Edition. Copyright 1962 The Confraternity of Christian Doctrine and reprinted by permission.

the transitory, perishable sphere, to show its imperishability: "Heaven and earth will pass away, but my words will not pass away" (Matt. 24, 35). Here, at an otherwise unattainable height, the paradox of tradition is revealed: in total openness to anonymous decline and death there is the widest opening up of history to be shaped royally and prophetically by one's own word.

There is a word by no means only divine, but also human. This is a word which is not only divinely powerful and at the same time humanly powerless, but also manifests the paradox of human freedom—which Christ has in his human nature—in its simultaneity of yielding and of dominating. Otherwise, the divine Word would not have become man, the law of the transcendence of the human word into the sphere of history would not have been included. The word of Christ takes up the challenge with other human words for dominion over history.[3]

Christ's word possesses its transcendent, self-extending power not through a power of the Holy Spirit, a power innerly strange to him and given him only from outside and from above and which after his death saw to the organization and propagation of his word. Rather is the depth of Spirit inherent in the word of this man from the beginning; "it is not by measure" that he is given the Spirit (John 3, 34). Indeed, he "taught as one who had authority" (Mark 1, 22), which means that out of the consciousness of this power he finds the power to make his word outlast heaven and earth. And this precisely because his life, as no other, is a life for death, and his word as no other is a word for death, a word face to face with destruction, a word that demands in advance the last drop of blood and the last drop of spirit. Only thus does the word obtain insight into the ultimate openness of being and its history.

Only through this kenotic, eucharistic consecration to earthly destruction do Christ's words acquire their incomprehensible, and yet evident, superiority over all things past and present. They are analogous to the poetic words that last through all time because they not only see the tragic before them, but also bear it in them in order, however little it is understood, to affirm and transfigure it in advance. If the word flees from fate or else defies it, no artificial refinement will prevent it from having no effect. It finally acquires its halo of glory which makes it last, openly or chastely hidden, on account of the defenselessness of the heart. This is something far deeper than Stoic impassivity. It is an untouchability in the middle of suffering which—Antigone! —can only be defined as fidelity.

RE-UNION

The word of man retains its human shape even, and especially, in its reaching beyond the barrier of death. Such reaching out is effective in history in spite of the barrier of time, of the allotted measure of finite duration. It is effective even more keenly in spite of the fear of the uncontrollability of the moment of death, or, as Christ says, the "hour." The branches of the word reach out powerfully only where the trunk is deeply rooted vertically in the soil of its time. Man and his language can certainly "abstract," but only as the tree draws its sap up from the earth. Every spreading of the upper leaves requires a deeper taking root below, otherwise the top breaks, like a superstructure, and everything has to start growing again from below.

The vertical dimension of man reaches without a break from the spirit through the soul and the living body down into matter, and "soul" and "body" are the stages and modes in which spirit takes root in matter, and matter blooms into spirit—a single, ultimate, dually moved life: corporalization of the spirit, spiritualization of the body, neither existing without the other. If the body strove one-sidedly to become spirit, without allowing the spirit correspondingly to penetrate the body and become one with it, then man would be striving away from himself into a chimerical self-alienation. But in this dual movement man is suspended in the middle, since neither the Dionysian drive back to the material origins, nor the Promethean drive to pure spirit brings him nearer to himself, and the two tendencies cannot be made into one. As a product of maternal earth and paternal heaven he has to turn his face toward both, without being able to see both at once. He cannot find his ground or take his rest in either, or in both at once, but only in him who has created heaven and earth, spirit and matter, day and night.

Language, as the expression of the existent world and of man, can only live in the resonance of this dual motion. It must not harden into a crystallizing "image" or "symbol" halfway between heaven and earth, spirit and instinct, and, thus, attribute to itself a false divinity (to which especially literature is prone). Language must, in the animated descent of the concept into the example, of pallid generality into the individual case of flesh and blood, and in the rising out of the limitations of a single instance into the breadth of the universal, remain close to its origins. In this movement it will cross again and again the point of image and symbol, but each time create it anew, enrich it, confirm it.

The middle itself becomes dynamic and dramatic: through and beyond it the concrete and actual is placed under the judging light of the spiritual logos, and, vice versa, under the same light is placed that which is undecided and generally is called into the challenge of the here and now.[4] This crosswise movement can proceed, in suggestion and without ultimate radicality, where matter and logos are seen in their contrariety, but are ultimately related to the image center of language, as in the myths and parables of ancient peoples. These, tied to the suspended middle, can neither quite reach the naked earth of existence, nor quite reach the height of the divine idea. The myth and its language remain, in this sense, "aesthetic." Even in its clarification in philosophy the latter remains close to the "middle" (at the same distance, the Aristotelean "mean"), which is wisdom. But there is, also, the fear, learned by experience, of approaching too near to those depths which are beyond the control of man.[5]

Only where the ground of spirit shines through, in a transcendent, personal way, does the word from the highest height break through the image center (which above all is the realm of the "typical") down into the material and individual in order to choose it and raise it up as something worthy of the height of personal uniqueness. Both are raised together; against the timelessness of the middle there are posed the truly eternal and the truly temporal, the latter through and for the former.

Hence, the full measure of language was sounded out by Christ for the first time, since "the Word became flesh," and, thus, the ultimate word is heard in the world and in man. Not at all through demythologizing—by dissolving the image into something rational or ethically and existentially "logical"—but by the acquisition, through the limited rhythm of the spirit-matter motion in mythical language, of the widest possible swing between heaven above and the abyss beneath. The words of scripture as a whole and the word of Jesus in particular always break through the middle of the image and symbol, in order to let through the maximum of "spirit" into the fully attained, everyday earthly sphere which is revealed in all its naked, realistic actuality.

The biblical parables do not relate neutral, typical, average human "cases"; they are always aimed as a unique flash of lightning from heaven directly at the immediate now. This gives them their weight which transcends the inner dimensions of poetry. And the weight of this vertical descent from heaven to earth (and ascent from earth to heaven), from soul to body (and hence from body to soul), is the condition of the possibility of a similar, even identical weight horizontally through time. Anticipating, we may say that because this word not only speaks to death symbolically, in aesthetic transfiguration, but penetrates it with its weight and as it were spears it, it is able, when rising from the dead, to take it prisoner up into eternal life and really "transfigure" it. And therefore this word, instead of speaking over the actual extendedness of time, timelessly healing, is able to capture, in the form and power of its word, the historical temporality of man and the world altogether and redeem them from within from all fallenness and alienation.

If the historical power of the word is ultimately based in the free vertical swing and suspension of spiritual-corporeal finitude, then it can be shown that human history as a whole has a human shape whose measure cannot in the least be altered by any historical evolution or be adjusted in favor of the logical and abstract to the disadvantage of the spiritual-corporeal image. All such alterations are accounted for in the range of variation of embodied spirit, crowned by the Word as flesh. The vertical presentness of the latter, hence, remains the measure for all other possible historical present times. Man would be fleeing from the true historical present if he thought he could alter his vertical axis to a horizontal one, if he believed he could leave his "origin" in "matter" behind him as the past and strive forward to "spirit." That would be to abandon the most precious and personal thing he has and, moreover, to deny Christ as well, because it would make his incarnation impossible.

By man's keeping himself open in his suspended center to movement toward the depths, his language is constantly enriched from heaven and earth. In his open gaze toward both one secret of the depth of his being becomes clear to him—the incomprehensible difference between being and what exists, between what exists through all things and that which is existed through. Language acquires its depth, its infinite significance, its poetic, prophetic, lawgiving power from the knowledge of this mystery. When the mystery of the ground of being fades, then the expressive power of words fades also. All great literature, all prophetic and philosophical interpretation of existence, all legislation which shapes history, is rooted, without qualification and without exception, in the religious, in the reverent vision of ultimate incomprehensible differentiation. And this is true of the individual statement of a poet, of the wise maxim, of the single law. It is not on the philosophical plane that the language of a people matures toward its valid statements, but on the religious, where the openness to the depths of being and the moving human equilibrium produce in a fruitful reciprocal effect the historical "great moment." Such *kairoi* are then like preparations for the all-fulfilling Incarnation.

And certainly one can say—and almost assume it *a priori*—that the displacements around this ideal middle range from an impoverishment of spirit dominated by matter to a rationalistic excess of spirit, the hubris of which is avenged by a sudden collapse into impoverishment. But this collapse is (as Vico saw) at a deeper level a compensation by nature and, thus, is a new chance to establish the ideal condition. Nor should one forget that the center itself is in motion and can displace itself rhythmically toward either side. Moreover, the relationship between spirit and image and matter creates a vertical central axis through which passes the axis of the Incarnation, which comes from higher and goes deeper. This central axis remains the measure of everything in the horizontal extent of history which could be taken as alteration, development, and "progress." The ordering Word sent down by God to man, the Word that raises mortal man to God, is exactly the same one that is the force which directs history toward an end at which the same Incarnate Word, who was always its guiding center, awaits it.

SUSPENSION AND THE GROUND OF BEING

As all that exists draws its meaning from its relation to being—to the unconditional in which it is grounded, to the fullness of the other, the coexistent in which it has its life and is co-possible—language too gains its significance from the recognized relation that all things are grounded in an ineffable ground. Thus, language is always born from silence and is constantly rooted in it; in order to exist properly, it must refer to it, interpret it, lead back to it, not because words are meaningless and vain, but because the fullness of their meaning always transcends them and only in this transcendence makes them possible. Just as the fullness of the existent is not a falling away from the fullness of being, so the fullness of language is not a falling away from the fullness of silence. In the recognition of the difference between being and the existent there is always "pre-given" (Max Picard[6]) the possibility of significant speech for the mind which knows the existent as a whole. There is given language itself (which man could never learn if it were not already given to him). With the gift of language is given insight into ontological differences, in which are founded the relation of speech to silence, of the expressed to the inexpressible. Beyond being and mind, beyond nature and freedom, there is the mysterious ground which gives them a common foundation and in which consequently silence exists as a "super-word." If God expresses himself in the being of the world, and man understands the language of this being, then man not only shares, through his knowledge, in the eternal reason, but as a knower is always addressed by the voice of God, and what he says is, in fact, a reply.

Thus, man is by nature endowed with the power of utterance and of response. He is not only capable of hearing the essential utterance of things as they differentiate themselves from the surrounding silence of being, of apprehending them through his reason, and of giving them appropriate names; he can also grasp these utterances of things as the elements of a language addressed to him, of which he himself, together with his reason, is an element. Man was " 'spoken' into the light of the truth of the existent out from being and out from God before he himself spoke. Only because he dwells without speech in the existent, i.e., that which has emerged from the luminous depth of being, is he able to 'receive' his inner word and pronounce it as an 'outer' one." (G. Siewerth[7])

This is the most hidden truth, that the luminous depth is not only the silence of being—so that all the activity of speech must be rooted in an open, receptive contemplation, if it is to be true —but also beyond this silence there is a word from the last depth of being itself: the word "man" that God speaks, so that man becomes a question to himself because he is asked. This ultimate truth can be discerned only through the bible, which does not limit the range of contemplation, but deepens it by making it hearing and obeying. The bible turns the openness to hidden being into the open love for the self-revealing God, and "open reason" into the responding love choice which includes one with the only beloved.

This mystery is known to man only because in Jesus Christ that union was shown as actual and, therefore, possible: the union between the silent super-word, of which all existent things partake in order to be an expression of being, and the word of man, addressed and responding, whereby he acquires his nature and is endowed with speech. He is not deprived of his utterance by the super-word which reveals itself as the eternal word of the Father—as if man's utterance no longer counted beside the complete power and exactness of the all-carrying, almighty word (Heb. 1, 3)—for language can exist only in the light of freedom, and the totally free word of God gives man's utterance its freedom. Nevertheless, man can answer this eternal word only by giving himself over to it freely and responsibly. Freedom from hearing becomes freedom in obedience. This freedom unites in a sovereign manner the free choice of the appropriate expression and the exactitude in the choice. The former because the eternal word is "Spirit," not the letter. Answer to the spirit can only be spirit, "and where the Spirit of the Lord is, there is freedom" (2 Cor. 2, 17), even in the creative manner and attitude of response. The latter, since "we all, with unveiled face, beholding the glory of the Lord, are being changed into his likeness" (2 Cor. 3, 18), not approximately but exactly.[8]

Here the mystery that we considered above in our discussion

of "open reason" culminates: the open is undetermined only as long as the act of knowledge and of love is still unfulfilled and incomplete. When it reaches its full measure, it becomes determined without ceasing to be open; it gains its final form which integrates all the earlier sketches and fragments. At the stage of the sketch the eternal word remains in the mode of surrounding silence; at the stage of fulfillment it includes all its holy silence within its super-word. Thus, the bible represents the surpassing fulfillment of all the mysticism of the wordless silence. Every fresh, pregnant utterance with which man responds to the God who lovingly reveals himself is heard and formed out of the infinite, silent firmament of being which arches above all that is existent—and at the same time out of the striving, suffering, and resurrecting dominion of the Incarnate Word of God.

But that the eternal Word can become flesh and a human word —a human word that will always have the speechless silence above it as its origin and its return and its ground—reveals an even profounder mystery of the eternal word. A word, even in the eternal, can only be something that is suspended and mediated, the product and the possession of a speaker who as such is not the same as the word spoken, and who, because he is "before" the word, therefore expresses something in it which lies beyond it. The Platonists and the Arians, who had the same way of thinking, placed the Father—as the "inexpressible, silent One" —beyond the multiplication of the word and, thus, applied the categories of philosophy too hastily to theology. In order to see that which is distinctively Christian, one must listen to the word of Christ and the way in which it refers back to the "greater" Father who is expressing himself in the Word he has sent. He must listen to the way in which Jesus, as this Word, rests in the Father, childlike even in the extreme exposure of his temptations and in the night of the agony. He stands as a man not in his own divinity but is related as a whole, indivisible God-man to the origin of the Father. The relation of his origin is necessarily the relation of his return: Jesus, as the Word of the Father which points back to him, now as a man performs this movement in the gesture of his ascension.

And yet in the word of a speaker there lies at the same time what is "meant," which, when one "expresses" oneself totally and, thus, "gives" oneself, can only be love: the "Holy Spirit." The Spirit rises freely from the Incarnate Word without itself being incarnate. And as every word implies spirit and can only be understood from and through the spirit, so the Spirit is truly and effectively that which rises from the Word, interpreting its infinite significance. And equally, just as every word is the expression of the creative speaker, and the latter does not conceal behind the word that he is its origin, but rather is revealed by his creative utterance as its origin, so the Father cannot be, nor wishes to be, known elsewhere than in the Son. The Son as the Word is the center of revelation by transcending himself "in both directions," and yet the transcendence is really the same, for in returning to the Father he breathes out the Spirit which the Father had already in the begetting of the Son also intended and breathed.

Therefore, not only human attitudes of possessing knowledge, but also, with the same power and dignity, the attitudes of trustful rest and acceptance in both directions point to the divine Logos: to the supporting ground "below" and to the independent, perfecting Spirit "above." The example that Jesus gives here is not only an "economic" model for created man, but is also the offer of a share in the life of God itself. The creaturely way in which Mary receives the Word of God spiritually and physically, and in the Word—without understanding it or foreseeing its consequences—agrees to everything that the Spirit will freely form and draw out of the Word, is the "following of Christ," the unique God-man. Her formability by the Spirit (in her feminine acquiescence), which is essentially readiness and devotion and the renunciation of any forestalling self-shaping, is the only valid and fruitful Christian way in which man (in his lifetime and after it) can, in God's sense, "make history." Formability does not mean empty passivity, because every seed of the Word and the Spirit that is sown always invites and makes possible a sharing in the shaping and in the responsibility.

KEEPING THE WORD AND BREAKING IT

Theo-logy—the speech of God, and in this speech also the speech of man in God—always comes from the highest height. Thus, a theology of the word about the word can consider the nature of language only from the ultimates which lie beyond the horizon of philosophy. If man is ultimately gifted with speech because he himself is a word of God—spoken by him as a unique invention and as such also addressed and invited to answer—if man, as the quintessence of the world, has his openness to everything and to God finally only in his having been chosen and in his responding choice, then as a spoken and as a speaking word he is only whole in this height.

Held by God in being, he is the word that God has kept. The saying "God keeps his word" is unimpeachable so long as it is God that is the subject of the proposition (for his word is eternal and changeless). It becomes even truer and more obvious in the light of God's triune relationship. The word that God keeps can—if the word is man—be broken only by man; but the breach can go so deep that it could almost become a temptation for God to break the breaking word on his side. In the Old Testament such breaches are apparent: when because of the wickedness of man "the Lord was sorry that he had made man on the earth, and it grieved him to his heart" (Gen. 6, 6); when "the Lord repented that he had made Saul king over Israel" (1 Sam. 15, 35); when God "repents of the good" which he had intended to do Israel (Jer. 18, 10). And yet God regrets this repenting and makes the eternal covenant with Noah and will be reminded by

the rainbow, in spite of any temptation to regret, of this eternal
covenant (Gen. 9, 15). And again, he regrets and makes the
eternal covenant with Israel (Jer. 26, 3), "for the gifts . . . of
God are irrevocable" beyond all historical repudiation (Rom.
11, 29).

Man is so near to the heart of God that the broken word of
God breaks God's heart, and yet, because he keeps his word, even
when it breaks itself, he keeps it whole, although it is broken.
One cannot fail to see the place reserved here that Jesus Christ
will fill as the Incarnate Word of God (and of man). Beyond all
breach of covenant and breaking off of dialogue he is the perfect
covenant and the dialogue that can never be broken off, into the
course of which God sets all that is fragile. The whole that he
created and that he found at the beginning "very good" can be
shattered into fragments only within this abiding wholeness.
Human poetry and religion sense on their level something of the
eternal wholeness of that which is not whole, but only as if by
transfer. In order to know how God heals that which is not
whole, one must learn from him himself that man is his creaturely word which has its existence in his eternal Word, and that
God, so that his covenant and his dialogue with man should not
be broken off, would rather let the heart of his eternal Word
break on the cross. Thus, the whole *in* the fragment only because
the whole *as* the fragment.

Man, to be whole, must make himself (and hence the total
cosmos, which is whole in him) the answering word. In order to
affirm himself, in order to advance to the fullest consciousness of
himself, he must express himself toward God as he whom God
has created in love and addressed. He can do this only if beyond
his separated possibilities he lives in the area of the riches of
God and draws on them in order to be himself. In the house of
these riches he is eternally safe and satisfied, and he, a temporal,
because material, being, finds a present which cannot be erased by
the future and cannot be lost into the past, but remains open in

promise toward every direction. He is not dominated by this
present, for language requires distance, free play, and the dignity
of a free decision to be faithful. Only in this freedom is there
mutual truth as absolute openness with each other. As long as
this truth lasts, man is beyond all concealment, and, thus, he
needs no flight into the future from an unpresent present, because its genuine presentness always becomes his past. The covering over of the fulfilling present is at once the discovery of empty
and vain temporality and, hence, of death. As freedom emerges
as mere indifference out of fulfilling decision through integration,
so out of full, "eternal" time emerges empty time which has death
in it.

The hiding of the truth by the tempter, which makes possible
the abstract, hypothetical persuasion to disobedience and seduces
one to an imaginary discovery of good and evil, has its counterpart after the Fall in the sinful couple's hiding from God and his
searching call. Even their evasive answer, which puts the blame
elsewhere, serves to conceal, while God's punitive words point
openly to what is revealed of pain, suffering, and death. The
covering fig leaves are exchanged for full-covering clothes made
from animal skins; Adam is cast out of Eden, which has now
become a contradiction, in order to till the earth from which he
had been taken before he was put in the garden and to which he
must return. Even the relationship between the man and the
woman now assumes a quality of concealment which makes the
other person truly other. God says to the woman "Your desire
shall be for your husband, and he shall rule over you." The
natural form of love comes under the sign of personal nonlove
(as drive and as power). It includes the total picture of pain in
childbearing, of life with a curse upon it, of the eternal loss of the
original Paradise, now guarded by a flaming sword.

We now know the word only in its deprived, depotentialized
state. It has lost its power over God, power given to it from the
strength of the word of God and as an answer to it. In this highest

empowering through grace lay also power over the cosmos: the naming of the animals made them open to Adam and put them at his disposal. The object and the word were one: "and whatever the man called every living creature, that was its name" (Gen. 2, 19). Before they were named and known by Adam they were unfinished. Not until they were raised into the light of his knowledge of the world and of God did they acquire a share in the spirit, which gave them with their name their final mental and sensuous form and released them from their closed inarticulateness.

After the Fall the power of the word no longer reaches into this sphere. It reaches at most only to the openness of being as a whole, from which the word draws the power of its significance, its universality, the fullness of the relationships illuminated in the free survey of possibilities and shades of meaning. But when it comes to the ineffable quality of being which can never be understood, then the word fails. It is now no longer transitional, in the trinitarian sense, but is more ephemeral. And where occasionally it is successful and reaches the heights, as in "immortal" poetry, it is darkened most by the sadness of finality and of death. Every outline which it cuts out of destiny and offers to the reverence of men moves us because of its fragility, because of the mere chance that snatches it from decay and makes it endure.

Only with the element of mortal fragility can the poet celebrate in song a supreme moment in the wholeness of the world. He can accompany his hero, dramatic only when he is vowed to death, but transfigured and reconciled by it; he can write epically only of fate. And if the laughter of comedy is not to appear distorted and a hybrid (in a forced turning away from the threatening abyss), then it is given to the poet by a redemptive grace which—vicariously for those who laugh—knows about death and darkness.[9]

The human word can sing of death, accept it as the unavoidable, and affirm in it the cosmic law of expiation, to bow to which sanctifies the mortal. The word, then, celebrates death, but only by transferring it into song, not by penetrating it. And if it pretends to transcend it and look down contemptuously from above—in the idea of eternal fidelity—then it is saying more than a word can contain, and the daring flight of the heart is not confirmed by things. What the poet is saying must collapse, become separated from the words it has presumed to use, and leave them powerless. Through this collapse all words lose their rich fullness; something hollow has come into them.

A weariness seizes the whole language. It is of no value to words to approach objects; they cannot hold them or save them from their fragility. The ultimate senselessness of dying blows like a cold wind through all the rooms of speech. Words, once seized by this weariness, fade and droop, and finally, detached from the trunk and the supporting branches of language, they whirl away on their own, driven together by the wind and then blown apart again. They no longer have any meaning; no one relates them to that which is whole. They are abstract "ideas," pitchers that one can empty and fill again at will. Finally, they are, perhaps, only "logical" signs for a finite, strictly limited content—assuming that in such finitude there would still be significant content.

Now it is true that a strong, trusting heart can, even in a time of the most extreme decay of language, swim against the tide and, as far as he is able, seek to give words new depth and richness. It does not have to be impossible, even if it is very difficult in such an age to be a poet and a philosophical contemplator of truth. Yet, it is more apparent in this age than in others that ultimate wholeness can be assured for the human words only by the divine-human Word. The wholeness which the human word always inevitably seeks amid the fragmentation by time and death is only possible if God implants within time and death a power which is able to focus the contrary forces in order to produce meaningful words. Death itself must be compelled to yield up from its frightful depths the woes of eternal love: *mors eructavit verbum bonum.*

Notes

1 The theology of history relating to language in the sense used here is a science which has hardly begun. There are beginnings in Hamann and Franz von Baader (e.g. his letter to Jung Stilling of September 5th, 1815), in Ebner (*Das Wort und die geistigen Realitäten*) and Theodor Haecker (*Essays*, 1958), in Leo Weismantel (*Der Geist als Sprache*, 1927), in Max Picard (*Der Mensch und das Wort*, 1955), in Gustav Siewerth (*Philosophie der Sprache*, 1962, particularly the section *Wahrheit und Sprache*), and in Paul Schütz (*Die Kategorie der Sprache* in *Parusia*, 1960, 529–591). Essential for the background are the philosophies of language of Wilhelm von Humboldt (*Schriften zur Sprachphilosophie*, ed. by A. Flitner and Kl. Giel, vol. 3 of the new study edition, 1963) and of Martin Heidegger (*Unterwegs zur Sprache*, 1959). For older theology see H. Paissac, *Theologie du Verbe. S. Augustin et S. Thomas*, 1951. For Protestant views see Friso Melzer, *Unsere Sprache im Lichte der Christusoffenbarung*, 1952; Edmond Ortigues, *Le Temps de la Parole, Cah. théol.* 34, 1954.

2 For the Greeks, cf. Gerhard Steinkopf, *Untersuchungen zur Geschichte des Ruhmes bei den Griechen*, 1937; Walter F. Otto, *Tyrtaios und die Unsterblichkeit des Ruhmes*, in *Die Gestalt und das Sein*, 1959, 365–398. For its revival in the Renaissance, cf. Jakob Burckhardt, *Die Kultur der Renaissance in Italien*, 2nd section.

3 Compare with previous chapter's treatment concerning the proportionality of power.

4 Erich Przywara: *Bild, Gleichnis, Symbol, Mythos, Mysterium, Logos* in *Analogia Entis*, II, 1962, 335–371.

5 Claudel quotes with approval what Chesterton says in *Orthodoxy* in this connection: "Christian truth differs from all other teachings in that it does not see wisdom in a certain mediocre neutrality, but in apparently contradictory states, which always seem to be pushed to their greatest extremity: joy and contrition, pride and humility, love and renunciation etc. As if stretched on a cross man experiences its uttermost tension and stretching power in every direction . . . That was the great teaching of Christian art and culture and made of Europe something other than this absurd 'kingdom of the middle.' " (*Corresp. avec J. Rivière,* April 28th, 1909).

6 Cf. Max Picard: *Man and Language,* translated by Stanley Godman, Regnery, 1963. The whole work of Picard is relevant to everything we are saying here. He also sees historical existence in an ultimate tension between a good (of the creation) and a bad (based on the "flight from God") diastasis,

as a "destroyed and indestructable world." Thus, he reads "the face of man," knowing at the same time the "limitations of physiognomic study," which lie in freedom and in its hiddenness. The historico-theological insight in his work is the continuous reference to the fallen existence as it pertains to the present. But it does give the saving element: not only the grace of God but the faithfulness of man which is helpfully allowed him and through which he can live, even fragmentarily, a whole existence.

7 *Philosophie der Sprache*, 1962, 80. Cf. also Claudel's philosophy and theology of language in his *Cinq grandes Odes* and *Ars Poetica*.

8 "Language is clear because of the clarity of the Logos and it is mysterious because of the mystery of the Logos. 'Language is both revelation and mystery' (Hamann). Language is mysterious even when it reveals; man's speech is even more mysterious than his silence" (Picard, *loc. cit.*, 71).

9 Ulrich Mann: *Vorspiel des Heils, Uroffenbarung in Hellas*, 1962.

8. MAN AS THE LANGUAGE OF GOD

MAN, THE LANGUAGE OF GOD

Jesus Christ is the Word. He is the word and language as such, the word and the speech of God in the word and speech of men. As mortal man he is the speech of the immortal God. The form of his word carries its own conviction, just as much as, and even more than, the words of a great poet are their own witness. The words of a great poet cannot be affected by philological criticism: they are what they are, and achieve what they intend, unconcerned by the praise or blame of philologists. Praise and blame will pass away, but the words of Shakespeare will not pass away. Equally, and even more so, is the word of God exalted above all positive or negative, analytical or systematic exegesis. It tolerates these activities, but they will pass away whereas the word will remain.

Christ considered that his words carried more conviction and were more effective than all his (miraculous) works, which were something like a substitute for those hard of hearing (John 10, 38) and, ultimately, only prove the words and are proof when taken together with the words. They demonstrate the active side of the word, the fact that it is only the word as the truly active Son. Word, power of action, and enduring suffering are identical in him. As Matthew says, "He cast out the spirits with a word, and healed all who were sick. This was to fulfill what was spoken by the prophet Isaiah, 'He took our infirmities and bore our diseases.' " (Matt. 8, 16–17). Thus, the word's outliving of death is identical with the resurrection of the Son of God and of man from the dead: "I am the resurrection and the life" (John 11, 25) is the same thing as "Heaven and earth will pass away, but my words will not pass away" (Matt. 24, 35). He has changed the silence of death into a word that is his word alone, the word of God.

Here God's might is perfected. Now as an immeasurably great power (Eph. 1, 19–20) God not only finishes speaking his own word of creation, but also takes as well the *no* of man and fashions out of it his own and man's *yes*. The dialogue between God and creation, Yahweh and Zion, becomes, in the incarnation of the Word, a single word which resumes everything in itself. It reveals the internal dialogue of God, it represents the world's affirmation of God, and in that affirmation it wipes out every contradictory *no,* not only symbolically, but also really (in the truly vicarious suffering for sinners on the cross).

Thus, in the one word there are two witnesses speaking (John 8, 17)—God and man, Father and Son—and in order to understand the one word, it must be heard and seen stereoscopically. "The Father who sent me has himself borne witness to me. His voice you have never heard, his form you have never seen; and you do not have his word abiding in you" (John 5, 37–38). And when the two witnesses "have finished their testimony, the beast that ascends from the bottomless pit will make war upon them and conquer them and kill them, and their dead bodies will lie in the street of the great city which is allegorically called Sodom and Egypt" (Apoc. 11, 7–8) for the philologists to feed on. "But after the three and a half days a breath of life from God entered them, and they stood upon their feet, and great fear fell on those who saw them . . . and in the sight of their foes they went up to heaven in a cloud" (Apoc. 11, 11–12).

The Word of God, which at the same time is the last word of man and the world, dies and is resurrected. He is contradicted, he is murdered, and he rises from the dead, in order to rise in the sight of his enemies in an obscuring cloud of glory to God. A philological method appropriate to this divine-human perspective does not exist. As one is able to describe the rhythm of a great poet's language by sensing it, so one can in faith (there is no other way) catch the divine-human breath of this Word. The Gospels are not painstakingly compiled collections of "sayings" (*logia*). Max Picard is right when he says, "In the bible the word moves always from the speaker to the object, back again to the speaker, and then back to the object. It is as if there were barriers between the individual words because of this vertical structure; one always has to pass over a barrier to get to the next word."[1] The words are not to be read horizontally in order to be intelligible; they refer vertically to the depth of the subsisting Logos. Thus, the parables do not make up a system of truth themselves, for the eternal truth cannot be divided up in this way. They all stream out of the same divine center.

Again, it is essential to see that man as a spiritual and bodily creature is already the utterance of God, which experiences itself as such and, thus, has the power to answer. This creaturely element is important in the words and being of Christ. But beyond this utterance God had held hidden in his heart a last word, like a last card which, just when man seems to have lost the whole game, makes him win—for man, in man. In the divine-human

Word man will always have to recognize that not he, but God, has spoken; man, with all his mythical foreknowledge, could never have hit upon the idea of the resurrection of the dead. And, yet, man will know also, humbly and happily, that this was not something that was just done to him, but that a man, one of ourselves, has performed the deed, and God could perform it only in man himself. The Church Fathers always noted that with admiration.

Thus, the cross shape of the Word made flesh becomes finally apparent: the Word descends vertically from the highest height, deeper than a mere human word can descend, into the last futility of empty time and of hopeless death. This Word does not poetically transfigure death, playing around it; he bores right through it to the bottom, to the chaotic formlessness of the death cry (Matt. 27, 50) and the wordless silence of death on Holy Saturday. Hence, he has death in his grip: he dominates it, limits it, and takes from it its sting. Thus, he has passing time also in his grip, not through a poetic, legislative transcendence of time, but by dominating the inner time structure.

Because of a temporal future the men of the Old Testament are already stretched beyond their finitude into a total historical destiny. In the uncountable stars of heaven Abraham *sees* in advance the number of his descendants (Gen. 15, 5). He is to be given in the distant future the land in which he is living (Gen. 17, 8). He "rejoiced that he was to see my day; he saw it and was glad" (John 8, 56). But the man of the New Testament has, in Christ, death for sin behind him (Rom. 6, 4; Col. 2, 12). The true life comes to him as his future in order to consign his sinful past to oblivion and make room for a lasting present. Edmond Ortigues[2] had a profound insight into this: the working word of God, the drama of the justification of the sinner, the movement of his conversion, each has time for its inner dimension, but in such a way that now the emptiness of time serves the experience of plenitude. Whatever the content of historical time in the past or the future might be, this content, seen from the point of view of creation, will always be embraced and measured by the form of the salvation time of Christ and, thus, by the form of his substantial, human-divine, dying and resurrecting word.

But now the vertical descent of the Word into the deepest state of the flesh is identical with the flesh being filled with the eternal Word of God: it is the rising of the flesh in the power of the divine Word. As "flesh" the dead Son is awakened by the divine speaking power of the Father (Eph. 1, 19), which is nothing other than himself (Rom. 1, 4). He himself is God, and in his humanity is dependent on God, so that this raising of the flesh can in no way be referred back to human strength working itself out cosmically. Dependent on God in this way, he provides for the course of time and its futility the way into "eternal life."

His temporal utterance, spoken or lived, has always been "the words of eternal life" (John 6, 68), the words of God which with temporal and mortal sounds and contents (with the help of man) pronounce eternal truths. This language is to be the next subject of our consideration. It consists not only of fragmentary sayings that offer glimpses in time and space of the whole which the whole, always richer than its parts, can never say at once. It even consists of words which have been debased, which have strayed into the *regio dissimilitudinis*,[3] the sphere of vanity, from which, however, the whole can be joined up. What does the joining is the fidelity to the mission of the Father, changeless through all the variations of human fate. This fidelity is enough. It is what can write straight on crooked lines. One can also call it faith, hope, and charity. It liberates the temporal from all sinful fallenness. It makes the foreign land into a home in both directions: heaven on earth and, therefore, earth in heaven.[4]

PASSAGE THROUGH TIME

The Word of God passed through time. Everything in his passage was the word and revelation of the Father, but also revelation of the truth of human existence. God wished to show himself in this life, but God wanted to manifest himself as the eternal Word to men and in this way, not just incidentally, but necessarily, show as an answer what man is before God and in God.

Man's life is development in time: he is seed and sapling, child and boy, man and old man. He cannot be both of these pairs simultaneously. His nature which passes through the changes of the years is subject to a mysterious law: in every stage he is a full and complete man in the creative thought of God. The child and the youth, in spite of their "immaturity," are not, as was inevitably believed outside Christianity, incomplete, simply half-realized adults. In his development a man does not *become* a man; he is that already. And if ages have characteristics which exclude one another, than the "mature" man, even the old man, will always long to get back to what he possessed as a child and a youth, but which he has now irrevocably lost. Nevertheless, the ages are not lined up timelessly and absolutely, like perfect pictures in a gallery; they are joined together in the stream of time, and the flowing itself has its meaning in just this progress with its irreversibility. The loss that this entails is balanced by the gain which the passing of time brings, even if it finally leads to the deprivations of age, the helpless wisdom of its poverty, and even to the clouding of reason.

People who have mastered the art of living manage to some extent to integrate the seasons of life: to take their childhood with them into their youth, and their youth into their maturity. Generally, it is in the second and third generations that the aging person is refreshed because the sadness of his leave-taking is transfigured by his moving renunciation for the sake of the young. Full integration of temporal life, however, could only be hoped for in a super-time in which with the eternal significance of every moment there would be given the sense of direction of the river of time. This hope springs from the dreaming longing of mankind—all the myths play around making the temporal immortal, free from the limitations of growing old and dying.

But today, now that the mythical friezes on the temple walls of human memory have faded almost to unrecognizability, who could concede even a shimmer of probability and proof to the fulfillment of these myths?

It is different when the Word of God becomes man. Then every period of his life acquires, even within its continuing unfolding, the character of a revelation of eternity. If the eternal Word becomes a child, then the child becomes in the framework of providential revelation the full expression of eternal truth and eternal life. This is true not only in a revelation or intensification of those eternal values that lie hidden in human childhood or are read into it by men, but also in a new way that transcends the human. The eternal Word could not have made himself intelligible to temporal beings by speaking in the form of their existence unless this temporal existence had something like a sense of the eternal: of having come from God and of going to God, a creaturely fullness of meaning and beauty, which reflects the eternal.

The Madonna and Child are, for the Christian, the unique, incomparable pair which places every mother and child relationship within the radiance of eternal grace. Even to someone who is not a Christian, who does not know about this uniqueness or consciously represses it, the picture is not wholly dumb. He hears something like a stammering sound, for sound and gesture are as much prerequisites for the clear word as the alphabet is for words and sentences. Thus, even the crucified Christ speaks to him though he considers him to be a mere man; but in Christ man as such appears to him. The resurrected Christ, the Christ ascended into an invisible heaven, speaks to him also. For the believer, however, the power of the utterance does not have its basis merely in a vague analogy between life in general and the life of the Word that reveals God, but in the far more effective analogy which sees the whole of concrete creation already designed in relation to this unique, overwhelming victory, and in advance chooses all children as playmates of the Christ-child and all men as brothers of the Son of God.

If Christ at every stage of his earthly life is the fully valid Word of God—not only when he preaches publicly, but also when he talks to individuals; not only when his word is written down, but also in the far more frequent cases where, not written down, it is lost; not only in what he says, but also when he is silent or prays—then human life shows that it is fitted in all things, apart from sin (Heb. 4, 15), to serve for God to speak through. In a far higher sense, then, since the purely human is involved at every stage of one's life, every condition of the Word made flesh is a final self-manifestation of the fullness of God, and in each of these this fullness is apparent. And yet the mutual complementing of earthly conditions is not removed by this: full-ness passes into fullness; fullness, without being subdivided, un-folds its richness in the stream of time. That his passing life is always a demonstration of eternal life gives the Son of Man on earth a highly mysterious relationship to time and to life. Truly, and not just apparently, subject to the flow of time, he, neverthe-less, is not swept away by it like us. Of course, he experiences like us, because he is a man, the emptiness of time; but he does not resign himself to this emptiness, but into the hands of the Father. His weariness and his occasional heaviness of heart are, even without his knowledge, filled with an unchanging fidelity of love which can appear more convincingly in weakness than in strength.

And, thus, because in his earthly life and all its changes there is already eternal life revealed, it becomes apparent that in rising and ascending to heaven he is able to embrace all the forms of human existence within the eternal. What the myths showed as a human longing, without being able to guarantee or achieve it, is achieved here once and for all: enfolding the already enfolded in the temporal. The individual figure as well as the sense of direction are enfolded in the eternal. This is true of both in such a way that the Son receives God's sovereign freedom and power over all his temporal forms and can pour out from eternal life his fullness into these forms, now made eternal, as he chooses, without doing violence to his human nature. He comes to some as a child, to others as a man: both forms are equally true, neither is just a condescending accommodation to the mental capacity of men sunk in temporality.

But the important accommodation does not take place now: it took place when the Son became man, when he decided to become man, when the eternal being took a temporal nature upon himself, and in himself, in his own unique person, undertook the translation of the divine into the creaturely, which he never sought to go beyond, even in his ascension. The various images that came to mystics in visions during the course of the history of the Church—sometimes the child, another time the Son of Man in Nazareth, or in the temple, or on the cross, or risen in his glory—each has its essential, and not just "phenomenal," truth, both individually and collectively.

True, the Son on the right hand of the Father is now no longer the child, in a physical, transitory sense, that lay in his mother's arms on earth. But he is the eternal child who has assumed into his eternity all the forms and stages of his earthly childhood existence because his earthly childhood was already the word of revelation concerning his heavenly one. True, the Son no longer hangs bleeding on the cross. But since the three hours of agony between heaven and earth were already the breakthrough of time into the eternal, as of eternity into the temporal—hours which cannot be measured by any chronological time, by any psychological feeling of time ("Jesus is in agony until the end of the world"—Pascal)—so the divine-human suffering is the most precious relic that the resurrected Christ, now free of pain, takes with him from his earthly pilgrimage into his heavenly glory.

Apparitions of Mary have drenched cloths with visible tears. When the parish priest of Limpias went to the altar to touch the crucifix that those standing round saw bleeding (but he did not see it) his hands were covered with blood. One might say that in the sight and the touch of this blood or in those tears of the Virgin, God had worked "wondrous signs" which were to "call to mind" the past suffering of the Son. But the visions themselves had no real connection with the present state of the persons concerned. But to say this is not strong enough. It is necessary to combine two things which are difficult to imagine simultaneously: the visions and their physical manifestations (obviously symbolical) are temporal translations—hence, intelligible for us—of experienced earthly states which went to heaven; they are no longer in "fleshly" and transient forms, but in "spiritual" and eternal ones. They now reveal themselves in a christologically adequate manner.

It is true that Christ in heaven no longer suffers, but it is also true that the phenomena of his suffering are real, and not fictitious, expressions of his heavenly being. This being is not a quantitative intensification of the joy he knew on earth with all the sufferings excluded. It is not related to his earthly life at all in this partial and antithetical manner—with the same proportions of joy and suffering—but, rather, in the form of a total transfiguration and making eternal. For us sinners it is true that we shall have to lose the worthless part of our being and our life in judgment and purification. In Christ, and through his grace, also in his mother, the model of the spotless Church, is everything that they lived eternally potent because containing eternity.

What else could "eternal life" be for a creature of time than an enfolding of his imperiled, exposed, and continually lost existence in the eternity of God, in which, by God's inviting, opening, admitting grace, he is given a share? This vision of the eternal remains unshakable, even when no cosmology of any kind can offer any clearer view of it. Indeed, now that this resting in God is withdrawn from human "imagining," it can be thought of without hindrance and envisaged by the mind in all its necessary radicality.

Infinitely varied are the ways the Word chooses to make himself intelligible to us. His humanity is an instrument on which every melody can be played; even silence, the pause, can become a striking means of communication. But just as varied as its melodies are the ways of understanding those melodies that the Word offers us. The multiplicity which is seen in the experiences of the mystics is here only symbolical and introduces a similar or even greater multiplicity of modes of encounter in faith and in prayer. One does not have to see, with the eyes of the mystic, the Word of God as the child Jesus in order to encounter him, by faith, in his childlike state. The content of the gift of the Word can be the same both inside and outside mysticism, and can be understood at the same depth, providing the believer opens himself and gives himself to the Word in humility and serenity.

THE WORD AS A CHILD

God's eternal Word was once a child—and hence he has always remained a child. He became a child of men because he was never, nor ever will be, anything other than the eternal child of the Father. Because he was once the child of men, he can constantly reveal his eternal childlikeness in a form that is human and intelligible to humans. We are able to see into the world of the child and make it transparent, without leaving it, into the appearance of God.

Man begins his life in the silent hermitage of his mother's womb, totally invisible to start with, but then known to the mother by indirect signs and later by direct experience. Later still, he becomes for others a living reality, again indirectly, through the visible changes in the mother's body. He advertises his presence long before his first sound is heard. The mother does not produce the child by herself. The "seed" of the child is given to her from without, in love which opens her up and calls her to give herself. The child is nourished from the beginning by the life of the mother. Without the warmth and moisture of the womb and without the system of feeding which is built up around the child, he would perish. The foreign seed unites itself with the maternal ovum—like the Word coming from the outside with the supernatural grace held ready in Mary—in order to form from that moment a unity which becomes the model of all the unity in the world.

The spiritual individual is characterized in word and fact by his indivisibility. That he has features in him of his father and mother does not matter. He is a reflection, in creation, of the Holy Spirit of love which comes from the Father and the Son and is, in its sovereign freedom, the eternal triumphant mark of the divine fruitfulness. But who, in whose soul the Word of God rests and grows, can decide what is grace from without and what is grace from within, what is Word and what is assenting response made possible by the Word, which is again food for the growing Word? The Word seeks to relate himself to obedience as a child relates himself to his mother (Matt. 12, 50; Mark 4, 35; Luke 8, 21). This relation does not affect the brother and sister relationship.

Both the Word and Man obey the same eternal Father in the same community of blood. Man as the fruitful, receptive, and bearing soil for the Word (Matt. 13, 23; Mark 4, 20; Luke 8, 15) is drawn into the laws of essential fruitfulness, independent and inclusive of each conscious individual act, which is the fruitfulness of the Word growing in him: "The seed should sprout and grow, he knows not how. The earth produces of itself, first the blade, then the ear, then the full grain in the ear" (Mark 4, 27–28). That is the secret of the supernatural fruitfulness of the soul: that it is aroused entirely by the seed of God (1 John 2, 9), and yet cannot do without the assent of the natural powers of the mind; that its willing cooperation, once the Word has been received, is the *sine qua non* of its growth.[5]

Hence, we find the use of the images of motherhood and childhood in relation to the faith of the soul most impressively in

German mysticism since Eckhart, but even clearly in Origen. Whoever takes God's word into his soul becomes its mother and can, through grace, help to bring it forth. But he can do this only because he is at the same time drawn into the eternal birth of the Son from the Father, in which, through grace, he becomes the brother or sister of the Word.[6] The Father "of his own will . . . brought us forth by the word of truth" (Jas. 1, 18). The Father does this from the free choice of grace, not from his nature, as he bears his Son, the Word. Yet through the word that he addresses to us and lays in us, and in such a way that there is no creation, but rather "giving birth," we become "a kind of first fruits of his creatures" (Jas. 1, 18), raised above other creatures by a special mark of distinction.

If, however, God the Father gave his Word in the Holy Spirit to the Virgin as the fleshly seed, which grew in her and became perceptible, which claimed her totally and toward which she could and did regard herself as a mother—precisely because her Son drew her into the same child-relationship with the Father— why should not the Word be given to us also as a child? The Child-Word in his quiet powerlessness can be so easily and by a thousand means rejected and got rid of, almost without believers noticing it (in the same way that human society is built on the tacit, thousandfold murder of the unborn, as if there were no need to waste words over that). The Child-Word clings to us and seeks warmth and protection from weak human flesh. "He did not come as a conqueror, but as one seeking shelter. He lives as a fugitive in me, under my protection, and I have to answer for him to the Father" (Bernanos). This is also the language of his kingdom.

The secrets of pregnancy are incomparable in their private sweetness and private pain. The new life, of which all one knows to begin with is just that it exists, becomes something independent and personal at a point that no one can know. Its emergence from God is just as mysterious as the resurrection of the Lord. It separates itself from the life of the mother in such a gentle manner that it is like the blossom which opens, swells to become a fruit, and, when it is ripe, drops from the tree. But that which nourishes itself so carefully has a law of its own. It assumes an ever more magistral attitude toward the law of man and makes it ever more serve as a handmaiden, just because it clothes its divine superiority ever more in the laughing helplessness of a tiny child. Omnipotence asks through a child; it uses the child's irresistibility, the unconscious charm of the child's gestures, in order to gain that which can only be given freely. This is an everyday experience. These charming little tyrants keep adults occupied all the time; their mother is busy with them the whole day. Even when they are asleep, one has to be quiet; and when they play, they often take up the whole house, and nothing is safe from them.

Sleep and play are the two activities of the Word that fascinated Thérèse of Lisieux, who like a real mother was constantly drawn to the divine Child in wonder and reflected in a quite sober, practical way about her relation to him. "The baby is asleep" means that it is not available, it must not be disturbed; one must be quiet, save questions and requests for later. It is not even the moment for demonstrations of affection. It was a mistake for the disciples to wake the Lord when he was asleep in the boat, although they were in a storm and the Lord commanded it. Children sleep longer than adults also; sleep is one of their normal occupations. Even in their withdrawals they make claims on the adults. And if the Child is the Word of God, then he cannot be left alone like an ordinary child even for a little while so that his mother can do something else; he holds his mother in a constant relationship to himself.

Because the child is asleep, the mother is awake. Because he gives himself freely, the mother is alert and watching. Because he has apparently broken off contact, the mother redoubles the communication. And when she has to sleep herself, then she must be

turned toward the child so that she wakes at its slightest movement. "I sleep," says the bride in the Song of Solomon, "but my
heart wakes." The mother's capacity of attentive readiness has
been activated by the child. She only has to open herself to her
maternal nature which guides her. Her readiness echoes the helpless dependence of the child. And, thus, it is again seen that the
divine Child, in becoming man, draws us into his childlikeness
by making us mothers. The grown-up son will look back at his
own childhood, which is still with him, and taking a child in his
arms will embrace the eternal state of childlikeness and emphasize above all its helpless openness to the will of the Father, to
the kingdom of heaven that is coming: "To such belongs the
kingdom of God . . . whoever does not receive the kingdom of
God like a child shall not enter it" (Mark 10, 14–15; Matt. 19,
14–15; Luke 18, 16–17).

Apart from sleep there is play. In play the child freely creates
its world. And the creative wisdom of God becomes, according
to its own words, a child, who, while the Father was working on
creation, "was daily his delight, rejoicing before him always"
(Prov. 8, 27–31).[7] But the divine play, either of the Creator or of
the Redeemer, is not something whose rules are known in advance. The rules belong rather to that fairy-tale world which
children, when they are among themselves or alone, build up for
themselves. They pull the strings, but at the same time watch,
fascinated, overcome by the charm of their own creation, and
enchanted by the fact that what they have invented has its own
laws. (An adult experiences this unity generally only in dreams,
when the controls of reason are relaxed and the imagination is
given free rein.)

Little Thérèse knew what it meant to be subject to the caprices
of the divine Child. Woe to the person who plays with him according to fixed rules and protests against the unfathomable
decisions of the Child! If that person truly wants to play, he
enters the world of the Child which is built up and transformed

as he goes along. Only one thing is necessary: a readiness to comply with the strangest demands. Now one is a tree, now a bird or a red balloon, then suddenly a horse, a dwarf or a giant, or the famous ball that is thrown and caught, fondled and then left lying in the corner for days or finally slit open in order to satisfy curiosity as to its contents. Children at play are often cruel, not from malice, but from the excitement of adventure. The objects and plans that are drawn into the game are treated roughly. Play knows only one law: itself. He who does not recognize that is automatically excluded; he is too old. He has strayed too far from the whirling spring of life into the arid fields of static reason.

But the child is also a master of contemplation. He lies in the cradle or in a meadow and watches. He watches for hours. One does not know for certain what the child sees or whether he is consciously aware of the object on which his gaze rests. His contemplation hardly detaches itself from the identity which the subject and the object made up originally in God. Thus, never in his life will a man have this look again, except perhaps at the end of his life when his eyes open wide, with intense silent attention, in order to see again that from which he had turned away as he strode into life. A man as he dies must turn his gaze back in a way that utterly humbles his freedom and his adulthood. This is what the Lord meant when he put the child in the middle: "Truly I say to you, unless you turn and become like children, you will never enter the kingdom of heaven. Whoever humbles himself like this child, he is the greatest in the kingdom of heaven" (Matt. 18, 3–4).

The Word in the condition of his humility becomes also as a child the Word of contemplation. The deprivation of all power of one's own, the incapacity of the child to act, even to express himself—this total poverty is the way and the condition of true contemplation. Here are gathered the masters of contemplation among the Fathers of the Church who were the lovers of childhood: Jerome, the man who prays at the crib of Bethlehem, Chrysostom with his childlike soul, St. Francis, whose vision of God was transfigured by the Christmas poverty of the Christ-child, Bonaventure, Anthony with the Child in his arms, St. Bernard, Tauler, and the author of the "Book of Spiritual Poverty,"[8] to whom poverty is the necessary prerequisite for all contemplation.

The "French School" has a harsh, almost sombre, picture of the nature of childhood and its fourfold "lowliness": smallness of body, dependence on others, lack of freedom, uselessness (Condren). Bérulle describes "the extreme poverty of childhood where Jesus is hidden and caught in us, whereas Adam lives and rules where the Holy Spirit is silent, while sin works itself out." Renty speaks in brighter colors: we must be "like a tool in the hands of the Christ-child, to do anything he likes with, in great innocence, purity and simplicity, without regard or concern about anything."

Then there are the founders of the cult of the childhood of Jesus in modern times. The Carmelite Marguerite de Beaune[9] radiated devotion to the crowned *Petit Roi de Gloire.* The image of the Little King was to slip from the horrified hands of Gertrud von Le Fort's and Bernanos' Blanche de la Force and be smashed. Jean Garat's biographer says of him that he "saw Jesus as a 'child in spirit,' not only in his early years, but throughout his whole life, and even after his death, his resurrection, and ascension."[10] Jeanne Perraud[11] sees the Child with the instruments of his torture; the secret of childhood is combined with that of the Passion. She even sees the man of sorrows celebrating the feast of his holy childhood with an enormous gaping wound in his side. This concept opens the way for "Thérèse of the Child Jesus and of the Holy Agony," and also for Bernanos, whose profoundest intuition is the identity of birth out of God and death into God, of the fear of birth and the fear of death, as the truth of existence in its Alpha and Omega.[12]

In this Bernanos has been helped by perhaps the greatest

glorifier of childhood, and the childhood of Christ in particular,
Charles Péguy. Even more profoundly overwhelmed by the child's
closeness to God than his more obscure successor, Péguy pours out
an unending hymn of praise to childhood, a hymn which passes
into the praise of night: sleep after all passion, sleep after all
adult experience, even that of the divine Son. After all his bitter
days on earth he sleeps in the arms of his mother, in the cool
shroud of night, in the hands of the Father which he cannot
feel.[13] Charles Péguy has captured in his poetry the true Christian
conquest of the night of Schopenhauer and *Tristan,* and of all
the desolation of the bottomless physical and psychological
abysses of modern science. Toward these abysses even today
Christians often have a defeatist attitude, but they are abysses
over which Christ not only reigns as Pantocrator, but also as the
helpless child that floats on the waves of slumber.

The regions that Péguy opens up to Christian devotion and to
the Christian sense of the world and of existence are of a richness and a fruitfulness that has not yet been explored. The spring
that has started to flow here pours from the eternal mystery of the
childhood of God through the eternal mystery of the childhood
of Christ into the eternal childhood which is given to men:
eternal hope. The language of Péguy's prayer has caught something of the tone of the eternal Word; it suggests in its flow the
life of eternity, which gives infinite joy at every moment, but
says infinitely more than can be said and, hence, would require
an infinitely greater number of words. The inner eruption of the
inner fountain becomes an outer stream, but in such a way that
it constantly returns to itself "and flows and rests." Faith and
love pour out as hope, hope flowers in faith and love; all three
are eternal, circling life, happily sealed in innocence and in the
untouchable, unconscious quality of a child.

For Péguy, God the Father is the Ancient of Days who is constantly moved by the divine Child to merciful love—the Child with
its tears melts hard justice; the Father eternally agrees with the

Child, and lets himself be conquered by the triumphant divinity of the Child, who is right because he is young. This is the picture, stimulating and moving, which arrests the poet, as it arrested Thérèse. The contemplation of faith will absorb it profoundly and go beyond it only insofar as it sees in the childlikeness of the Son ultimately the reflection of the eternal newness of the whole trinitarian life: of the eternally young, potent richness of the Father and the "youngest one" in God, the Spirit.

On no other point, perhaps, does the gathering act of the Incarnate Word become clearer than here. For everywhere outside Christianity the child is automatically sacrificed. Because time flows in one direction and irreversibly, the way leads away from childhood, and the thought of forcing one's way back up time against the current seems absurd.[14] Time in the Old Testament runs in a straight line toward the future; that is why there is no room there for the child. "How can a man be born when he is old?" asks the Pharisee, not only amazed, but shaking his head at the idea. "Can he enter a second time into his mother's womb and be born?" (John 3, 4). It is the same with the vertical, cyclic time of the Gentiles. For physical birth comes from below, from *natura naturans*. The return to the spiritual origin demands in any case distance from what involves one in the wheel of birth and death. The child still clings to it with every fiber; it is only the mature man who attains the height necessary to detach himself.

The eternal Word is the eternal Child of the Father. This idea casts an eternal light onto the human child, gives the lie to all the delusions of adulthood, and revolutionizes the whole of the philosophy of history. Now the backward look to lost childhood— as cultivated by Christian poets[15]—is no longer a romantic dream, but the longing for a lost innocence and oneness with God that Jesus and Mary never lost and which through the depths of grace of baptism and of the ever-renewed forgiveness of sin also always lies before us. Only the Christian view of the mystery of

childhood can offer a counterweight today to the heedlessness of
the belief in progress, whether it appears in anti-Christian, or
neutral, or even Christian guise.

Every child begins at the same point, in the absolute newness
of being, in the same absolute wonder which is the basic attitude
of philosophy. He engages in the same play, which is the complete superiority over all things, but without the cooling, resigned distance from them. Every child knows, or should know,
absolute security in the bosom of the mother, the father, and the
family. All the later activity and suffering of the adult has to
nourish itself from the inexhaustible store of this security. Every
child understands, or should understand, his speech as the answer
to an awakening word of love, as an expression of thanks so
obvious that it does not need to be even fully spoken.

Thus, the holiness of the highest grace descends into this forgotten sacred region of creaturely existence, overshadowed by the
period of original sin. The temporal, all too temporal, is made
secure beyond all perishing in the eternal childlikeness of God.

THE WORD AS A YOUTH

One ought to be able to follow the Word in the subtle changes of
his daily existence, from the emergence of reason to the discovery of the world—of love and hate in that world. To the
discovery of his own self—and who this self is! To the gradual
recognition of his own mission, with the youthful, shy circling
of its mysteries in prayer, through all the shades of human mat-
uration. Current christology makes it hard for us not to see in
the boy Jesus one of those infant prodigies who are able to
know and do things "in advance of their age," and, hence, appear
somehow sad and old, cheated of their youth. This is even more
so when one considers the episode of the twelve-year-old Jesus
which seems to confirm this picture. After this incident there is
no other description of the mental state of the boy as he grows

up.[16] Perhaps the secrets of this development are too private for the Father in heaven to expose them to the misunderstanding of men. It is, perhaps, already too much to hand over the strong mature Word to be broken and fed on. Nor is it possible simply to assume that the God-man had more or less the same experiences as fallen man, experiences purified of the coarser elements.

There, however, are two methods of feeling our way forward from what we know as the most intimate, precious experiences of maturing life—deeper than all the levels of obscuring guilt— toward what God desired to experience as man. Then, as it were from above, from the fullness of the Word of God, we can sense those attitudes and behavior—visible in the adult Jesus—which express eternal adolescence. The two methods cannot be separated, they must be undertaken together. Where the one breaks down, the other can help us on. Our experience, even as Christians, must be experienced beyond itself in relation to Christ. His experience, unknowable by us, must be made knowable by us, must be made knowable through christological grace and our experience.

Even so, the fifteen- and twenty-year-old Jesus is harder to know than the little child that has been depicted countless times in his mother's arms or playing with his friend John. But who is the youth's friend? To whom does he open his shy, burning heart? The passionate friendships of that age do not prevent an almost unconquerable loneliness. The youth Jesus was probably the loneliest among men. He has his Father above and his converse with him. The clearer his approaching task becomes, the less he is able to confide even in the people closest to him. The highest hours of youth are not those of communication, but the more difficult ones, when one discovers how little of the best, most important, and most pressing can be communicated. How much deeper everything is than "what the day thought," in the words of Nietzsche.

The child swam over this abyss, slumbering, unsuspecting.

Now he measures its extent: boundless! It is not primarily the experience of being lost in a world that is far too big—although there can be something of this in it as well—but the fearful, yet delightful, discovery of the depth, above all, of *being:* of one's own, of other people's, of that of nature around one. Existence, itself unintelligible, is woven from the stuff of wonders. Not the existence of the child in a fairy-tale world which veiled the sad reality of the adults. No, reality itself is what is wonderful: frightening and seductive, burdensome to the point of melancholy, yet inviting one to a secret, continual feast.

The shells of things break open, and at the same time the shells of the heart: the secret of love emerges from all forms and all levels. This becomes dangerous and fateful for the man bound by original sin. The lower, destructive forms overpower the others. Overhasty freedom becomes a new net; depression and a nameless feeling of guilt weigh on the soul. What should be a leaping flame becomes a low, creeping smoke. And yet, the fire breaks out again; enthusiasm dispels the fog.

Enthusiasm means being taken over by the Spirit, literally "having God in one." This is called more pallidly idealism—living for an idea. We may project this, beyond opacity, into the experience of the young Jesus. This enthusiasm or idealism is subject to the inscrutable hypostatic transformations from which it returns divinized and, yet, still recognizable. To be a Christian means not only being a child, but also, in a supratemporal and completely human sense, to be young. The Christian stands on the threshold of life where everything opens up, everything is promise, everything is bathed in a profound, not superficial, in a true, not "rose-colored," transfiguring light. For most people the curtain of cloud does not ever lift entirely in their earthly life. The sun shimmers through, but the full horizon is only rarely seen. It is even more difficult to keep the horizon clear when one is stepping out into life for the first time.

He who can do it is a poet after the age of puberty, when

everyone writes poetry. The others, if they still feel homesick for what they once saw, cling to the poets in order to let their spiritual wine restore them to a condition of openness. Through the reading of poetry the hardened soul becomes soft again, remembering what it was once or could have been. But whatever these means of renewal might be—poetry, music, country walks, journeys, change of environment, ways of training one's body, one's memory, one's senses, and one's perceptivity—time does its work, and even most poets are compelled, when old, to broach their emergency rations of stored youthfulness and use them up.

It is just at this point that the Word of God reveals his eternal, youthful power. He is youthful by nature; he does not simply put one into an enthusiastic mood which will pass. He imparts substantially that Spirit which makes all things new. It is, inseparably, also the Spirit of Jesus who was always young. And the youthfulness which he gave to his Church and his followers has nothing to do with that of those unfortunate people who have stood still and fixed the center of their lives in constantly relived youthful experiences and problems. These are the old men who are scouts or youth hostelers, whose lives seem frozen in an attitude of youthful activity that should have long passed away. Rather, one can observe the true youthfulness of the Word in the saints, who all live from the Word of God. There is hardly anything which is as common to them all and at the same time distinguishes them from other great men as this mysterious youthfulness. Here we already come upon the puzzling fact that Jesus was snatched away in the fullness of his strength, in the middle of the period of his life that the Romans called *iuventus* —between twenty and forty—so that he never knew old age.

Growing old can be a humanly rich and dignified experience, but it cannot, strictly speaking, be called specifically Christian. To grow old means that one has passed beyond the peak, one is descending toward the physical end. This descent can and must be filled with the moral strength of renunciation, which, as it

were, moves always one step ahead of one's losses, so that, if one's
mental powers are still free, he assents to them in advance. Human aging is unthinkable without resignation. But resignation
is not a Christian virtue. Christ was not resigned to his death,
nor were any of his saints to theirs (if they were truly saints), not
even when they were old. Thomas More on the way to the scaf-
fold was not, nor has any martyr been. Resignation involves an
idea that time is irrecoverable; this concept is alien to the time
sense of the Christian. The youthfulness of the Christian, even if
he is very old, prevents his childlikeness from becoming childishness.

What keeps him young is the youthfulness of the Word of God.
That is the flame that blazes in the Gospels and prevents the
word of Christ from ever being completely at home in the dis-
enchanted world of the grown-ups. Does not the Sermon on the
Mount, with its utopian, uncompromising idealism, appear odd
among all the other ethical systems of mankind? Do not the
moralists have to adapt it a little and interpret it *ad usum
delphini* in order to make it acceptable for ordinary people?
"This discourse is to be understood in a spiritual, figurative
sense, that is, as oriental hyperbole!" And how remote from life—
if life means culture, politics, government, and business—are all
these stories of the apostles, these stammering sentences of the
eternal youth John, and finally these flaming speeches of Paul!

Christianity established itself in the world of that time, which
did not lack maturity, virility, and strength, on the basis of its
youth, simply because the Christians were in their being always
a generation younger than everyone that surrounded them, opposed them, and persecuted them. Like boys who throw away
their lives recklessly and without counting the cost, for the sake
of an adventure that is fun, they faced death. Youth is used to
conquering. The glow on its face and the soft strength of its tense
limbs always arouse admiration and indulgence from age, even
against its will. Before the fascination of this phalanx of young-

sters, with Christ's seal upon them and his spirit in their hearts as a guarantee (2 Cor. 1, 22), before this "proof of spirit and power," human wisdom and politics fall back, as the Philistine army fled before the young David with his sling.

In his *Christentum als Neuheitserlebnis* (1939) Prümm describes this victory of the Christian on all fronts, inevitable from the nature of his being; the victory does not depend entirely on militant activity. The Christians knew that newness was not based on a temporal condition, but only on the being of Christ, the new eternity which has broken into time. Irenaeus was, as so often, the spokesman. To the Gnostic objection of what could be new in what Christ brought, since the Old Testament had foretold him down to the smallest detail, he replies, "Know that he brought all newness with him by bringing himself" (Haer. 4, 34, 1). And Hippolytus says in an Easter sermon,

The Virgin brought forth, the source of life lay on his mother's breast, the light received illumination, the ruler was tried, the judge judged, he incapable of suffering suffered in his flesh, the immortal died, the heavenly one was buried and rose from the dead. Are they not new things? What has never been part of the life of the world before, that is what is new. . . . But if it happens with Christ for the first time, then it becomes a new mystery: new because of the New Covenant, because of the new Church, because of the new salvation, because of the new kingdom, for your sake, that will save you and lead you by new paths. For your salvation is new, the way is new in which you are redeemed by the cross and the nails of God (*Achelis* 259 ff.).[17]

It is not a matter of counting up the various single truths which worked together powerfully toward this consciousness of newness: the redemption of the world made old by sin, the appearance of God as a child, baptism as the new beginning of life in the radiant purity of the newborn ("*Quasi modo geniti infantes*," 1 Pet. 2, 2), the transvaluation of pain, sickness, death, suffering, and labor in the world to liberating ways into eternal life. This newness promotes the walking of unsuspected paths whose spiritual fruitfulness is shown by Christ and Mary—the paths of virginity, obedience, and poverty. Marriage is sacramentally ennobled. Men are made new through the mysteries of rejuvenation: penance and the Eucharist. Pervading this "new" era is the whole eschatological feeling of time to which the future belongs. It is more important to conclude from this utterly radical revolution of all ideas about the world and living the Christian's attitude to life. It is that of a man who stands *before* life, in front of whom are spread incalculable riches that are truly to be his: "All things are yours whether . . . the world or life or death or the present or the future, all are yours" (1 Cor. 3, 21–22).

This basic feeling, which bursts out in the first centuries with an external vehemence visible in its political and historical consequences, continues also when Christians living at the close of the ancient world—such as Augustine and Gregory the Great— start to sigh under the burden of the world's age. Christian newness becomes more inward, without losing its extent, at least in all those who give their whole soul to Christianity and let its newness flood over them as did the first generations.

When faced with the saints one can understand why Bernanos refused to accept the "mature man" as the center and norm of life. He is "that legendary animal whom the moralist has thought up to help him make his deductions. This mature man does not exist, for there is no neutral stage between youth and age. He who cannot give *more* than he receives is already starting to decay. Even a careless observer can see that a miser at twenty is already an old man." For Bernanos the Christian is essentially the man who gathers together and leads the youth of the world. He is like Joan of Arc, who refused to be daunted by the "old foxes," the "people composed of old men," the politicians and casuists who burned her; she triumphed over them in death. "The gospel is eternally young, but you are so old," he says to Christians, "even your old people are older than other old people." But the poet's heroes, who are always saints, are, above all, young.

They are fifteen years old, even if, like the "country priest," they are crushed by the weight of physical and moral death. All their thinking flows from their youthful spirit.

It would be fascinating to trace the youthfulness of the saints through the centuries. Not only that of the great utopists like St. Francis, the adventurers like Mary Ward and St. Francis Xavier, and those who died young like Stanislaus and Aloysius, but also that of the theologians with their strict and virile work. A basic formula, like the one Anselm used for his conception of God, *"id quo majus cogitari non potest,"* is markedly the idea of a youthful heart. That idea, not of the "greatest," but of the "always greater," counters every possible opponent in advance. The same feeling comes with Gregory of Nyssa's "ineffable splendor" as a description of God, so awesome that it daunts any hope of grasping it entirely with the mind, let alone of putting it into words. It is the enthusiasm of Nicholas of Cusa, to whom mathematics offers the right alphabet for love and infinity.

This is the enthusiasm of the innocent pilgrim whose heart continually threatens to burst at the paradoxes of the inventions of God. Such is the enthusiasm of St. John of the Cross, who, in the age of discoveries, traveled through the lands of mystical experience, like islands of the Far East, and brought back strange accounts of them in verse. We must include the enthusiasm of Newman who, as an old man, resisted to the end the spirit of aging and ever more daringly challenged the world and its spirit. All of them (standing here for the countless others that could be named) have encountered the youthful Word of God, who has imparted to them his youth. Their youth is only the reflection and the proof of the youth of the Word that inspires them.

No one has perhaps fought more bravely for true youthfulness in relation to the Word than the contentious Jesuit, Jean-Joseph Surin. The kernel of his doctrine developed when he saw with horror that a large part of his fellow novices during their studies and later in their apostolic work dropped the manner of their original encounter with the Word under the pretext of the maturity they had attained. They held the view that the former direct comforting and overwhelming emotions they had experienced as youths were then appropriate to their age and to their just starting along God's path. But, according to their view, it is part of the prudence of adult living to overcome these emotional reactions in favor of "solid virtue." In opposition to this view Surin wrote:

They are making a great mistake. Just those true demonstrations of favor lead to holiness. Paul speaks of these experiences of fullness when he says *"ut impleamini in omnem plenitudinem Dei."* These men have a clear conscience in many ways, but they depend on their learning and their reason, and therefore they no longer savor God and do not share his visits. They are people who have a high opinion of their own views and believe that in order to come closer to God, all you need to do is to argue like the philosophers. In discourse with truly devout people they always have the last word, thinking that the open heart and tenderness toward God the others show can make them credulous and exposed to many deceptions. Their secret thought is that the soul is strengthened if it is less weak towards God. When they find that their devotions are arid they ascribe this to their strength of soul. They are not like women, they say, and God does not treat them like novices any more. When they were young they too had such moments of emotion, but now the reflection of their reason is enough to guide them in their behavior.[18]

Have not all the saints, after appropriate tests, followed the inner movements of grace and the touch of the Holy Spirit? That is what those too often fail to see who walk the path of the senses and of pure reason. That law is speaking all the time, but because it is very gentle and very deep, it is seldom heard. Only he who is inward, detached, and dead to all else, who is used to seeking God in all things, listens to it, gives it its right value, and lets himself be led by it, without letting his obedience suffer.[19]

The tears of the saints (Surin refers constantly, and rightly so, to Ignatius) are not something to be ashamed of. Their burning souls and their enthusiasm do not make them appear immature, and the sad adulthood of which their sons boast is in truth nothing but incipient, or even advanced, sclerosis of the heart. It is possible that the religious emotions of the novices contain a certain amount of a dubious sensuality, but these emotions are later purified and deepened. It is also possible that the Word leads one in prayer through ever new nights of self-abnegation in order to bring him to a state of pure, selfless listening. But to outgrow the Word, to acquire knowledge gradually and be content with what one knows, to manage a kind of technical mastery (corresponding to the work methods of an adult), instead of letting oneself be overwhelmed ever afresh, of listening always attentively, of burning ever anew with melting, helpless love, of looking up in wonder at one's divine teacher and master—that is not Christian. One must be led by the Word in the attitude of contemplation as in the response of active prayer, in apostolic action as in suffering with him.

The Christian has the privilege of remaining to the end, and in everything he does, a "poet." In the eyes of the children of this world he is a dreamer, not in the sense that he lacks the discipline of the Church and falls into childishness, but in the sense that he has youthful enthusiasm for a model which he has discovered and which he has made the idol of his heart. This model, this ideal, seems, for the moment anyway, perfect. His deeds, words, and actions are admired and imitated to the last detail. Of him one dreams, to him one swears faith and discipleship without telling anyone. He is an ideal which, if a mere man, soon reveals himself as an illusion, but if God in human form, keeps fresh and ever renews, even into old age, the heart's delight.

THE WORD AS A MAN

If St. Thomas thought that a man thirty years old was a fully developed man, we can agree, providing that the unique quality of his previous and his subsequent life is preserved. Christ revealed himself to the world at this age: the fullness of man becomes the vessel for the fullness of God. In this human fullness, though, the essence of childhood and youth has not been lost; yet, it is a fullness that still needs completion, because it is the fullness of a man and not of a woman. It is a fullness also that pours itself out in the kenosis of the Son of God, a fullness that, finally, is overshadowed by approaching death, for—as if it were incapable of further earthly growth—it is snatched away at the moment of highest potency. There is no experience of the process of growing old.

Jesus appears before the world at thirty, at the age of full maturity, beyond which no essential development could humanly be expected. The fullness of man becomes equivalent to the divine Word in him. But that means above all that he carries the burden of this Word with his whole, undivided existence. He assumes it with the sense of responsibility that an adult man has for his task. The long period of preparation has caused this fruit to ripen slowly to its full maturity. He has prayed, seen, been silent, fasted, and worked. He has loved his mission above everything and, at every stage in his life, has submitted, adapted, and assimilated himself to it ever anew. He begins his ministry with the quiet assurance which knows that it has behind it, as a tremendous source of strength, the rightness of the mission and his election to perform it.

In his life he has made actual the Word that he is. If he now approaches men with his word, and if they will experience it first and foremost as a demand, then he is able to justify this demand from the strength of his being filled by and sustained in his mission. He knows that without this he would have to offer men proof of the truth of the word. The demand would then be so evidently excessive that they would obviously reject the message as something which hardly came from God. It becomes credible for men only if he lives it out for them, not only now at this moment, but also from the beginning of his life. His existence is the basis of his teaching: that is the adult seriousness of the word. And yet, this is simply the basis for his even more serious, more daring activity. He applies the yardstick by which he measured himself to his followers as well. He does it constantly because he loves them, because they are to be drawn into the truth of his life. But he can do it only by vouching for them, substituting himself for them, paying for them. He makes up the difference which there will be till the end of the world between the theory and the practice of Christians. He pays for everything he says with his life.

He will do it visibly for everyone once and for all in his bloody passion. But the passion toward which he goes, with his face set (Luke 9, 51), and which is so surely approaching that it is as if it were already present, throws back the light of its fire into his previous life. In the incarnation itself he placed himself beneath its law: he must pay the ransom for every fulfillment of the word and every appearance of glory. The raising of Lazarus he pays for with his troubled spirit at the grave and with his tears (John 11: 33, 35, 38). By observing that power has gone out of him he recognizes that he has performed a miracle (Mark 5, 30). That is why the evangelist is able to venture the same conclusion: "he cast out the spirits with a word, and healed all who were sick. This was to fulfill what was spoken by the prophet Isaiah, 'He took our infirmities and bore our diseases.' " (Matt. 8, 16–17; Is. 53, 4). That is so much the law of his life from the start that it had to end on the cross.

But that does not prevent everything from happening in the most human way; there is the full, pure hope that the people of God will accept God's word, and that Jerusalem will be converted. And at some point at the peak of the struggle between the Word and the people, the human awareness breaks through that Israel will not be converted. The Word of God experiences in a human way that he is not converting, but hardening, the hearts of men. That is the hour in which he weeps for the city of God, the terrible hour in which he experiences the uselessness of the most extreme human effort. From this point he pays for his truth not only with his life, but also with these bitter tears. From them the Church is born, whose brittle, institutional side will be as it were the crystallization of this liquid agony.

But in all his extremes of humiliation the Word remains unconquered, and reveals increasingly his glory. The divine directness is translated into the highest human openness: there is no fear of men, no concessions in order to engender a favorable atmosphere, no diplomacy to reach by roundabout ways what could not be reached by straight paths. This human directness of Christ is so total that it reveals what Paul calls "the foolishness of God" (1 Cor. 1, 25). It stakes everything on one card, it calls on those who will not simply accept that which they cannot understand to "go" (John 6, 67). He can throw out his word like a challenge to those who do not believe and has no fear of rousing them to extreme anger.

Christ does not have two kinds of teaching, an esoteric one—higher and more difficult—for his friends and an easier one for the people. The same words about the cross and the need to follow him, to leave everything and everyone, which one evangelist presents as spoken to the disciples (Matt. 10, 37 ff.), another says were spoken to the "great multitudes" (Luke 14, 25 ff.). And he speaks in the knowledge that so far he is the first person on earth to proclaim the truth he does. All the truth of the Father is concentrated in him; he alone is the master of all the treasures of wisdom and knowledge (Col. 2, 3). This consciousness rings through all his words.

The Church will always retain the sound of his word, and since the word is given it to be passed on, it will speak in the same tone:

Beloved, you know very well: scripture does not conceal anything from us, God does not flatter us. You can judge yourselves how freely we speak to you from this pulpit, and even if I myself, or everyone who addresses you from this place, did not speak with absolute openness, one thing would still be certain: the word of God is not afraid of anyone. So whether we are afraid or not—we, who are compelled to preach him whom no one fears—does not matter, since not men, but God gives you the power of hearing through turgid preachers the voice of directness (Augustine, *En. in Ps.* 103, S. 1, 19; PL 37, 1351).

The failure of Christians, even of the official proclaimers of the word, can never, in the Church, be a pretext for softening down the uncompromising nature of the word. Its swordlike sharpness (Heb. 4, 12; Apoc. 1, 16; 2, 16) cannot be blunted. It will never be able to talk of holiness, virginity, poverty, and obedience any differently from Christ. And there will always arise in the Church men whose mission is to reemphasize the hard, virile integrity of the word: men like Irenaeus against the Gnostics, Athanasius and Hilary against the Arians, Augustine against the Donatists, Ignatius against the Renaissance and the Reformation, and Newman against the sentimentalities of the nineteenth century.

And then, there is the man—the young man—the last face of the Word of God on earth. We always tend involuntarily to imagine Christ as older than he was, because the weight of the word, its finality, suggests a man of fifty. But this was not the case. Perhaps Origen was right: by his brief appearance and then disappearance God spares the world. What devastation would he have caused if his fire had burned here for centuries? And yet, he does not go by himself; he is violently killed. His death is not natural, it is the opposite. Men shall stand eternally before this most fearful cutting off and know: *we* have murdered God, we have forced God's Word to be silent. He is not, like the Greek heroes, a man cut off young by the envy of the gods; his Father would have let him be longer with men. His death reminds us of nothing but his own guilt. Nor is he a sacrifice offered to propitiate the anger of the gods, like Iphigenia; those who killed him were not thinking of making reparation. John quotes Caiaphas' remark about the value of one man dying for the people only in order to make the contrast between the intention of the slayers and the secret salvation significance.

In the legends of the peoples the human mind tries to discover a tragic, purifying sense in the death of a young man. In the death of Christ there can be no question of any tragedy. It is simply the revelation of what sin is. "Tragedy," like "guilt," is surrounded by a certain sublimity. "Sin" is deviod of any greatness; it is repulsive, dirty, and contemptible. Here it is out of place to weep for the dying hero who is sacrificed. "Weep for yourselves and your children!" Nor is there any way of drawing the Resurrection on the third day into the structure of this "drama." Iphigenia is killed in order to propitiate the gods. Her death has an immanent religious significance. The meaning that the murderers of Jesus see in his death is simply "Away with him! Away with him!" That of vicarious suffering is expressly excluded by the derisive "He has helped others."

That this horrifying end is made by grace into the beginning of all beginnings has nothing to do with what the men are actually concerned with. Only from the retroactive power of this transcendent grace can we see the continuity, which the Word establishes through his prophecy of suffering, between the abyss of death and the Resurrection, so much so that he can even ask his friends in advance to give assent to his death.

The important thing to note here is the violent nature of his death. From the human point of view his murder is only crass sin, and yet, the sin is transformed by God into a boundless, longing remorse at having driven from our world the Word of God which had barely had time to be heard. Forever exists the inconsolable attitude of the weeping Magdalene at the grave, as she looks into the empty cave. But—beyond all the bitterness of Peter's tears— we can let ourselves be moved by the fact that the Word died as a young man and returned to the Father; that the curve of growing old was spared him; that there is no Christian wisdom of age; that Christ does not grow old with the old, but accompanies their aging with his eternal childhood and manhood. That his life breaks off at its height is in him finally itself a word of God: the word of his power over time. He has freely submitted to it; he has given his life freely and by his own power. But he never, neither in this life nor in death, neither in the soul nor in the body, saw corruption (Acts 2, 31). The human countenance is absorbed by and returns to the divine countenance.

Notes

1 *Der Mensch und das Wort*, 87.

2 *Le Temps de la Parole*, 1954, 8, cf. 13: "The structure of justification is identical with that of salvation history."

3 E. Gilson: *Regio dissimilitudinis*, in *La Théologie de S. Bernard*, 1947, 48–77.

4 For the whole, cf. *Gott redet als Mensch* in *Verbum Caro, Theologische Skizzen I*, 1960, 73–99.

5 For the motif of fruitfulness see J. Bommer: *Die Idee der Fruchtbarkeit in den Evangelien*, Diss. Rom. Angelicum, 1950; Franz Bockle: *Die Idee der Fruchtbarkeit in den Paulusbriefen*, Diss. Rom. Angelicum, 1953.

6 Hugo Rahner: "*Die Gottgeburt*," *Zeitschrift für katholische Theologie*, 29, 1935, 335–418.

7 Cf. Hugo Rahner, "*Der spielende Gott*," in *Der spielende Mensch*, 1952, 15 ff.

8 Published by H. S. Denifle, 1877.

9 Cf. Bremond, *Literary History of Religious Thought in France from the Wars of Religion down to Our Own Time*, 1928–1936.

10 *Ibid.*

11 *Ibid.*

12 Cf. the articles "*Enfance de Jésus*" and "*Enfance spirituelle*" in the *Dictionnaire de Spiritualite*, 1959, and the literature listed there, together with Zimmermann's *Aszetik*, 2nd ed., 303, and Karl Rahner, "*Gedanken zu einer Theologie der Kindheit*," *Geist und Leben*, 36, 1963, 104–114.

13 Péguy: *La Porte au Mystère de l'Espoir, La Mystère des Enfants Innocents*. Cf. also *Herrlichkeit*, II, 1962, the chapter on Péguy, 767–880.

14 The ancient image of *puer senex*, which Augustine also takes up again (*in Ps.* 112, 2) is not the equivalent. Cf. Epicurus, *Letter to Menoikeus, Diog.*

Laert., X, 122, and E. R. Curtius, *Europäische Literaturgeschichte*, 2nd ed., 108–115.

15 This was the basic theme of all Albert Béguin's books. Cf. his introductions to the works of Bernanos and Péguy, as well as *L'âme romantique et le rêve*, 1939, *Poésie de la présence, Cahiers du Rhône*, 1957, *Essais et Témoignages*, 1957.

16 Cf. Peter Lippert's meditation in his book, *Der Menschensohn, Bilder aus dem Seelenleben Jesu*, 1926.

17 Cf. O. Casel, *"Die 'Neuheit' in den Weihnachtsorationen," Liturgische Zeitschrift*, 4, 1931–1932, 83–87.

18 *Les Fondements de la Vie Spirituelle*, 1682, 273, 134 ff. But that was never the way of the saints.

19 *Traité Inédit de l'Amour de Dieu*, 190.

9. CHRIST AS
THE LANGUAGE OF GOD

THE PASSION OF THE WORD

The sequence of the natural conditions of the Word finishes with
the Man of Sorrows; the new sequence—the passion, the resurrection, and the ascension of the Word—lies in the region of divine
activity, which makes use of nature and extends it beyond its
possibilities.

To a still greater extent than before, the conditions of mankind become transparent to the conditions of the Word in its
divinity. And in the Passion (which here leads to the kenosis of
the Incarnation in its greatest intensity and obviousness), through
the sufferings of humanity, are revealed both the victory and the
power of God and the will of the divine person of the Son (and in
him the will of the whole Trinity) to let himself be affected by
this suffering. The subject of the suffering is the person who is

the Word (and the Son is the Word precisely as a divine person, not as a divine nature, which he shares with the Father and the Spirit), even if he requires human nature in order to suffer.

Rupert von Deutz looks at the subject entirely from the viewpoint of power when he speaks of suffering. In the guise of impotence he contemplates power:

He not only looks at the reed that is given to him in place of a sovereign's staff, but regards the true fact, of which the other is a sign: the highest power on heaven and earth, because with that reed and for the sake of that reed on that same day "all authority in heaven and on earth has been given" to him (Matt. 28, 18). He does not regard merely that handwoven purple which was laid about him as a mockery, but meditates in this purple on the purple Church, purified by his blood and ready to shed its own blood for him. . . .[1]

This way of looking at Christ's passion is perfectly correct; but it must be supplemented by the way of Origen, who sees in the passion of the flesh the passion of the Word itself. Three layers of thought lie one on top of the other and, finally, make up an indissoluble total picture.

First of all, there is the unity of word and sacrament, particularly in the Eucharist. Blood and water, which flow out of the wound in his side and fill the chalice, are the poured-out substance of the Logos, which gives himself in this effusion also as the word which we receive in the Church, the sacrament, the homily, and the scripture.

The bread which the Word of God declares is his body is the word which nourishes souls, the word that proceeds from the Divine Word, and the bread that comes from the Divine Bread. And the drink which the Divine Word declares to be his blood, is the word that quenches the thirst and fires the soul of those who drink it. It is the blood of those grapes that were thrown into the winepress of suffering and produced this drink, as also the word of Christ is the bread prepared from that wheat which had to fall into the earth in order to bear much fruit.[2]

Thus, we receive the word like the sacrament from the wound in the side of the Lord.[3] The "teaching" had already been identified with the "blood" of the Word by Clement.[4] For Origen the spiritual blood of the Logos circulates in scripture.[5] Augustine sees it in the same way: "The scourging of Christ is doubled and repeated, for his word is scourged, 'they heaped their blows on me and they knew it not' (Ps. 34, 15). He was beaten by the scourges of the Jews, and now he is scourged by the calumnies of the false Christians: they multiply their blows against their Lord and do not know it."[6]

Overlying this is a second thought. There is an aspect of the passion which is expressly related to the Son's essential nature as the Word: the tearing up, the defiling, the murder of his gospel of the Father, of his truth and unity. "That is why 'all the righteous blood that they have spilt' by perverting the truth of scripture will be upon them, for the scriptures are truly called blood and life."[7] The murderers here are above all the sectarians and the heresiarchs:

They crucify the word of truth in the scriptures by their false interpretations and kill it by their lies. They would like to kill it and, as it were, break it in pieces, because they cannot grasp its total immensity; their own vessels are too small for it. They are many who scourge him and beat him with rods, but he is silent and says nothing, and from then until now Jesus has not turned his face away from the shame of being spat on.[8]

Thus, it is a passion of the Word which lasts through all time, in the same mystic sense in which Pascal saw the agony of Jesus as lasting until the end of the world. But here Origen ventures the third and final step, by seeing the inner, spiritual passion of the Word of God as antecedent to and the cause of the external fleshy passion and by not letting one take simply the latter as the true, genuine suffering, and regard the former merely as suffering in a metaphorical sense.

He came down to earth out of compassion with humanity. He underwent our sufferings before he underwent the cross and before he took
our flesh upon him, for if he had not already suffered he would not
have entered on the course of human life. First he suffered, then he
came down and became visible. What was that suffering that he went
through for us? It was the suffering (*pathos*) of love. And the Father
himself, the God of the universe, 'slow to anger and abounding in steadfast love' (Ps. 102, 8), does he not also suffer in a certain sense? Or do
you not know that when he involves himself in human affairs in the
shape of providence that he suffers the suffering of humanity with it?
'The Lord your God bore you, as a man bears his son' (Deut. 1, 31). God
supports our misdeeds, just as the Son of God takes our pain upon himself. The Father himself is not without compassion (*impassibilis*). If he is
implored, he is merciful and shares in the suffering, he undergoes something through love and by it is transferred into those beings in which
he cannot exist while seeing the sublimity of his own nature.[9]

It would be wrong to call Origen a patripassian on the ground
of such words. He is only drawing the logical conclusion from the
words of the Psalm, "He who formed the eye, does he not see?"
and, at the same time, denying a physical interpretation of the
suffering of God.[10] For Origen the important thing is that, like
everything else in the human life of Christ, his suffering also is
truly the Word of God. His suffering is an expression of the
living, streaming love which—quite apart from the "occasion"
offered by the sin of humanity which had to be borne—could find
in all creation no better language in which to express itself than
the Passion. The Greek idea of *pathos* (which the philosophers
kept carefully separate from God) unites splendidly the meaning and the expression.

It would be the proper exposition of these insights of the great
Alexandrian if one were to follow them—at the three levels we
have shown—through the whole Passion and translate them into
the visual images of contemplation. One would understand to what
degree the Word of God, who gives himself as flesh and blood

and is slaughtered on the cross, is, simply as the Word, in a condition of sacrifice. He would realize then how near the unending flow of the farewell discourses is to the blood flowing away to the last drop on the cross. He would comprehend how much the cutting protest of the Pharisees (at his time or today) resembles the thrust of the lance. He would have an idea of how much of the thinking of Christians, particularly of the physically-minded theologians, amounts to an imprisoning and fettering of the Word, or the dragging of him before the court of human reason, or the betraying him, even by a kiss, or the delivering him up in order to release Barabbas in his place.

In this, so as to strike the Word at his most vulnerable spot, the word of the scripture is used. Knowledge is played off against divine wisdom, the recognized openness and weakness of love against the divine devotion, one aspect of the truth against another, against the total truth. How often the word of the Old Testament in some form is used as a weapon against Christ, as if this "sword" were not one of the swords of Christ. In the Passion itself there is murder after murder of the Word through the word. What Christ said about himself, his kingdom, his destruction and rebuilding of the temple, is turned back against him. The profound truth of the cross, that the doctor who helped others cannot now help himself, falls back as scorn upon him. The word about his being abandoned by God is misheard— intentionally, we can be sure—and turned into a joke. It is as if here, where all the elements are shattered and all light is darkened, even the alphabet of the eternal word is so fractured that no saving word can be formed out of it.

No one has ever dared to work out a "logic of the passion: to face the fact that that Logos, in which everything in heaven and on earth is gathered and possesses its truth, descends into darkness, into fear, into nonfeeling and nonknowledge, into the inescapable, into the abyss, into the absence of any relation to the Father who alone supports truth, and, therefore, into a hid-

denness which is the exact opposite of the truth-revealing nature
of being. One would then have to understand the silence of Jesus
in the passion as a falling silent, a failure of the Word of God to
say or answer anything. He would have to see the great flood dry
up and become just drops, but also see how unspeakably precious
these drops have become, condensed to the uttermost. Each one
of the seven words from the cross is a kind of totality of the
gospel, just as rich in the world and in God as the sacraments.[11]

One can almost sense how the Word changes its specific gravity: the streaming blood thickens and coagulates, and, soon, of
the unending flow there will be only the frightful rigidity which
shows that the vessel is empty. *"Stetitque oleum"* (2 Kings 4, 6).
The pitcher of the Word is empty because the source in heaven,
the speaking mouth, the Father, has dried up. The Father has
withdrawn. And the words of abandonment, shouted into the
darkness, are, like standing water, condemned to evaporate, or
are like the convulsions of amputated limbs. The question of Job
and of Jeremiah resounds in its ultimate form, but it resounds
only where it can, by its very nature, no longer hear any answer.
The indicative mood has been lost; statements are possible only
in the interrogative.

The end of the question is the great cry. It is the word that is
no longer a word, that therefore can no longer be understood and
interpreted as a word. It is the monstrous thing that still remains
after everything moderate, understandable, and attuned to the
hearing of men has faded away. In truth, one should hear in
every clothed word what breaks out naked in this cry. It is something literally unsayable, which comes from infinitely further
than is comprised in the finite dialogic situation, and is directed
infinitely further than can be expressed in the creaturely word in
fully formed words.

Many times before in the life of the Lord this cry smoldered
latently beneath the words, mostly in St. John's Gospel. There is
the writing in the sand—he is unconcerned about those about

him, who do not hear but only, as it were, see the lips of the Logos moving: "And as they continued to ask him, he stood up and said to them, 'Let him who is without sin among you be the first to throw a stone at her.' And once more he bent down and wrote with his finger on the ground" (John 8, 7–8). Out of an incomprehensible context in the invisible writing there emerges for a moment, as an interruption and an almost incidental reply, the audible word, and it dies away again. There is also the "crying out" of words and messages into the multitude: for example, the knowledge of the Father which only he has, and not those listening to him (John 7, 28–29); the promise of the rivers which will flow out of his heart and which all who thirst can drink (John 7, 37); the renewed statement that he who believes in him does not believe in him but the one who sent him, that he does not see him but the one who sent him. (John 12, 44–45). All these "cries" point to the transcendental relationship and origin of the Word.

There is that *vox magna* which calls back the dead Lazarus from corruption, a sovereign, and yet shuddering, weeping cry into the realm of death. There is the dialogue with the thunder, with the voice of the Father that he hears, but which the people do not understand (John 12, 28–29). This is a true dialogue which shows how much thunder there is repressed in the voice of the Son. "His voice was like the sound of many waters" (Apoc. 1, 15). Thus, one cannot gainsay the words of Nicholas of Cusa when he sees the life of the Son as the uninterrupted growth of this power of the Son which is more than the Word:

We have a Redeemer, who is a mediator who includes everything, fulfills everything, and is the firstborn of all creatures. This Jesus . . . spoke with one voice, from the beginning of the world, which gradually swelled until it reached its climax in him at the moment at which he gave up the ghost. This one voice proclaims that there is no other life except life in the Word, and that the world, proceeding from the Word, is

sustained in its existence by the Word and guided back to its origin. . . .
After this mighty voice had grown continually louder through centuries
up to John, the voice of one crying in the wilderness, it finally assumed
human form and after a long succession of modulations of teachings
and miracles which were to show us that of all frightful things the
most frightful had to be chosen by love, namely death, it gave out a
great cry and died.[12]

That the Word goes beyond the sayable, as breaks through in
the naked dying cry, though it was always potentially there, is the
justification of Christian mysticism. Nicholas of Cusa argues from
Dionysius up to St. John of the Cross; he also sees (at least in
outline) that the superabundance of the Word is expressed not
as a gigantic shout, but in the dying cry of a man brutally cut off
from living and speaking. It is the death rattle, to which the Holy
Ghost gives this incomprehensible power; it is a sub-word, the
sound of impotence which by the power of heaven, which reveals
itself in it, is chosen to be the bearer of the eternal super-word.
Therefore, all Christian mysticism of the "bright darkness," of
the failure of words before the majesty of God, of falling silent
after everything that can be said in Church teaching—all this
mysticism of the "abyss" and the "desert of God" is seen inevitably as true mysticism of the cross, as mysticism of a sharing
in the helplessness of the Word of God. Only as seen in this way
can mysticism have a place in the Church.

The inarticulate cry of Jesus on the cross is not a denial of his
articulate teaching to the disciples and the people, teaching
which lives on in the "articles" of the Church's faith. Rather, it
is the end of all these articulations, in which the cry is taken for
granted and sealed—*consummatum est.* The sprinkling of the
blood consecrates and speaks loudest where a formulated statement is no longer possible. The centurion "who stood facing
him" recognized in this cry that the Word "truly . . . was the Son
of God" (Mark 15, 39). But in the same sense in which the cry is

the end of the articulated Logos on earth, it is, as the cry of redemption, the new beginning of true speech on earth. As Omega this cry becomes Alpha, the cry of birth with which the new man breaks through to the light of the world. Thus, Baader can say, "After man by his fall lost the power to address his Creator and preserver as Father and his power of speaking to God atrophied, this voice—the lost word—had to be given to him again by the Redeemer as the Son of Man. That last bursting cry on Golgotha as it were loosed the tongues of men, and the earth quaked, the rocks split, the graves opened, and the veil of the temple was rent."[13]

But the cry is followed by the wordless Saturday, the great, silent Sabbath when the Word rests from its labors, following exactly in the footsteps of the Father. The body of the Word, wrapped in cloths and spices, rests in a cave in the rock, and seals on the grave prevent all entry; but the soul of the Word passes through the realm of death, the only "paradise" that there is before the resurrection of the Word. Again the mystics have contemplated on this and sought to make their own the sabbatism of the Creator and of the Redeemer, as one of the conditions of the soul in grace on the path between cross and resurrection, between the serene renunciation of the earthly world and the admission into the heavenly world. Maximus the Confessor brought these various ideas together in his *Gnostic Centuries* and developed them in striking interplay: The "grave of the Logos" is then, after my "being crucified to the world and the world for me," the quieting of all discursive mental activity, "for when all the natural power and movement of the understanding is removed, then the Logos rises alone, existing for itself, as if rising from the dead, comprehending everything and possessing in itself that which was created for it."[14] Or, expressed in another way, "The grave of the Lord is perhaps this world and the heart of every believer, the linen cloths the kinds and ideas of sensuous things, the sudarium the uniform knowledge of mental objects including the knowledge of God: the Logos was known by these things before; whereas, deprived of them, he cannot be grasped at all."[15]

Once more it is the bright night of Dionysius: not only the sensual man, but the mental and noumenal, must be buried. Even the Logos, who assumed the form appropriate to him, must lose his shape. The Resurrection goes into the shapeless darkness of God. "The peace of the seventh day that God took upon himself for our sakes" is the only way to the "divinization of the eighth day";[16] it is almost to be equated simply with contemplation. Gregory the Great completes this equation: "Divine contemplation is a burial of the mind in which the soul is buried. The saints never stop killing themselves with the sword of the sacred word and hide away from the face of God in the womb of the ground of the mind."[17] And like Maximus, Gregory speaks of a "double grave," that of the active and that of the contemplative life. Meanwhile, however, neither this mystical contemplation nor the medieval veneration, fraught with armed conflict, of the Holy Sepulcher, has penetrated to the deepest region that must be reached, and perhaps does not break out until the horrified cry of Nietzsche's Madman, "God is dead!"[18]

God's Word in the world has fallen silent; he does not even ask in the night for God; he is laid in the ground. The night that arches above him is no night of stars, but a night of dull distress and self-alienation in death. It is not a silence pregnant with a thousand secrets of love that come from the sensed presence of the beloved, but the silence of absence, of turning away, of empty abandonment, which comes after all the agonies of leave-taking, after such weariness that it can no longer make the effort of pain. And so there is the dull emptiness of purely human talking and thinking about God. Such talking has become a mere clatter of formal logic, empty syllogisms, because the breath of faith, hope, and charity no longer blows through it. There is no indication that God hears this talking nor that it is still in contact with the speaking God. Such a logical and mathematical skeleton is an expression of the fact that the Incarnate Logos is dead and buried, and that the logic that formulates truth is suspended for these three days.

THE RESURRECTION OF THE WORD

The passion of the Logos up to his death in this world, even if there took place in it an agony and death of logic, still seemed somehow expressible in the words of this world. But in what words are we to describe the logic of the Resurrection, whose nature is to burst open the graves of our ideas, to surpass our conceptions of time and space, to pass through in sovereign manner the closed doors of our minds. It is so spiritual that all the laws of matter are suspended, and yet so physical that the Son of God not only appears, not only speaks, but also lets himself be touched and felt, and he eats and drinks in community with his own.

The Word has become wholly divine, has remained wholly human. This humanity which was always an expression of his divinity and has now been taken back into the heavenly sphere is so naturally credible in a physical earthly way that no distance separates it from this world. The whole past of his earthly course is, as it were, gathered in the stigmata he shows and has taken into eternal truth. The stigmata are more than an external sign, a kind of honorable distinction for having suffered; they are, beyond the gulf between death and Resurrection which reaches to the bottom of hell, the identity of the subject in the identity of consciousness. It is always this man who suffered this life, this cross, and this death. "See my hands and feet, that it is I myself" (Luke 24, 39).

This christological logic, which, though based on the principle of the Incarnation, reveals itself most strikingly in the death and Resurrection, has been most fully developed by Bonaventure. Christ becomes for the logician the perfect syllogism, since out of the major of his divinity and the minor of his crucifixion he draws the conclusion which only he could draw, and to which all the power of logic reduces itself. . . . For the theologian who contemplates the return of all things to God and the reconciliation of the world with God, Christ becomes through his eternal blessedness the everlasting Mediator, for through the Lamb in the middle of the throne is all blessedness mediated.[19]

Thus, Christ is *"logica nostra."*[20] An unknown author (Kilwardby?) also called the God-man the *medium enuntiabile,* since he

unites the infinitely separate extremes in the simplicity of one person, which is why theology surpasses every other science, especially as no other can discover a mediating principle of such quality. He unites what would otherwise be impossible in nature, he joins up things which are wholly foreign to each other—virginity and motherhood in a single woman, God and man, Creator and creature, the simple and the complex in the simplicity of one person.[21]

Within the framework of this logic of the Resurrection there is a particular logic of the forty days, whose laws, just because of the tangibility of the resurrected Christ, defy formulation. This logic is removed at the Ascension into heaven and given to the Church as a mode of its experience. The eye witnesses created it, but the faithful can share in it according to the measure of the grace given them. From the touching and worshiping of the reproved Thomas there goes a direct way—exclusive and inclusive —to those who do not see and still believe. Similarly, in the turning away of the Magdalene, who wishes to touch (in the middle of the concreteness of Easter), there is an exclusive and inclusive way to all those who are not to touch, but have to let ascend. If the mystery of the Ascension is, thus, set within the Easter mystery—just as the Pentecostal mystery of the breathing of the Spirit into the Church is already present at Easter (John 20, 22)—then this proves that situation of the Logos at Easter will pass into the situations of the Ascension and Pentecost, and, thus, the full concreteness of seeing, hearing, touching, eating together, and walking together (Luke 24, 13 ff.) passes into the later figure of the ascending Christ. But then does everything else pass into it as well: all that the Logos was on earth—child, youth, and man—in the variety of his experiences among us?

The Logos of the resurrection which springs from the miracle of the display of the Father's power, integrating in himself everything that he was on earth, in order to take it away into the sphere of this miracle, to translate it, to heighten it, thus preserving his continuity with the realm of history, by refounding history from this new beginning—this Logos, understood in its newness, cannot possibly be understood from the categories of the old relationships. "The unspiritual man does not receive the gifts of the Spirit of God, for they are folly to him, and he is not able to understand them because they are spiritually discerned. The spiritual man judges all things, but is himself to be judged by no one" (1 Cor. 2, 14–15). Here we come to Paul's doctrine of the believer's being buried and resurrected with Christ, even of ascending to heaven with him, in order to make it possible for him by the "formal" articulation of the logic of Christ to understand something of the contents of this logic. The less one depends in this articulation on anything known from elsewhere, even if only by an analogy, but rather bases everything on the single, undeducible behavior of the Incarnate Word, which becomes the "syllogistic form" of Christian thinking and living, the more profoundly one possesses the truth.

Certainly the Father has set within nature likenesses of the unique events which surpass all nature, images which Jesus uses (in the parables of the seed, of the dying grain of wheat which bears fruit) and which Paul takes up and elaborates (1 Cor. 15, 35 ff.). But these likenesses find their developed sense only in

Christ, who is the unique gathering together of everything. That is why he and the Apostle demand a true, not merely imaginary or symbolical, death, burial, resurrection, and ascension with Christ, in order to receive, as "the body of Christ," a share in the fate and the truth of Christ.

The Mystical Body must be "built up in him" (Col. 2, 10); it must be "buried with him in baptism, in which you were also raised with him through faith in the working of God, who raised him from the dead" (Col. 2, 12). "The bond which stood against us with its legal demands" was nailed to the cross in him (Col. 2, 14), and thus "one has died for all; therefore all have died" (2 Cor. 5, 14). "One man's act of righteousness leads to acquittal and life for all men" (Rom. 5, 18).

To have died with Christ "to the elemental spirits of the universe," (Col. 2, 20) means, therefore, already to "have been raised with Christ [and to] seek the things that are above, where Christ is, seated at the right hand of God" (Col. 3, 1–2). It is living in the breakthrough which Christ performed and only in this way made available to us: it is to "have put off the old nature with its practices and have put on the new nature" (Col. 2, 9–10). This action of "putting off" and "putting on" is not Gnostic or contemplative, remote from the world, but arises in the concrete and active performing with Christ of his act: "Put on then, as God's chosen ones, holy and beloved, compassion, kindness, lowliness, meekness, and patience, forbearing one another and . . . forgiving each other; as the Lord has forgiven you, so you must also forgive. And above all these put on love, which binds everything together in perfect harmony" (Col. 3, 12–14).

Ethics flow from the christological logic of death and Resurrection, for logic gives one the capacity to recognize them as credible and to undergo them with Christ. The "new creation" (Gal. 6, 15), the "new man" (Eph. 2, 15; 4, 24) on "the new and living way" (Heb. 10, 20), receives not only a new spirit, but also new senses with which to grasp the resurrected Christ and his spiritual-bodily reality in commandment, word, sacrament, and life: new wine in fresh wineskins (Matt. 9, 17). Only the new man has sufficient powers of understanding to hear the word of the Resurrection. He must be capable of accepting it in all its concreteness and physicalness, without spiritualizing it and, at the same time, without holding on to it. He must allow it every form of ascension and spiritual existence. Indeed, he must always let himself in this process be ever newly made physical and spiritual with Christ.

As, however, he himself has not yet been resurrected in the body, he shares in the Resurrection only through a daily "wasting away" of his old nature (2 Cor. 4, 16). He gains the necessary power only if he is daily assimilated to Christ through grace. Earthly men often fail to recognize the risen Lord; they walk along talking to him without seeing the person that is speaking to them. Resurrection-eyes are not set in us like a natural organ, but only lent to us every time the old grave is broken open, and the new truth shines forth.

The Magdalene does not only speak, through her veil of tears, with the angels; she even turns around the first time and still does not recognize Jesus, whom she takes to be the gardener. She does not recognize his voice or his form (John 20, 14). Only when she turns round for a second time (John 20, 16), only when the Word of the Resurrection addresses her directly, does the veil of Holy Saturday fall from her eyes. The Emmaus disciples felt their hearts burn within them as they were talking to the Word as he interpreted scripture, but the mist before their vision was not dispelled. Only as he vanished did the Word take away with him the bands from their eyes and ears. The fishermen by the lake go further than that, in that they not only answer the Word standing on the shore and giving them instructions, but also expressly obey him, though with their minds clouded until the miracle gives them understanding. Their understanding is not complete, since at breakfast "none of the disciples dared to ask him, 'Who

are you?' They knew it was the Lord" (John 21, 12). Their attitude is one which alternates between intimate understanding and
a hesitant feeling of strangeness.

The obedience of those fishing in Peter's ship, confirmed and
given to them by the resurrected Christ, is present, calm and
constant, in the depth of their souls; but it does not penetrate
with the same force into their conscious minds. The senses and
thoughts of the outer man, turned toward the world, share in the
world of the Resurrection only fleetingly. Thus, the disciples
doubt the message of the women; Thomas doubts the testimony
of his fellow disciples. Even on the mountain in Galilee to which
the Lord has directed them and where, confirming and rewarding
their obedience, he appears to them, "some doubted" out of the
eleven (Matt. 28, 17). It is a not-being-able-to-believe in the
middle of faith: whether it is from fear and shock (Luke 24, 37),
as in the storm on the lake of Galilee, or afterward from the
superabundance of the evidence given to them of sight and of
touch ("they still disbelieved for joy, and wondered" Luke 24,
41).

The Church is reproached by the Lord for its unreadiness for
the Word of the resurrection. In the Gospel of Mark the confusion is so great—the women fail to deliver the message of the
Resurrection from sheer fear (16, 8), the mourning and weeping
disciples do not believe Mary Magdalene (16, 10–11), nor even
the disciples returning from Emmaus (16, 13)—that the Lord,
when he appears to them in the middle of a meal, "upbraided
them for their unbelief and hardness of heart, because they had
not believed those who saw him after he had risen" (16, 14). He
uses similar words of judgment to the Emmaus disciples, words
that he used formerly to those whose minds were on fleshy things:
"O foolish men, and slow of heart to believe all that the prophets
have spoken!" (Luke 24, 25). The joy and closeness of Easter
require a simultaneous word of judgment, as is given finally in
the epistles of the Apocalypse: seated at the right hand of God,

the Word, as a Bridegroom, judges, until the end of the world, his bride, the Church, with the sharpness of the sword.[22]

The whole judging function of separating out, of acceptance and rejection, is performed within the love relationship itself, in the fire of purgatory, which assumes that the "keys of . . . Hades" are in the hand of the swordbearer (Apoc. 1, 18). Thus, the Church is constantly adapted and assimilated anew, in all its various historical forms, to the Word. Here we can see how much the grace of the Church, in its ontic, sacramental side, involves a commitment to the Word, because of the Word's commitment to the Church.

The sovereign freedom with which the resurrected Christ reveals himself to his own again confirms the accommodation theory of Origen, which emphasizes two things: the freedom of Christ's choosing to be seen, as opposed to the lack of this choice with the material things of this world of the senses, and the freedom of the shape in which he desires to be seen. "Physical things cannot do anything about being seen by some one. Higher, divine beings, however, are not seen unless they want to be, even if they are present, and it is their free decision whether they are seen or not." All were able to see the physical body of Christ. "But that which made him Christ they were unable to see in him. Only those saw Jesus whom he considered worthy of seeing him."[23] "Perhaps the Word of God appears in different intensities, according to the capacity of the various souls seeing him. . . ."[24] The apparition stands in an essential relationship with the consciousness into which it shines.[25] The expression that Mark uses for the Emmaus disciples justifies this view: "After this he appeared *in another form* to two of them, as they were walking into the country" (Mark 16, 12); and, in view of Luke, one would like to translate it as "in a strange form." But what is accommodated is always the real, risen man in God, and even the choice of the form depends partly on the integration of his really lived earthly existence into the glory of God.

THE ASCENSION OF THE WORD

Although the Resurrection can take place only in the heaven of the Father, and, thus, already contains in itself the Ascension, the latter is shown by the Word to be a separate event. It is an event which does not so much redetermine his own relationship to heaven, as rather his relationship to the world. The period of the forty days with the particular tangibility of the Resurrection appearances removes it, together with the rest of the earthly life of the Lord, to heaven. To describe this as a "spiritualization" would be inaccurate, at least as long as one is thinking of the human spirit and not the Holy Spirit.

The Ascension is the final "divinization" of the completed mission, its passage into the eternity of the Father. It is the lifting up of the whole cycle of actions and suffering into the potency of God, apparently in distancing it from earthly events. But the Ascension is not a turning away or an alienation from earth; rather, it is a regular relationship to earth, but one no longer bound to specific times and places, and high enough to relate all times and places to itself. Without the Ascension it would inevitably have seemed as if the Word of God which was heard between the years one and thirty-three of the new reckoning were subject to the laws of historical effect. Without the Ascension it would have appeared as if, for example, the land where Christ appeared were truly a "holy land," or as if one had some kind of advantage over other Christians if one had been to Palestine, or as if it mattered in whose hands politically the "holy places" lie. If there had been no Ascension it would have seemed as if those people were privileged who happened to be the contemporaries of Jesus, or who stood nearer in time to early Christianity, because the historical working-out of an idea is a wave moving out concentrically, spreading, but slowly losing its force as it does so.

But the Ascension was no vague end, trailing away into the infinite, for the mission of Jesus. It was a clear-cut, historically exact, and identifiable event which took place on a walk together from the town to the Mount of Olives. It happened after a particular conversation, a commission, and a promise to remain always to the end and to return visibly at the end. It was an event of tremendous physical plasticity, particularly because of the cloud which receives him. The word of Christ was followed by the word of the angels, who take up the word as it fades physically and translate it into the new form of the word of the Church. This conclusion has none of the emotion of leave-taking about it: sadness, like the old leaven, was swept out at Easter (doubting Thomas is a straggler).

The Ascension leaves behind in the souls of the disciples a "great joy" (Luke 24, 52). Grief at the departure of the Lord belongs chronologically before the Passion: here the disciples are grieving like the woman whose hour has come, and the Lord comforted them by saying that his going away was for their good (John 16, 6–7). "So you have sorrow now, but I will see you again and your hearts will rejoice, and no one will take your joy from you" (John 16, 22). It is the reunion of Easter, and the joy of Easter is not darkened by the Ascension. For it promises the pouring out of the Holy Spirit, which can only take place when the Word, returned to the Father, transforms, through his human nature which had entered into the one breath of the Father and the Son, the outpouring of the Spirit within the divine nature into world history for salvation.

Thus, the spirit can become the perfecting representative of the Word:

I have yet many things to say to you, but you cannot bear them now. When the Spirit of truth comes, he will guide you into all the truth; for he will not speak on his own authority, but whatever he hears he will speak, and he will declare to you the things that are to come. He will glorify me, for he will take what is mine and declare it to you. All that the Father has is mine; therefore I said that he will take what is mine and declare it to you (John 16, 12–15).

This extraordinary continuation, this passage of the Word into something even greater and ultimate, the surprise of the trans-figured end becoming a new beginning, the sending of a new divine person, outshines anything that might suggest an "at-mosphere of the end." In God there is no end, only a breakup of what appeared to be final and finite, showing that it is really infinite; and it is to be understood not only backward in time, but forward, prophetically. The sending of the Spirit marks the beginning of the prophetic interpretation of the Word. Because the Word is interpreted by the Spirit, which constantly proceeds afresh from the Father and the Son, there is no danger that the age of interpretation will become decadent.

There is nothing of resignation about Church history. What-ever "fullness," whatever "height and depth, breadth and length" may lie in the word of the Son, the Spirit that "searches the depths of God" and moves, thus, in its own element, will profess it, as and when it pleases to blow. It will bring forth things which lay hidden, confined in the letter like the tree in the kernel of the fruit, hidden even from the Church which was made the storehouse of faith and to which the seeds of all the truth to be sown were entrusted. It is as if the truth of Christ, even the truth of his earthly life, suffering, and death, could only bloom fully when his humanity was translated into the life of heaven. It is no artificial transplantation which the Holy Spirit performs in the Church, by, say, drawing a moral from past history or even from supratemporal, eternally valid truths. It can read from the heavenly presence of the Incarnate Word, from the eternal unfolding of his earthly existence, what it has to com-municate to the earthly Church at every stage (and thus "take what is mine"), without, to the end of the world, fear of ever having to say the same thing.

The event of Pentecost remains connected to the Ascension, to the precise event.

And when he had said this, as they were looking on, he was lifted up, and a cloud took him out of their sight. And while they were gazing into heaven as he went, behold, two men stood by them in white robes, and said, "Men of Galilee, why do you stand looking up into heaven? This Jesus, who was taken up from you into heaven, will come in the same way as you saw him go into heaven." (Acts 1, 9–12).

The event is the indication of the border, the making evident of the vertical transcendence of time together with its contents into eternity. The earthly becomes suspended; its course can be followed for a little while, but then it is removed from sight by a veil. Eyes remain lifted, held by the rising movement; they follow, without seeing, what is enfolded in the cloud, and beyond it perceive the goal. But heaven, embodied by the angels, is already standing "by" the ecstatic watchers and in bringing back their attention calls them to their earthly mission. The cloud, as on Tabor, in the old temple, and the tabernacle of the covenant, represents at once both the manifestation and the concealment of the glory of God—a manifestation through concealment, an experience through nonexperience, an assured presence through apparent absence. It is the world of sense trying itself in nonsensuous transcendence, but also transcendence trying itself in a transformed world of sense.

Luke adds three features in his gospel: the blessing of the Lord as he departs, the worshipping of him by the disciples (not attested by all the manuscripts), and the great joy as they return —three features that affect and refer to one another. The Word of God disappears with a blessing, and this disappearance is the last in the succession of Easter disappearances, in which the Word gives himself as he departs, lets himself be grasped as he slips away, as it were, through the mesh, so that blessing and withdrawal make up, for those looking after him, a single gesture. And the fixed upward look, where sight fails, becomes adoration. Indeed, all adoration and all contemplating has here its foundation and home: in this following up of the Word, whose earthly form shows by its movement the way toward God. As he departs he indicates the direction in which the faithful must look in order to observe the heavenly continuation, the divine translation.

Every word of God must be looked at in this way: moving away out of the fullness of its earthly reality into the fullness of God— *ut dum visibiliter Deum congnoscimus, per hunc in invisibilium amorem rapiamur.* None of the three stages can be dispensed with: the visible, the cloud of the Kabôd, then the invisible, indicated by the first stage, but concealed by the cloud. There is, too, the corresponding tripartite contemplative organ of faith: vision, the breaking-off of vision, and the continuation of vision in nonvision, in worship, where the divine form of the Word takes over. And this vision passes into the joy of the earthly task, whether this is active work ("to the ends of the earth"), or liturgical prayer together ("and [they] were continually in the temple" Luke 24, 53), or, within this, contemplation ("All these with one accord devoted themselves to prayer" Acts 1, 14).

The masters of the contemplation of the ascending Word are the Greeks, with their *eros* of the transfiguring rise into the divine and the boundless. The idea of the "gardner" and the *"noli me tangere,"* as not holding on to the Word on earth, but letting him ascend, is charmingly and passionately worked out by them in variations.[26] Augustine joins in with the idea of the completion of the Ascension in one's heart, as a longing for the home where Christ lives:

As if the Lord were saying to the apostles: "You do not want to let me go, just as everyone likes to hold his friend back and says to him, as it were, stay with us just a little longer, our soul delights in the sight of you—but it is better that you no longer see this flesh and are mindful instead of the divine. I am removing myself from you outwardly, but I am filling you with myself from within." Does Christ, then, enter the heart according to the flesh, with the flesh? In his divinity he possesses the heart. In his flesh he speaks to the heart by the sight of him, and he exhorts us from outside us, but inside us he takes up his dwelling place, so that we are converted and vivified inwardly by him and fashioned out of him, the uncreated model of all creation.[27]

The man who translated the Greek approach to the Ascension into the Western world is Duns Scotus. He considers the ecstatic upward look of the apostles and contemplates the passing of the humanity of the Word into the dimensions of divinity.

I tread unhesitatingly in the footsteps of those who soberly declare that the humanity of our Lord Jesus Christ is so united to his divinity that, while still preserving the essence of the two natures, they form in and with each other a single unity . . . and as his divinity transcends all reason, so does his humanity, which has been raised above the totality of visible and spiritual creatures, above all places and times, above all description and definition, . . . [it] has been raised, as it were, above being, ungraspable and indiscoverable by all creatures.[28]

Scotus is taken up by Nicholas of Cusa. The latter is concerned to show that the raising of the Word of God puts him at an equal distance from and an equal proximity to all creatures, places, and times. In fact, this transcendent position makes the Word the basis of all the world's resurrection and ascension.

His ascension takes place beyond all the motions of the transient world and all the influence of the heavenly spheres, for although he is in his divinity omnipresent, his place is properly that where there is no change, no suffering, no grief, as there is in the world of time. We say that this place of eternal joy and eternal peace exists above the skies, although it cannot be perceived, described, or defined in terms of place. This place is the center and the inclusive periphery of all spiritual beings, and it is above everything, because the spiritual power of reason penetrates everything. Thus, Christ has ascended above every place and every time, since he is truth itself and does not sit, as it were, at the edge of (the cosmos), but in the center—as he is the center of all spiritual, reasonable beings—as their life.[29]

From Nicholas of Cusa on, the ascended nature of Christ can be seriously considered as the canon of all creaturely existence. This is, for example, the justification of the visionary world of Hildegard, who sees the cosmos, its whole terrifying reality and brutal facticity, as raised to a heavenly potential. The foundation is given also for baroque and modern spirituality, insofar as they strive particularly to see the separate mysteries of the Word's earthly life as integrated into his timeless state: the devotion to the pierced and flaming heart, the devotion to the ever actual Passion (from Pascal's *Memorial* to Casel's theology of the mysteries), and Bérulle's devotion to all the stages of the life of Christ.

The Ascension, which eternalizes everything about Christ that is of time and place and offers it to contemplative eyes in a timeless simultaneity, is the basis of it all. It opens up that dimension that St. Paul called the "pneumatic." But precisely because the whole bodily life of Christ is raised by the Ascension to the potency of the man in heaven, the mystery of this festival cannot be a one-sided contemplative one. How could one by mere contemplation obtain a share in that life, which was such an active, fully-lived one? Being taken from the earth is the prerequisite for the new, final sending of the Holy Spirit to Christians throughout all the world. As the ascended Christ is raised above time and place, in order to reign over everything from this "center above" everything, so he renews also, in the order of the second Adam, the commission to the first Adam to rule and order the whole world. The apostles are not to wait for the end of the world and the coming of the kingdom, but "you shall receive power when the Holy Spirit has come upon you; and you shall be my witnesses in Jerusalem and in all Judea and Samaria and to the end of the earth" (Acts 1, 8).

THE WORD IN THE CHURCH YEAR

After following the Word through all its human and salvational transformations, we might easily feel dizzy, or even frightened, at the boundlessness of this depth and fullness, which opens up and gives itself to us according to an unknowable law. He gives himself first as the Word of the crib, then as the Word of the cross, then again as the Word of the Resurrection. He does not give himself merely according to the natural circumstances of our own life—when *we* are sad, that gives us the right to understand the Word as the Word of the Passion, or when *we* are happy, the right to see the Word as the festive Word of Christmas or Easter. Rather is it that the Word, because of the sovereignty of his choice, independently of any situation in the hearer, can choose *the* language, *the* mood that he pleases. Are we not, thus, exposed to the arbitrary power over us of this superabundance which threatens to break our human measure?

In order to banish this fear the Holy Spirit has channeled the fullness of Christ into the order of the Church and its "year." The Church year offers an appropriate framework which is suprapersonal, social, and available to all the members of Christ; it is sufficiently solid to avoid shapelessness, but wide and airy enough to allow that "blowing of the Spirit where it wills." The Church year brings down among men through the Spirit, within its plans and laws of construction, the Word that ascended to heaven. It makes present the Word in his one inseparable divinity and humanity, his spirituality and corporeality. Thus, its function of bringing Christ down again is inseparable from the Church forms of making Christ present again: scripture and the sacraments with their center, the mystery of the Mass. Just as the sacraments, and most clearly the Eucharist, are completely immersed in the qualitative time of the Church year, so scripture, which belongs to the Church and to her alone, is, in the homily and the liturgical prayers of the Church year, a book which is constantly unsealed and translated from the letter to spirit and life.

There is the adoration of the eucharistic presence, but only in conjunction with the Mass which is part of the Church year. And there is the private contemplation of the Word in scripture, but only in conjunction with the homily and the preaching that is colored by the Church year. No Christian who wishes to be a member of the Body of Christ can isolate himself from the life rhythm of the Body, under the pretext that his personal rhythm does not correspond—ever, or just this year, or even just today— with the rhythm of the Church. No one can presume either to say that the yearly repetition—the continual curving back of the end into the beginning, of maturity into childhood, of transfiguration into the renewed confusion and agony of the Passion—is no longer appropriate for the stage he has reached; that he has through his own development reached the spiritual point at which he responds only to certain aspects of Christian truth.

The Church year[30] is the solid, yet suspended, center between the limitless destinies of men on earth and the limitless fullness of the triune God in heaven. The relation between God and man is mediated through Jesus Christ, who like no one else lived through the whole dimensions of human destiny, in order to extend it to become a vessel of the limitless fullness of God. It is also mediated through the Holy Spirit, which transmits this double fullness, human and divine, from heaven to earth and back again. The important thing is that no partial vision of the total fullness should be forgotten or abridged. That means that man must not withdraw himself from what is offered him, but, letting himself be turned constantly, he must expose himself on all sides to the light of God. This happens in such a way that the uniqueness, the "this-ness," of Christ is many times sunk into the "this-ness" of man, whereby the unique creature is gradually filled with the uniqueness of the divine man, i.e., with the uniqueness of God.

Because the uniqueness of Christ—his childhood, youth, and manhood; his death, resurrection, and ascension—is from the beginning divine and, hence, beyond time, eternal, no man can outgrow him, but must always go back again from the end to the beginning, in order to find the Alpha again in the Omega,[31] the Omega already present in the Alpha, together with all the intermediate stages. A Christian has to learn to see the suffering Christ and the glorified Christ already in the child, the eternal child. Made a child ever anew, he must grow into eternal childhood. It is the same with the adult Christ, suffering and glorified.

But if the Church year reproduces in some measure the course of Christ's natural life, which becomes ever more the course of the successive stages of redemption, it is not in order to imprison that life within a closed cyclic time or an eternal return. Rather is every feast, every new stage, always an immediate opening onto eternity. At every moment the stone can, and must, fly from the whirling sling into the infinite.[32] So as to impress more deeply the entry and the indwelling of the divine through the individual feasts and their moods, the Church has distributed among the "historical feasts" suprahistorical ones, points of perspective at which the "eternity content" of a period emerges.

For instance, in the Epiphany, we are invited to see the Lord of all glory, the king of kings, the miracle-worker (of Cana), and the revealed Messiah (in the epiphany of the Trinity at the baptism in the Jordan) in the Christmas baby. On feasts like the Most Precious Blood, the Exaltation of the Most Holy Cross, and the autumn feast of the Seven Dolors, the mystery of suffering is renewed in the middle of a time of transfiguration or of peace, in, as it were, a heavenly perspective (that of the Epistle to the Hebrews). At the end of the historical succession of feasts, giving everywhere a supratemporal and eternal setting, stands the feast of the Most Holy Trinity. This eternal perspective does not make the earth disappear nor our task here inessential. Indeed, in the feast of Corpus Christi everything is tied back again to the mediating center of the hidden and revealed Christ, Head and Body, in eternity and in time.

Thus, as the Church year comes to an end, it shows him again timelessly as Christ the King. The temporal feasts seek to assimilate us to Christ, whereas the supratemporal ones seek to put away a too-earthly-conception of Christ and prevent our stopping at the physical crib, the physically seen risen Christ. "Let me ascend to the Father!"

If God were not true God and true man, the center, it could never have been shown that we are able to remain completely temporal beings and, at the same time, can already begin to share in the laws and the habits of eternity. And yet, the eternal penetrates our life in such a gentle, human way that we cannot make any objection from the human side when it adapts us inexorably to its own rhythm. The Word that resounds out of the Church year is both the highest glorification of all the mysteries of human existence—of the tenderest and of the hardest, of even those of treachery and abandonment and death in naked suffering—and the most pressing call to live alone for God, to die to the world, to return to the world only from God. This Word is not a formula or a definition. As such it could speak only dialectically, showing two sides which could never be made to overlap. But it is the Word of a fullness which bursts all formulas, which cannot be unfolded except as an outpouring through time in the ever-changing reflecting identity which turns around an immovable axis of the divine love as it shows itself in the life of man.

The changing movement of the year often cuts across our private inclinations and seeks to envelop us in an atmosphere which we find disturbing. Perhaps we regard ourselves now as adult and mature, and we are expected to behave like children beside the crib. We prefer to be withdrawn and thoughtful, and the Church expects us to feel the jubilation of Easter. We should like to continue in the peace of the time after Pentecost, and have to go back to the beginning, to Advent. This movement makes us supple in our faith and vitally alive as human beings. For it corresponds to our own growing life:

> The directions, the tendencies that rule it now, did they not already exist in the child? And was not the child's game the man's work embryonically? Thus, it is true that we no longer live in Advent, nor in Christmas, nor in the horror of Gethsemane and Golgotha, nor in the jubilance of Easter and the fire of Pentecost, but are members of Christ, who sits at the right hand of the Father, and we with him "in hope," so that the peace of the eternal Sabbath already breathes into our life. But this ripeness of the time after Pentecost draws its life from Advent, and Christmas, and Lent, and Easter, as a plant and a tree grows in the strength of its root; and the annual repetition of these seasons is only this welling up of the life of the root.[33]

The Greek Fathers had thought too one-sidedly away from the flesh toward the spirit. The necessity for the constant redescent into the flesh and the constant redirection out into the world and to the activity that is involved in that could not be as clear to them as it is for us. The repeated working through of the Church year has an effect on the consciousness of the Church, in the sense of an insight, growing through the centuries and extending in every direction, into the mystery of Christ, whose "breadth and length and height and depth" is ever more comprehended, that it "may be filled with all the fulness of God" (Eph. 3, 18–19).

In the order of the Church year even the unmanageably vast ranks of the saints acquire something of an order. This is true not only in the sense that a few of them have their own Church feasts and that a few have even found their way into the daily liturgy, but, more important, in that they have a relationship to specific places in the cycle of the festal mysteries. They are not, on that account, narrowed down, nor do they cease to share in the completion of the annual cycle. We can also learn from them that every man can have, as it were, a place in the cosmos of the mysteries. This "place" can even be a "constellation" of "feasts,"

304 *Man in History: A Theological Study*

a particular way, a particular view. But it is found all the more correctly, the less it is chosen according to natural consideration and desires. This place is found the more surely, the more it is received in obedience to the Word, even against one's natural inclinations. This is not to say that these "places" must remain unaltered all one's life; after all, everyone who receives a place in the fullness of Christ has admission to every other place—to every star in the communion of saints.

Notes

1 *De Victoria Verbi Dei,* XIII, 2 (PL 169, 1479 AB).

2 Series 85, Klostermann XI, 196.

3 Cf. the texts 716 ff. in *Origenes, Geist und Feuer,* 2nd ed., 369 ff.

4 Cf. Staeh. III. 211, 214.

5 Cf. *Fragm. in Cant.* (PL 17, 269–272, cf. 141 D); *Exod hom* 11, 2 Baehr. VI, 254.

6 *In Joh,* tr. 10, 4 (PL 35, 1469).

7 *Origen:* Series 27, Klost. XI, 48.

8 *Geist und Feuer,* Texts 407 ff., *loc. cit.,* 240.

9 *Ezech.* h. 6, 6 Baehr. VIII, 384–5. Cf. Gregory of Nazianzen's poem about human nature, v. 121 ff. (PG 37, 765).

10 *Peri Archon* II, 4, 4 Preuschen V. 131, line 25 ff.

11 Cf. Adrienne von Speyr: *Die sieben Worte am Kreuz und die sieben Sakramente,* 1956.

12 *Excitationes* 1 3, opera Basel 1565, 411–12. Quoted from de Lubac's *Katholizimus als Gemeinschaft,* 1943, 404–405.

13 *Drittes Sendschreiben an Prof. Hoffmann,* Collected Works, First section, IV, 1853, 406.

14 *Centurie* I, 67. Cf. v. Balthasar: *"Die Gnostischen Centurien,"* in *Kosmische Liturgie, das Weltbild Maximus des Bekenners,* 2nd ed., 1961, 629.

15 *Ibid.* I, 61, 626.

16 *Ibid.,* I, 60, 625.

17 *In Job,* 1 5, c 6 (PL 75, 684).

18 Cf. the fine analysis of Eugen Biser: *"Gott ist tod,"* Nietzsches Destruktion des christlichen Bewusstseins,* 1962.

19 *Herrlichkeit,* II, 1962, 331–332; Bonaventure in *Hexaemeron* 1, 12–13, (Ed. Quaracchi, V, 331–335).

20 *Ibid.,* 1, 30 (V, 334).

21 *Archives d'hist. litt. et doctr. du MA,* XIII, 1942, 307 ff.

22 Cf. *The Theology of History,* 140–149.

23 *Hom 3 in Luc,* Rauer IX, 20 ff.

24 *Series 35,* XI, 65.

25 *Komm. zu Matthew,* XII, 37–38 (X 152–154).

26 Cf. *"Die Gnostischen Centurien"* in *Kosmische Liturgie,* 552 ff.

27 *Serm.* 264, 4 (PL 38, 1215).

28 *De Divisione Naturae* V, 26 (PL 122, 921).

29 *Docta ignorantia,* Petzolt I, 1949, 107.

30 Cf. especially Erich Przywara: *Kirchenjahr, Die christliche Spannung-seinheit,* 1962, 277–321.

31 The Gospel for the last Sunday of the Church year and that for the first Sunday of Advent significantly proclaim the same *parousia. "Adventus"* was originally the Latin translation for "epiphany," "appearance in glory," whether the "first" or the "second" coming.

32 Adrienne von Speyr: *Die Pforten des Ewigne Lebens,* 1953.

33 Przywara, *Kirchenjahr,* 278–279.

10. GATHERED IN THE WORD

THE WORD AS MAN AND WIFE

As child, youth, and man, as a mortal, dying, and resurrecting man, the eternal Word underwent limitation in order to be still the whole within the fragment. The wholeness of his love for the Father and to men, since this love knows no limitations and transvalues every boundary from within, becomes an expression of the boundless. But there are three characteristics of man which seem to rule out such a transvaluation, because here man's perfection consists in three cases of being always one of a pair. He requires the existence of the other as one who is unalterably different in order to make his own perfection possible.

A human being can only be either a man or a woman; in the same interhuman relationship he can only be either a master or a servant; finally, in his relationship to the redeeming Messiah he

306

can only be either a Jew or a Gentile. In the dynamics of these three pairs of relationships, Gaston Fessard has seen the kernel of a dialectic of history and constantly returned to it in his thinking;[1] but he has also shown that these three pairs can be understood in terms of the theology of history, since Paul gathers them together as false opposites in a single statement: "For as many of you as were baptized into Christ have put on Christ. There is neither Jew nor Greek, there is neither slave nor free, there is neither male nor female; for you are all one in Christ Jesus (Gal. 3, 27–28).

Male and female are the elements of the dialectic of nature, and this is what gives the life even of animals something of an historical dramatic quality: the intensifying and transforming frenzy of the erotic condition, with its heroic and its idyllic varieties, its limits of mortal combat in one direction, and of play and song, almost for its own sake, in another, and the readiness to defend the family. How much this natural dialectic has influenced human history, particularly that of simple people and of the early periods of civilizations we know from legend and poetry.

At a later stage the second dialectic moves into the center: master and servant, in all the forms of domestic, clannish, tribal, and national existence, in all the gradations from brutal conquest, natural superiority, and voluntary submission from motives both high and low. Hegel described this dialectic in his *Phenomenology of Mind,* and Marx built on it and made it the center of his economic theory about the nature of man.

The third dialectic has meaning only within the world-view of Christian theology, but is essential within it: the Church (as the center of world history since Christ) consists of Jews and Gentiles. The fact that Jews and Gentiles, even after Christ, have stayed outside the Church shows that the Church itself cannot pass beyond the transition from the Old to the New Testament, but is essentially this event itself.

Man, as a natural being, exists as male and female. Genesis is concerned to place the statement of this relationship of opposition immediately after the supreme origin of man is stated, namely, the fact of his likeness to God (Gen. 1, 27). The male-female relationship is the object of a special concern of the Creator, who—in contrast to the creation of the animals—takes Eve out of Adam (Gen. 2, 18–24). There is here, in both respects, an immediate relationship to the divine source. In contrast to the unquestioned pairing off of the animals, Adam is at first alone and receives directly from God—and yet also out of himself—the companion who cannot be found elsewhere and who answers and completes him. Adam has this richness in him, but only God can release it from him—in the profound weakness of his slumber. Without Eve his richness remains poverty and—in the naming of natural things—roving discontent. Eve, however, becomes the cause of his fall; for her he leaves not only father and mother (Gen. 2, 24), but the wealth of his origin, in order to wander about the barren, thorny earth.

The Church Fathers have interpreted this scene again and again in terms of Christ and the Church. Truly there is no end to the perspectives that this viewpoint offers. The main thing here is that the Incarnate Word, who is the ground and cause of everything, enters into the narrow limitation of sexual difference. He becomes human in one mode of being human and not in the other. With this passing of the whole into the fragment, the limitation of being able to live only in one sex becomes apparent in all its implications for the first time. For it now does not lie, as with the other philosophical, religious, and mystical thinking of humanity, as it were beneath and behind the thinker, who turns away from the limited situation and raises his gaze to what is universal. Rather, it is situated at the end of the movement from God and is to be understood as an essential articulation of the language of God in human sounds.

We must first realize what the limitation is. The fact that the Word of God became a man and not a woman involves metaphysically a greater limitation than the nonuse of the sexual function—which is the Christian virginity established by Christ, and which Mary followed too. The Word assumed the characteristics of the king of creation who needed a partner in Paradise, but was profoundly humiliated by the Fall in order to play in this "character" the role given to him on the stage of the world. It is the natural role of a man to command, but in profound dependence on the planning, careful woman. He symbolizes freedom, but now, how wound round he is by clinging ivy, which often threatens to choke him—by wife and children, home and profession, a knot of cares.

It is part of the kenosis of the Word to have chosen this one sex, this natural superiority, and at the same time this dependence on the other. (This superiority is not fruitful in itself, but in the other, and receives its own fruit in return from the other.) The links here between Christ the model and man the copy can hardly be unraveled. The Word, who depends on nothing in the world, is, nevertheless, dependent on the response that men make, and he can return, fruitful, to the Father only if he bears that response with him. The vine that performs everything and without which the branches can do nothing is dependent on these branches in order to bear its fruit. The seed of the Word needs the field of the world; Christ needs the womb of the virgin Church.

Thus, natural sexual relations are suspended because the important thing now is not the succession of generations, but a vertical harvest that must be reaped. And thus, not only is virginity given precedence over marriage and the whole dignity of marriage raised to a "great mystery" between Christ and the Church (Eph. 5, 32), but also this mystery goes down into the sphere of earthly and bodily fruitfulness. The virgin who has heard the word of God becomes a mother. That is not a concession of the higher Christian order to the lower sexual order. It is part of the economic kenosis which is the essence of the Incarnate

Word. What Christ says about those who believe and obey being his brothers, sisters, and mother is not an allegory either, but contains the profoundest literal truth.

On the same plane on which Mary (the Church) is spiritual and bodily, at the same time, Christ (the Word) is eucharistic. The mystery of the Eucharist equally depends on the primacy of virginal renunciation in order to descend by this renunciation to the plane of fleshly fruitfulness and there produce immeasurable fruit through the sacrifice of flesh and blood. One need not hesitate to see the limited natural generative function of the male universalized in the eucharistic Lord and extended to his whole corporeal nature. The flesh sacrificed on the cross is the seed of new life throughout all the ages of the feminine Church and through her of the whole historical cosmos. This insight of Teilhard de Chardin is correct.

And because the bride, who constantly receives afresh this eucharistic seed, is always the visible Church as well, which in its members—in fact or, at least, in spirit—is virginal, something of this generative power of the new Adam in the new Eve passes also into the history of the Church and the world. Human history cannot be conceived without Christians' ever renewed witness to life, particularly the witness of those who practice chastity because of their marriage to Christ. Even the hatred that this witness of obedience to the Lord's command will always arouse is a sign of its presence and its fruitfulness.

The Head in heaven, the Body on earth: both are the one Christ. The bridegroom is in heaven; the bride is a pilgrim on the earth. She is in one sense a "widow" (Augustine, in Ps. 131, n. 24), and because of her widowhood is more secretly the "bride of Christ" (in Ps. 127, n. 11). She is a "wife heavy with child" (in Ps. 57, 5), "a wife in labor" (in Ps. 52, n. 1), "a wife giving birth" (in Ps. 126, 8). The reception of the heavenly seed means pain for her on earth. It means farewell to carefree untouchability; it means the cross, and does not spare her the pain of childbirth.

"She was with child and she cried out in her pangs of birth, in anguish for delivery (Apoc. 12, 2). No horizontal development can be substituted for this vertical relationship between heaven and earth. Perhaps as the birth pains of the earthly daughters of Eve are lessened medically and even removed, the pains of the second Eve are intensified: the more human beings refuse to share in redemptive suffering, the more falls on the Mater Dolorosa: Mary—Church.

The pains laid upon Eve (Gen. 3, 16), which refer not only to child-bearing, but also expressly to her relationship with her husband, are inseparably both a humiliating punishment and an ennobling expiation. The whole sphere of the sexual shares this ambiguity. He who tries to remove from it the element of suffering robs it as well of its sublimity, its relation to the nobility of the second redemptive pair. Man is king only if he is humbled; otherwise, not at all. This is also a law which stands forever in the theology of man in history. The seed, which bears fruit a hundredfold, is the Eucharist and the Word together. The Word, however, rang out once in the middle of history in a certain way and dominates history to its end and works through it like a leaven. No "evolution" can alter one jot of it; each rising or falling alteration in man can only show forth more clearly its sovereignty. For not only the Eucharist, as Teilhard de Chardin says, will undergo the "evolution" at the end, but also the Word, which is one with the sacrificed flesh and will judge heaven and earth and also the Church by itself.

For the Church as a whole comes from the Word; she is, like heaven and earth, living only in him (John 1, 3–4). She comes from the rib of the new Adam; only as his body, but his body as *bridal partner*, is she his bride.[2] A "partner," which he needs, both as man and as God, inasmuch as God, in creating a world, commits himself to it. "Bridal," as the other self into which he pours his fullness. Thus, in Ephesians 1, 23 it is not clear whether Christ "fills" his Body, the Church, which is his fullness, or "is

filled" by her. Both are true in the relationship between Christ
and the Church, which points down to the relationship between
Adam and Eve, but also up to the tremendous relationship of the
persons of the Trinity and their mutuality within eternal, complete fullness.

In this strange suspension between fullness and emptiness—
since woman comes from the man and yet fulfills the man's need
of completion—which in the Incarnate Word is the appearance
of a mystery of absolute love that is even more difficult to grasp,
lies the possible wholeness of Christian experience. Christ does
not need sexual experience in order to know his bride, the
Church, in the total way that the biblical use of "know" suggests.
He knows the force that goes out from him. He knows it both as
strength and as powerlessness. He, therefore, knows everything in
the bride (and in all her members, which we are) which not only
corresponds to his strength, but also—as contradiction and refusal—limits this power.

We must always remember this profound mystery when we
speak of the significance of Christian virginity. Taken in its materiality it is a limitation, a renunciation of a fulfillment in the
region of the Adam nature. Formally, it is—in a grace of faith
which cannot be calculated—existence in the fruitfulness of the
word and the flesh of Christ, thus also existence in the fullness of
the mutual experience which is fulfilled in the emptiness of
the cross. Where there is a renunciation of marriage in the
strength and the wholeness of the grace of faith, God responds
to him who makes the renunciation with an experience of
wholeness which transcends the fragmentation of existence. Thus,
he does not go without the essential experience of completeness,
nor does he appear to others as deprived or stunted.

Perhaps we can pursue the great Pauline analogy even further.
If Eve was taken out of Adam, then Adam had Eve within him
without knowing it. Of course, God created her and breathed his
breath into her; but God took the material for her out of

Adam's living flesh infused with the Spirit. There was something feminine in him which he recognizes when God brings him the woman. It is the feminine element that fashions creatures before the face of the Creator. And the Creator gives the man the power to be creative in this creaturely womb. But the woman is taken from the man; the substance from which she is made is masculine. She knows the man from the beginning. She is, together with him, feminine in relation to God, but she also has the actively responding power with him. She is able to give him the fully formed child that the seed can only indicate. Though his "help-mate" she does all the work, which he only, as it were, proposes and stimulates.

This profound mutuality, which here rests on nature, continues between Christ and the Church—but no longer chiefly on the natural plane. If the Church comes from Christ and, hence in everything which makes it the Church, lives from his substance, then the Son of God has this "feminine" element in him at the deepest level, not because he is a creature, but because he is the Son of the Father. He knows simultaneously what it means to be God and to be begotten of the Father. In this double relationship he becomes the origin of the Church. The Church comes from within him through the power of the triune God, but also through his "first-born" love of the Father, which makes room for innumerable other children of God. What he gives is wholly his own, and, thus, he recognizes himself in us, as the Father also recognizes him in us. And we recognize ourselves in him, since we are his "other" (his "feminine completion") only through the communication of his substance.[3]

Seen thus, the fragmentation of nature through sexuality ceases to be tragic. Even nature differentiates in order to unite; how much more so does the bridal secret between heaven and earth, which gives us a share in the differentiation of the trinitarian unity. On all planes the truth and depth of union depend on preserving the differences. "Equality" of the sexes prevents the

real interlocking of man and woman and levels out the organic
and constructive unity to one that is abstract (the identity of
human nature) and ineffectual. One sex is then unable to discover in the other, beyond the valuable difference, what is its
own. For if there is this "equality," each already knows simultaneously itself and the other. The same thing is true in a profounder way of Christ and the Church. The relationship exists
only beyond the always more deeply experienced difference between him and us, between the only one who has descended from
heaven (John 3, 13) and all of us who have not. When the
Church is raised to him as a bride, she knows and confesses herself ever more finally as a virgin.

If something of this vertical mystery were to appear in the
course of history, then it could only be a continually more
deeply experienced union in a continually more deeply and
finally experienced differentiation. If, therefore, Pauls says that
in Christ there is neither man nor woman, then that does not
mean that the difference between God and the creature is effaced
(in the sense of a pantheistic interpretation of "that God may be
everything to everyone" 1 Cor. 15, 28), nor that the earthly sexes
become eternalized (as in the Gnostic doctrine). It means, rather,
that the final form of the difference will be as an "economic
trinity" in the "marriage of the Lamb" (Apoc. 19, 7), which as
such is the phenomenal form of the "absolute Trinity."

In this marriage the law of virginity is the ultimate one ("For
in the resurrection they neither marry nor are given in marriage,
but are like angels in heaven" Matt. 22, 30). For this marriage
those "who have not defiled themselves with women" and "who
follow the Lamb wherever he goes" have already "been redeemed
from mankind as first fruits for God and the Lamb" (Apoc. 14, 4).
The Incarnate Word is virginal in order to take the sexual difference, with all that it contains in humiliation and glory, and
gather it into eternal life.

THE WORD AS MASTER AND SERVANT

If "male and female" is the dialectic of man primarily as a natural being, then "master and servant" is his dialectic primarily as a social and historical being. Whereas Genesis relates the sexual difference to the creative act of God and describes it as existing in Paradise (even if veiled and in suspension), the relationship of master and servant emerges for man only after the expulsion from Paradise. Or, more exactly, it comes into view for the first time in God's words rebuking Eve: "Your desire shall be for your husband, and he shall rule over you." Hitherto, only nature had been subject to man; he himself was its master. Now man sinks down to the condition of nature and is ruled over by his fellows. Both mastership and subjection are the sign of "fallenness." We do not know the form of a paradisal human society; a "primal natural justice" is unconstructible. We do not even know a primal relationship between the sexes, since children of the first marriage were born outside Paradise. Every speculation about master and servant, which seeks to go back behind the Fall, is pointless. We can interpret forward only, toward Christ as the gathering Logos.

Inasmuch as the difference characterizes the unredeemed natural condition of mankind, it is basic and irremovable. There can be no family without authority and obedience. Likewise, there is no tribe without leadership, loose or strict, by an individual or a "superior" group, however they gain power and however willingly or unwillingly their direction is obeyed. There is no people without a head and a more or less developed governmental system. Whatever the means whereby this power structure is established and sustained, these means will always be to some extent violent ones. That this use of force is connected with an original disorder and manifests a concessionary form (or rather, an already secretly kenotic form) of the divine dominion in the cosmos is clear from the way that Genesis differentiates.

From the act of creation man rules over nature, but in the allotting to him of the vegetable kingdom for food, the right to kill animals is implicitly denied him, although he still rules them (Gen. 1, 26–30). In the covenant with Noah, however, this right is specifically accorded him (Gen. 9, 3): now the "fear of you and the dread of you shall be upon every beast of the earth" (Gen. 9, 2). But there are two provisos: the consumption of flesh is allowed, but not of blood. Blood is the seat of life, and only God is master over that, so much so that whoever spills human blood will have to answer to God, who delegates to men his avenging power: "Whoever sheds the blood of man, by man shall his blood be shed; for God made man in his own image" (Gen. 9, 6). But then a new and final covenant of God embraces man, the violent ruler, and the ravished creature, whether animal or man (Gen. 9, 8–11). Both are enfolded in the peace of God.

This does not mean that God watched earthly happenings with indifference, with his eyes fixed only on the coming peaceful reconciliation to be performed by Jesus Christ. For even the first violent deed before the gates of Paradise, Cain's fratricide, is carefully noted and avenged by God, since Abel's blood cries to him as the only possible avenger. Cain is banished from fertile soil, but it is God who, nevertheless, holds the exile in his grasp. God's mark upon his forehead protects him, for he belongs to the terrible race of God, to kill whom brings sevenfold vengeance (Gen. 4, 15) and with whom it is better to have nothing to do.

Thus, authority, which wields the sword in the name of God and as his assistant, becomes "a terror" (Rom. 13, 3), particularly for the wicked who are directly threatened by it. But, because authority has power, it can become a terror for the good who "must be subject" to it (Rom. 13, 5) and must try to see through an unjust and violent order a gleam of the universal order. Equally, "Servants, be submissive to your masters with all respect, not only to the kind and gentle but also to the overbearing" (1 Pet. 2, 18). This obedience must come from inside themselves; it must be rooted in their conscience. It must be directed toward the state authority (Rom. 13, 6–7) and toward domestic authority, even if the authority is unjustly wielded (1 Pet. 2, 19). Obedience in such a case is, of course, justified only by considering the unjust sufferings of Christ. Here the covenant of Noah becomes an earthly reality; here alone the fearful dialectical knot of master and servant can be untied.

One can make profound statements like Hegel and Marx about the immanent historical logic of this relationship. The master, who commands the work of the servant and exploits him for his own advantage, places himself in a position of dependence on his tool and becomes a servant, whereas the servant, who manufactures the goods, becomes the true master and sooner or later declares it and fights for it. Because of this dialectical process the economic, social, and political situation is revolutionized, but never once and for all (as Marx states), but over and over again in an unending shift of the center of gravity. Even the new masters, who were servants yesterday and now rule their rulers, have to beware of the dialectic that brought them to the top.

One can transcend (with Hegel) this whole unstable sphere with a vertical movement into higher self-realizations of the spirit, but to fix it securely in itself (by unambiguous historical progress) is impossible. As an earthly reason and law it remains always in an inchoate state, because as Hobbes saw, it has, as its fundamental postulate, an unreasonableness and a lawlessness. Improvements in the relationship of master and servant, of him who wields power and of him who suffers it, so long as they remain within the immanent play of historical logic, can lead only to rearrangements which do not remove the basic evil (which they either cannot or do not see). It is different if earthly relationships are seen as a reflection of the dialectic that ends in Christ (as largely was the case with medieval chivalry and the Christian understanding of the feudal system). Here the important thing is to leave the model where it is, i.e., beyond *mere* ethics, politics, and economics, so that there is no mingling of the two spheres, either by drawing down the model into the earthly order, or by pushing up the earthly order into a directed, usurped Christianity.

We have already spoken about the model when considering the problem of power, so we need only remind ourselves of the essentials. Christ is Lord—he knows it and says so (Luke 22, 27); he is king—he knows it and says so (John 18, 37; Apoc. 19, 16). He underlines the distance between him and us even when he removes it, as is evident from the following scripture passages. "A servant is not greater than his master" (John 15, 20). "It is enough for the disciple to be like his teacher, and the servant like his master. If they have called the master of the house Be-elzebul, how much more will they malign those of his household" (Matt. 10, 25). "If they persecuted me, they will persecute you" (John 15, 20). And why? Because "the Son of man came not to be served but to serve, and to give his life as a ransom for many" (Matt. 20, 28). That is why he washes the feet of his disciples (John 13, 1–11), and cleanses our souls in his blood (Eph. 5, 25–27).

Only in the Son of God's becoming a servant, becoming poor and obedient (2 Cor. 8, 9; Phil. 2, 8; Heb. 5, 8), lies the manifestation of the divine masterhood and glory. There is no retreat from this manifestation; rather, the whole height and power and might of God has to, and seeks to, appear in this poor and obedient man become "sin" (2 Cor. 5, 21) and "a curse" (Deut. 21, 23; Gal. 3, 13) for us—here and nowhere else. His lordship lies in his taking upon himself, in the full freedom of his love, the place of a servant, the humiliating and finally killing task of a servant. There is no greater love, but also no greater freedom and power, than to give up one's life for one's friends.

Only in relation to this incomprehensible freedom of love—of being the absolute master and putting oneself in the place of the last of the servants—does the gospel dialectic of master and servant (as opposed to the philosophical) become clear. Christ in his absolute love is so free that he can allow himself to be a servant, while still being the master. And it is in this that he proves himself the true God, in contrast to all the other gods, who can never allow themselves this, because they spring ultimately from human ideas of what masterhood is. And yet, the revelation of lordship in the state of a servant is not an inner necessity of this God—as if this were the only thing in which he could outdo the other gods. It reveals the freedom of boundless love, and, thus, the way the true God works. As, however, the free love of the man Jesus, who kneels at the feet of his disciples and of all his fellowmen, proclaims the human victory over all the enslavements of fate, the "humiliated" God is, at the same time, man raised up, who in this sovereign freedom of his love shares in the lordship of God and becomes the epitome of this divine lordship in the world.[4]

Thus, one cannot say that Christ was the servant of God up to his death and the Lord after his Resurrection. Both before and after the Resurrection he is the same—the Lord as servant and the servant as Lord. In order to come into his glory, he does not leave the servant's work of the cross behind him, for it is precisely on the cross that he shows himself as the triumphant Lord (Col. 2, 14–15), who takes the "marks" of this triumph as his distinguishing marks with him into eternity (Luke 24, 40; Matt. 24, 30; Apoc. 19, 13).

So, for Christians there is no other mark of lordship than the cross. For the cross is not only a passing means, a tool to achieve a certain end which is separate from it; it is equally the permanent expression of that which is the only end, the freedom of love. Therefore, it is only half the truth to say that the master became a servant in order to make us servants masters, for it is the truth of the master that makes us free, and this truth will be done and is the love that enters freely into service and death. The freedom of the Christian lies exactly where the freedom of Christ lies. Anything else would be merely to "submit again to a yoke of slavery" (Gal. 5, 1; 4, 8–9) in order to endeavor to remove "the stumbling block of the cross" (Gal. 5, 11). To be "called to freedom" means "through love [to] be servants of one another" (Gal. 5, 13), namely to "serve not under the old written code but in the new life of the Spirit" (Rom. 7, 6).

Thus, the ideas of master and servant, without being dissolved, have passed into an infinite movement, a specifically theological dialectic. If this dialectic was already anticipated in the story of Jacob and Esau ("The elder shall serve the younger" Gen. 25, 23; Rom. 9, 12), Christ establishes it as a spiritual reality ("Let the greatest among you become as the youngest, and the leader as one who serves" Luke 22, 26), and Paul makes it the basis of the community structure ("The parts of the body which seem to be weaker are indispensable, and those parts of the body which we think less honorable we invest with the greater honor, and our unpresentable parts are treated with greater modesty, which our more presentable parts do not require. But God has so adjusted the body, giving the greater honor to the inferior part" 1 Cor. 12, 22–24).

The doubly dialectical words which Paul addresses to the Corinthians, both in earnest and in bitter irony, can now be understood properly: "Already you are filled! Already you have become rich! Without us you have become kings! And would that you did reign, so that we might share the rule with you! . . . We are fools for Christ's sake, but you are wise in Christ. We are weak, but you are strong. You are held in honor, but we in disrepute" (1 Cor. 4: 8, 10). The serious point is that the apostles, for the sake of the community, are "exhibited . . . as last of all, like men sentenced to death; . . . as the refuse of the world, the offscouring of all things" (1 Cor. 4: 9, 13). Therefore, it is all right if they are weak so that the community is strong.

But the ironic point is that the community sees and strives for its strength and wisdom and masterhood outside the law of the cross, in the spirit of integralism which seeks first of all to command and then subsequently perhaps to serve, but from this commanding position. The biting sarcasm of the verses is theologically all the more important as it is bedded in the deepest mysteries of Christian existence in the cross. This sarcasm is aimed at all who seek, or achieve, masterhood outside the stumbling block of the cross, in whatever Christian trappings this masterhood may seek to clothe itself. One alone is Lord, he who bowed his knee before heaven, earth, and hell, in humility and self-annihilation; before him alone, and in his spirit, are heaven, earth, and hell to bend their knee (Phil. 2, 7–11).

The dialectic of master and servant is different from that of man and woman in that the master can really become his opposite. And yet, the relationship between the two pairs is a close one: for the man (Christ) also takes the woman (the Church) from himself and is still himself outside her. Nor does the Lord cease to be the Lord when he becomes a servant. Because he "did not count equality with God a thing to be grasped," but in emptying himself let his masterhood go (Phil. 2, 6–7), he shows that he is the great Lord. However, whoever clings to his masterhood is already losing it. In letting go Christ clings to the one thing which matters: to "submission," to subjective submission in objective subjection, to the downward pull which is the true *catena aurea* that keeps the cosmos hanging in the sky. It is through this obedience that the Logos, who pours out himself, gathers back the world. He, who in his obedience has not ceased to be suspended in the will of his Father, collects around this obedience of his the fragmented world, the divided Adam. He dies "not for the nation only, but to gather into one the children of God who are scattered abroad" (John 11, 52).

The basic unity of master and servant rests in a reciprocity and circumincession of the two estates which transcend all philosophical and sociological considerations and are based in Christ alone. It is so complete that a removal of the natural differences of the two estates does appear immediately necessary from a theological point of view. Paul describes concisely this complete mutual interpenetration: "Every one should remain in the state in which he was called. Were you a slave when called? Never mind. But if you gain your freedom, make use of your present condition instead. For he who was called in the Lord as a slave is a freedman of the Lord. Likewise he who was free when called is a slave of Christ" (1 Cor. 7, 20–22). The letter to Philemon shows how both work out existentially.

Certainly, the new ethos will influence temporal social structures in the direction of more "humane," more just relationships between human groups. This effect, however, is not the immediate goal. It lies higher and continues to be reached even when there are relapses into brutal tyranny, into inhuman working conditions, which—with our knowledge of human nature—cannot be excluded *a priori* by "progressive evolution." What the Incarnate Word gathers in to the Father is always just as much suffering as deeds, trials surmounted as well as independent actions. There are always the services of servants, who have become masters in the master, for the master does not seek to rule except as the servant of all.

THE WORD AS JEW AND GENTILE

The Word, in becoming flesh, also took on himself the limitation of nationality. Indeed, he entered into the narrowest national grouping that exists, because it was and is the unsurmountable barrier which God himself set up: the Jewish race. Other nationalities can be changed, and the barriers between peoples can be practically swept away in the cause of a vague universal humanism. With the Jews this cannot be, despite all their attempts to break out from the Maccabees until today.

Jesus was particularly careful to preserve this barrier. It belonged at once to his natural humanity and to his supernatural mission. In his reply to the "Canaanite woman" (as Matthew calls her, in order to remind us clearly of the ancient difference between Israel and idol-worshiping Canaan) he draws the distinction: "I was sent only to the lost sheep of the house of Israel" (Matt. 15, 24). He instructs his disciples, "Go nowhere among the Gentiles, and enter no town of the Samaritans, but go rather to the lost sheep of the house of Israel" (Matt. 10, 5–6). His words of rejection to the woman are still words he directs at her, whereas before, "he did not answer her a word" at her crying. And the words speak of a lost Israel, and it is still an open question whether, and in what proportion, it can be found again.

The earthly mission is still subject to the laws of the limited measure of time and space available. If the limited strength available must be applied to his work for the "children of Israel," how could there be enough for the "dogs of Canaan"? But has Jesus not already—and why?—moved beyond the borders of Israel to the heathen region of Tyre and Sidon? Admittedly he "entered a house, and would not have any one know it," but "he could not be hid" (Mark 7, 24). The Canaanite woman has a wonderful answer. She sees the children and the dogs as part of the one "household," and the dogs exist on the crumbs that drop, as if by chance, from the table of the masters. Her answer is faith, emerging unexpected and welcome from the darkness—in the same way that the Word that is present, but hidden, cannot remain hidden. Jesus addresses her with that "O woman," which he uses otherwise only for his mother. Here the expression points to the feminine element of readiness, of faith, which the Church has: "O woman, great is your faith! Be it done for you as you desire" (Matt. 15, 28).

At this frontier—in constant "withdrawals" from positions that can no longer be held[5]—is lived the life of Jesus with his people. Because the plan to kill him is conceived early in his public life (Matt. 12, 14), he chooses obscurity, the muffled word ("Nor will any one hear his voice in the streets" Matt. 12, 19), the parable, which is heard but not understood (Matt. 13, 13). He cannot perform many miracles because of the unbelief (Matt. 13, 58). The people honor God with their lips, but their hearts are far from him; their worship is vain in the eyes of God (Matt. 15, 8–9). Their rulers are blind (Matt. 15, 14), infectors of the crowd (Matt. 16, 6). The people form a generation that commits adultery against God (Matt. 12, 39; 16, 4). The Messiah can hardly continue to bear with them (Matt. 17, 17), and they cause him to weep over the unholy city (Luke 19, 41). He knows that they are going to crucify him (Matt. 16, 21; 17, 22; 20, 18–19); he prophesies his death in the parable of the vineyard (Matt. 21, 38). Because they will kill him, the kingdom will be taken away from them and given to another nation (Matt. 21, 43). The murderers will be killed, and their city burned (Matt. 22, 7). The denunciation of the leaders of the people (Matt. 23) and the prophecies of destruction (Matt. 24, 1–36) speak already from beyond the broken covenant.

The whole gospel stands on this frontier, and if the Word of God is spoken for all times, then the situation of the frontier at which it is spoken is also valid for all times. That is why all the words of the Old Testament which lead up to this frontier and were spoken in relation to it are also valid for all times. The whole nexus of revelation, and hence of the meaning of history, is gathered at this point. Everything becomes clear from this point, which however darkens most the image of God.

God has sworn an eternal covenant with Israel: "My steadfast love I will keep for him for ever, and my covenant will stand firm for him. . . . Once for all I have sworn by my holiness; I will not lie to David" (Ps. 89: 28, 35). In fulfilling the covenant by sending his son, God breaks it. Even at the time of the psalmist, who put those words into the mouth of Yahweh, the covenant was obscured, perhaps already broken: "But now thou hast cast off and rejected. . . . Thou hast renounced the covenant with thy servant" (Ps. 89, 38–39). Here we hear the lament at being abandoned: "How long, O Lord? Wilt thou hide thyself for ever? How long wilt thy wrath burn like fire? Remember, O Lord, what the measure of life is, for what vanity thou hast created all the sons of men!" (Ps. 89, 46–47).

Could men be expected to be equal to a covenant with God? Was it worthy of God to break it on his side also because of that? The Word that he sends proclaims the end of this covenant and declares, at the same time, the most intimate and tender things about the faithful love of the Father. It is a Jewish Word, spoken from within Israel; the Word therefore, as Israel goes to its death, must also suffer unto death with it (Matt. 26, 38), and cry out for the lost God (Matt. 27, 46). Like Samson, the Word buries himself under the collapsing temple. That is the power and the hour of darkness (Luke 22, 53).

Of course, there follows the Resurrection and from it the command of Christ Pantocrator (Matt. 28, 18) to go out to all nations and all times, "to the end of the earth" (Acts 1, 8). The apostles turn first in brotherhood to the Jews and, only when they are refused, to the Gentiles. And Paul succeeds in wresting the "Gentile Church" away from any relapses to the old Judaism. But does that solve anything? Paul himself, the apostle of the Gentiles, is torn to the bottom of his heart by the split that goes through the divine covenant. He suffers through the salvation that is given to him, or practically thrust on him, and he longs to be back in the unity of his brothers without salvation. "I have great sorrow and unceasing anguish in my heart. For I could wish that I myself were accursed and cut off from Christ for the sake of my brethren, my kinsmen by race" (Rom. 9, 2–3).

In this sorrow Paul has to set about defending God against the charge of desertion. First he has to go back through the Old Testament to the promise to Abraham—which, though given to his bodily descendants, was only intended for those among them who were the "children of the promise"—in order to show the constant choosing of one and not of the other (Rom. 9, 6–13). Then he has to charge God with the responsibility for a compre-

hensive plan of salvation. In this plan the "hardening of the
heart" (as with Pharaoh) is also attributed to God (Rom. 9, 14–
18), who, because he is God, cannot be called to account for it by
man. The case of Pharaoh, who hardens his heart for the sake of
the Exodus, passes (in an uncompleted sentence, Rom. 9, 22–24)
into the case of Israel. Israel, long endured with patience, finally
becomes the occasion for the manifestation of the divine wrath
in order to make room for and set in relief the "vessels of mercy,"
the new and final exodus of Jews and Gentiles.

In this moment, when the whole weight of the responsibility
seems to weigh on the shoulders of God, the stone of guilt rolls
back again onto the Jews. They have understood their share in
the divine covenant as "works," instead of "faith." Their religious
zeal, not for God, but for their own justification before God, was
why they had to stumble over the crucial stumbling stone that
God had put in their way (Rom. 9, 32—10, 3). It was always true
of them that "the word is very near you; it is in your mouth and
in your heart" (Deut. 30, 14). This divine Word could have been
grasped in faith, and now that it has finally become flesh it can be
reached through Christian preaching (Rom. 10, 14–17). So why
"did Israel not understand?" (Rom. 10, 19). And again the
burden of guilt is rolled back from Israel to God: "First Moses
says, 'I will make you jealous of those who are not a nation; with
a foolish nation I will make you angry" (Rom. 10, 19, cf. Deut.
32, 21). Paul places this divine act in a light which stops him
from quoting the preceding verse: "They have stirred me to
jealousy with what is no god; they have provoked me with their
idols."

God takes the initiative in this interplay of jealousy. For it to
be able to reach its full extent Paul states in advance that God
has not rejected his people (Rom. 11, 1). God has chosen un-
shakably a remnant from the people for himself, for "the gifts
and the call of God are irrevocable" (Rom. 11, 29). But for the
sake of this remnant "the rest were hardened, . . . God gave them
a spirit of stupor . . . a snare and a trap, a pitfall" (Rom. 11, 8–9).

And yet their "darkened eyes" can see enough to know of the salvation of the Gentiles and to be roused to jealousy. Paul, a Jew and the apostle of the Gentiles, reckons with this jealousy and hopes to excite it, so that the Jews—or at least some of them—may come to salvation (Rom. 11, 11–14).

But if salvation comes through jealousy, then it will be a good thing to excite the jealousy of the Gentiles against the Jews. Paul, the chosen Jew, turns to the Gentiles and warns them that the root is holy onto which they who are unholy have been grafted. If for the sake of this event of grace some of the natural branches were broken off (which still remain holy, Rom. 11, 16), how much greater should be the fear of the Gentiles, who, as foreign branches, could be all the more easily cut off again (Rom. 11, 16–24). And if, before, man had to bow his head before the incomprehensible elections and rejections of God, then he must now finally sink into the dust before the abyss of the inscrutable mind of God, which in turn rejects some in order to choose others, hands some over to disobedience in order to send grace upon others, and so finally "has consigned all men to disobedience, that he may have mercy upon all" (Rom. 11, 32).

This unfathomable "play of jealousy," in which God shows himself "unfaithful" to this one and then to that one, is the only way in which God seeks to achieve his total goal: universal salvation at the end of history. It is not enough to say that the old special covenant has been widened to become a new universal one, for the old covenant was in its inner intention universal in the promise to Abraham (and before that to Noah). But the new covenant itself will become universal only when "all Israel will be saved," i.e., when the Church no longer lives by the light of a grace that is withheld from Israel for as long as the Church lasts. The light in which the Church stands is hers, and yet it is not hers. And the darkness in which Israel dwells belongs to it, and yet does not belong to it, because it is a vicarious darkness for the benefit of those in the light.

That is the God of world history, who conceals himself as

much as he reveals himself in this chiaroscuro. The manifestation
of his full love remains really an eschatological event. In the
meantime, some are loved at the cost of the others. But who has
paid all the cost of the love, if not the Son of Man, who as a Jew
was rejected by the Jews and crucified by the Gentiles, who was
betrayed, denied, and ignored by the Christians? He, who did
not belong to any party and was welcomed by none, like the
sacrificial animals who were burned outside the holy camp of the
covenant, was finally killed outside the Holy City (Heb. 13, 11–
12). Thus, by his being outside he did not found a new inside:
"Therefore, let us go forth to him outside the camp, bearing
abuse for him. For here we have no lasting city, but we seek the
city which is to come" (Heb. 13, 13–14). If Christ is condemned
by Israel and for Israel, then the judgment is passed in him on
Israel, on the cross, outside his own town and his holy enclosure.
But that is the place allotted to the Church also, which has no
other place than this nonplace (u-topia). The nonplace outside is
the cross, under which Jews and Gentiles stand side by side. The
crucified Christ alone tears down the dividing wall and calms
all hatred through his flesh, and he creates from both the Jews
and the Gentiles the one new man. He establishes peace, and
reconciles both in the one body with God (Eph. 2, 14–16).

As both are in the same place it is impossible for the Church
to forget Israel, and to be unconcerned about its fate. The presence of Israel in the condemned flesh of the Son of Man, on which
the Church is nourished, causes Israel's fate, its being judged, to be
resurrected constantly at the center of the Church, until there is
an indissoluble community in the judgment that is "to begin
with the household of God" (1 Pet. 4, 17). If Israel, according to
Paul, openly suffers vicarious rejection for the sake of the Gentile
Church, why should not the Church, at least secretly in the cross,
suffer vicariously for Israel and with Israel? Why should it not,
like Israel—and more profoundly, like him who was abandoned
on the cross for the sake of both—come to know doubt in God's
faithfulness and jealousy toward the other toward whom God has

been more faithful? And why should there not be in its love that subterranean current of fear that Paul hammers into the Church (Rom. 11, 20), the fear of being cut off, which is the fruit of self-confidence, i.e., of implicit unbelief?

Should this fruit not grow in the same measure as the faith of the Church in its own infallibility and immaculateness? This faith is given to her only when the sinful Peter weeps bitterly and when Mary sees herself as a mere handmaid and as a pure believer (because she does not understand). Is the Church, then, a "pure virgin"? "I am afraid that as the serpent deceived Eve by his cunning, your thoughts will be led astray from a sincere and pure devotion to Christ" (2 Cor. 11, 3). Thus, Paul strives for the Church "with divine jealousy."

At the point of absolute truth, where the inexorable light of God falls on Jew and Gentile, the transitions between the old and the new covenants become clear. The betrayer Judas is the old covenant which does not want to make the transition and defends itself, but equally he is the new covenant whose unworthiness is gathered in his figure, one of the twelve. As this synthesis of the general refusal he is equally without a proper place as the crucified Christ himself. There is no way back for him (Matt, 27, 1–9) and no way forward. There remains for him also, as for Jesus, to hang nowhere but between heaven and earth, and to spill, instead of his heart's blood, his bowels.

Thus, the two peoples remain, to the left and the right of the cross, like the two thieves, with a different place in history and yet related. But they are unable to reach out to each other and become united. There unity lies where the separating wall is torn down, but this place, which for God lies in the middle of history, lies for them at its end. The dialectic of Jew and Gentile is the theological center of history; their division is irremovable until time is swallowed up in eternity. In this diastasis alone the risen Logos gathers together all history, which already has its only focus in him, the crucified Christ.

Notes

1 Cf. his collected work, De l'Actualité Historique, 2 vols., 1959. In Germany no one has considered the dialectic of these three pairs more thoroughly and with more theological circumspection than Karl Barth in his Church Dogmatics: Jew and Gentile, especially in the doctrine of God's choice in grace (II/2); servant and master in the doctrine of reconciliation (IV/1)—"Jesus Christ, Lord as servant," 1956; man and woman in the doctrine of the creation (III/2)—"Creature," 1960; III/4—"Command of God the Creator," 1961.

2 Cf. in Sponsa Verbi, 1960: "Wer ist die Kirche?", 148–203.

3 Cf. Eugen Biser: Erkenne dich in mir, Von der Kirche als dem Leib der Wahrheit, 1955.

4 Karl Barth, Church Dogmatics IV/1.

5 Cf. the "departure" in Matthew 2, 12; 2, 13 ff.; 2, 22; 4, 12; 12, 15; 14, 13; 15, 21; in John 6, 15—as well as the departure of Jesus and his hiding himself in 12, 36, there is a withdrawal of Christ right in the middle of the Gospel.

CONCLUSION:
BELIEF AND ETERNITY

In Claudel's *The Satin Slipper* Dona Prouheze's guardian angel
shows her life on the frontier, the border:

> And who knows if you are not dead already, otherwise whence would
> come to you that indifference to place, that helpless inertia?
> So near the frontier, who knows from which side I can send you, back
> or forward at my playful will?

He detaches her gently from "this earth which you think solid
and is but chained down. A frail mixture, at every second thrilled
with being as well as not being." Prouheze sees herself from
above, from the angel's vantage point, lying on the shore like an
empty shell, and she no longer knows whether she is inside or

outside her body. "The body, am I within it or without it? I live simultaneously as I see it." So she lives in advance in eternal life and is to be the "hook" to draw back to God the man she loves. The angel throws her into the purifying fires of purgatory, so that she may, like a Beatrice, lead the man toward her through the flames.

When she is talking late with Don Camillo about the end of the fortress of Mogador, neither is thinking fully about that eventuality. "So all these things about us which seem present are really past, if truth were told?" And in the great final scene between her and Rodrigo she has already based both their loves beyond death in God. But the emotional grief of the man sounds out of place. After her death it will sound ever more false and hollow, the more he talks of world union and evolution (instead of humble Christian love). Only when all his grandiloquence ends in treachery (which it always was), does he regain his beloved in "pure faith."[1]

Only the Christian faith is able to fill the present with the future of eternity in such a way that the present is at the same time convicted of its emptiness and judged in it, instead of it being intensified idealistically to a false "moment of eternity." Yet, it shows this emptiness only because of the plenitude which is promised to it. The simultaneity of all this is possible only when Christ is risen and has given an eternal foundation to temporal life. Otherwise, the only way out of the fragmentedness of existence would be the flight into a temporal future, which is always overtaken and left behind by the knowledge of the heart. The power of the preacher is part of the revealed word of God. It cannot be replaced by any philosophy of history or any relativizing philology. Wisdom speaks thus:

> A generation goes, and a generation comes,
>   but the earth remains for ever.
> The sun rises and the sun goes down,

and hastens to the place where it rises.
The wind blows to the south,
 and goes round to the north;
round and round goes the wind,
 and on its circuits the wind returns.
All streams run to the sea,
 but the sea is not full;
to the place where the streams flow
 there they flow again.
All things are full of weariness;
 a man cannot utter it;
the eye is not satisfied with seeing,
 nor the ear filled with hearing.
What has been is what will be,
 and what has been done is what will be done;
and there is nothing new under the sun (Eccles. 1, 4–9).

Should this wisdom be demythologized? Does this speak of
man, who is ruled by cosmic cyclic time and has not yet worked
his way through to the rectilinear historical time of human
freedom—and, thus, broken through to a hope in the future such
as the ancient peoples did not know? Or rather, are not the words
of the preacher in the New Testament much more true? For he
who has once seen and understood and taken into his heart the
one picture of himself that God has set in the middle of history,
what picture of the future can still captivate him? Or does he
imagine that he is able to discover something beyond this picture
that is different and perhaps more beautiful? Perhaps a picture
that disavows the past one, since in the more beautiful future
mankind will no longer be crucified, but must also outgrow the
reverence for suffering? There is no Resurrection and no Eucharist without Gethsemane, no understanding of God's love without the cross. He who has been able to see and to read this picture is beyond everything; he is at the end of history. He cannot

and does not seek to hope for anything—beyond all human grandiloquence—but the flaming up of the silent halo of the Word "as the lightning comes from the east and shines as far as the west (Matt. 24, 27).

Faith alone contains a fulfilling hope—and no empty clinging to the future—because, beyond all intermediate stages in time, it grasps fulfillment, nay, is grasped by it. It reaches for the goal that has already reached it (Phil. 3, 12–13). Faith grasps the whole in every fragment because it is already grasped by the whole and incorporated into its body. Faith, therefore, has no occasion, like all the idealisms, to fly from time into an "eternal moment," for it is in time itself that it grasps the whole, as the whole grasps it in time. But faith has just as little cause to fly from an unfulfilled present to a more fulfilled future, for it would lose with the present, which it had let go as of little value, the eternity dwelling within it. It fills itself with this eternity only by fulfilling eternity's mission in present time: only in the today do time and eternity become one. But a mission unfolds with unfolding time; this mission involves and requires future time. This mission which is being fulfilled is one with the prayer "Thy kingdom come, thy will be done on earth as it is in heaven." As the mission fulfills itself, eternity comes by way of the future into time and, therefore, moves along time toward eternity, in which fulfilled time is already waiting as resurrected time. Through prayer and obedience we hasten the arrival of Christ. "For salvation is nearer to us now than when we first believed; the night is far gone, the day is at hand" (Rom. 13, 11–12).

Only the Christian has in faith a tangible hope which is capable of reaching out beyond the emptiness of time to the physical body of the beloved Lord. "Do not hold me," he says, "for I have not yet ascended to the Father." But he has ascended, and now he can and wants to be held by the groping hand of hope, by all who without him are without being.

"But one thing I do, forgetting what lies behind and straining forward to what lies ahead" (Phil. 3, 13). This reaching forward cannot be replaced by any direct reaching upward. This leads us back to the beginning of our study, to Augustine.

The *distentio* (diastasis) of time can be overcome only by *extensio secundum intentionem* (as Augustine says, remembering Philippians 3, in *Confessions*, XI, 29). This tread of the believer through time toward the risen Christ is the true progress of the world. It alone sets creation as a whole in true movement toward God. It implants into all the vanity of earthly activity an eternal soul. As faith it does not seek to replace sight (2 Cor. 5, 7); as hope it does not seek to take possession now, otherwise it would not be hope with patience (Rom. 8, 24–25). In this there is certainty, "If God is for us, who is against us? He who did not spare his own Son but gave him up for us all, will he not also give us all things with him?" (Rom. 8, 31–32).

Note

1 Paul Claudel: *The Satin Slipper*, translated by John O'Connor, Sheed & Ward, 168, 169, 191.

INDEX OF NAMES